EVOLUTION OF CONSCIOUSNESS

WITH CONTRIBUTIONS BY

Lionel Adey, R. H. Barfield, David Bohm,

Norman O. Brown, Colin Hardie, Cecil Harwood,

Richard A. Hocks, Clyde S. Kilby, R. K. Meiners,

Howard Nemerov, Paul Piehler, Robert O. Preyer,

R. J. Reilly, Mary Caroline Richards,

Shirley Sugerman, and G. B. Tennyson;

a Bibliography of the Works of Owen Barfield

Compiled by G. B. Tennyson

OWEN BARFIELD

Evolution of Consciousness

Studies in Polarity

EDITED BY SHIRLEY SUGERMAN

Wesleyan University Press

MIDDLETOWN, CONNECTICUT

The publisher gratefully acknowledges the support of Drew University toward the publication of this book.

The frontispiece photograph of Owen Barfield was taken by Carol Reck.

Library of Congress Cataloging in Publication Data

Main entry under title:

Evolution of consciousness.

    Essays in honor of Owen Barfield.
    Includes bibliographies.
    CONTENTS: Introduction, a psychography: Sugerman, S.
In conversation with Owen Barfield. — To Owen Barfield:
Harwood, C. Owen Barfield. Brown, N. O. On interpreta-
tion. Nemerov, H. Exceptions and rules. [etc.]
    1. Barfield, Owen, 1898-   — Addresses, essays,
lectures. 2. Polarity (Philosophy) — Addresses, essays,
lectures. I. Barfield, Owen, 1898-   II. Sugerman,
Shirley. III. Adey, Lionel.
B1618.B284E9   111   75-37592
ISBN 0-8195-4094-3

Manufactured in the United States of America
First edition

In honor of

OWEN BARFIELD

with admiration and affection

"Polarity is dynamic, not abstract. It is . . . 'a living and
generative interpenetration'. . . . Indeed we shall see that
the apprehension of polarity is itself the basic act of imagination."
— Owen Barfield, in *What Coleridge Thought*

CONTENTS

EDITOR'S NOTE

In the spring of 1972, in anticipation of the seventy-fifth anniversary of Owen Barfield's birth (in November of 1973), a number of his long-standing friends and colleagues enthusiastically agreed to celebrate the occasion by contributing to a volume in his honor. This book is the outcome of that impulse. Our wish is to honor a man the importance and profundity of whose thought is yet to be fully appreciated. We would honor him by honoring the originality of his thought, original in the sense that it goes deeply into that center from which human thought springs, into origins. By addressing themselves from diverse points of view to the theme central to his life and thought, the contributors to this volume want to acknowledge Barfield's intellectual contribution to our time, a contribution which has so far permeated primarily academic circles. Although these essays are testimony to his intellectual influence on his peers, they are not more than an indication of that impact, for unfortunately a collection of papers broad enough fully to reveal that was not feasible. Owen Barfield's thought ranges over many disciplines, reflecting his belief in the unity of knowledge — its "all in every part" character. A suggestion of that range is, in turn, reflected back to us in the pages that follow, through papers from diverse disciplines — scientific, literary, philosophical, religious.

There is no "early" or "late" Barfield (to accord with current intellectual fashion), he tells us emphatically in the interview with him that follows, "just the same Barfield all along." It is to that same Barfield that this volume is offered, as an expression of gratitude from those who have been inspired by his thought.

In expressing my appreciation to those who have made this book possible, I want first of all to say a special "thank you" to Owen Barfield for his thoughtful and patient efforts in connection with the interview he graciously granted. I also thank Maud Barfield for her hospitality during my stay in England at the time of the interview. To the contributors to this volume, whose enthusiasm and cooperation made what might have been a difficult task a great pleasure, I am most grateful. For his generous advice and suggestions, I want to express my appreciation to Reverend Walter Hooper. I would like to acknowledge my indebtedness to Drew University and my personal appreciation to the dean of the Graduate School, Bard Thompson, for making possible the context in which I prepared this volume. Beyond that, I would like to acknowledge the role of Drew University, to whom the scholarly community at large is indebted, in bringing Owen Barfield to this country originally and hastening a recognition of his work. My thanks go to the Drew Stenographic Services, to Mrs. Elizabeth Staples and her competent staff, for unscrambling my handwriting and my tape recordings with patience and skill.

S. S.

Drew University
November 1975

FOREWORD

The visible thread that runs through the essays in this volume is the persistent theme of Owen Barfield's life and thought: the evolution of consciousness and the idea central to that, the polarity of contraries. As far back as the early 1920s, he pointed out to me, he entitled an exercise book "Human Consciousness." No matter which of his books one has in hand, it is this theme that is at its core, and it was to the evolution of consciousness that he hoped, as a writer, to contribute, as he tells us in the conversation with him in this volume.

In a time when many are writing on the subject of consciousness, Barfield has rejected a superficial approach for a depth understanding of it and has arrived at what might be called a "consciousness ontology." The term is perhaps unwieldy or opaque, but I have wondered how else to refer to a theory of poetry that is admittedly a theory of knowledge, but most significantly, a theory of being. According to Barfield, consciousness and objective being are obverse and reverse sides of the same coin: there is a "unity of intelligence and nature" — a unity that recognizes, however, the independent, although interdependent, existence of each. In other words, he sees consciousness and objective being as distinguishable but not divisible. The nature of this interdependent relationship is that of a polarity of contraries, which is not to be understood merely as a "coincidence of opposites." It is rather that the two poles "exist by virtue of each other *as well as* at each other's expense."

It is on the dynamic interpenetration of polar opposites that the evolution of consciousness depends. In this Barfield follows Coleridge's dictum: "grant me a nature having two contrary forces, the one of which tends to expand infinitely, while the other strives to apprehend or find itself in this infinity and I will cause the world of intelligences with the whole system of their representations to rise up before you." The two forces that exist as contraries in polar tension, Barfield also identifies as the Poetic and the Prosaic. The Poetic tends to expand infinitely to create new meanings, while the Prosaic strives to apprehend and to identify distinctions in that infinity. The Poetic in isolation would be mere unconscious impulse without conscious awareness;

the Prosaic alone would be the existence of the machinery of analysis with nothing to analyze. The two counteracting correlative forces of the one nature coalesce and coagulate into the world of objects at one pole, while at the other pole, the self comes into being — a process of "separative projection." In this fundamental duality of self and world, of consciousness and nature, the two poles interpenetrate; consciousness and world evolve together. It is this awareness of our participation in the process of creation — the "unity of intelligence and nature" — which we lack, and which, if present in full measure, would amount to what Barfield calls "final participation."

The collection of essays in this book as a whole seems to be charged with a tensive polarity, so that the book is not only about polarity, but is itself a polarity — between two such extreme approaches as that of Mary Caroline Richards and that of David Bohm. Although the various essays represent distinct points of view, they are at the same time bound together in an underlying unity: the parts interpenetrate the whole by virtue of their relationship to Owen Barfield's thought. Even in those that are not papers on the subject of polarity, but are addressed more directly to Owen Barfield, polarity is implied: Norman O. Brown acknowledges implicitly the polarity of Poetic-Prosaic; Cecil Harwood recognizes the polarity in Owen Barfield's life; Howard Nemerov suggests the polarity exceptions/rules.

In this colloquy, David Bohm addresses himself to the core of Barfield's thought, and Coleridge's as well. He analyzes the "two forces of the one nature" and in so doing he describes the dynamics of the process of polarity itself. In the context of science, he writes of the polarity between "imaginative insight" — theory enfolded in an image — and "imaginative fancy" — the unfolding discursive process. He describes the two as aspects of what is one undivided mental movement. Since the implication of polar logic is that no form of insight remains relevant indefinitely, paradigms crumble and are reborn in a different form in the process of the evolution of consciousness. Harmony evolves from disharmony via imaginative insight and rational discourse and then falls back into disharmony as contradictions develop in fixed theory. This requires a new image or apprehension of the totality of the ratio, a "creative response to disharmony" that is dependent on the art of "intelligent perception."

On the one hand, Bohm is speaking of the process of polarity in the evolution of consciousness, in general, while on the other hand, Mary Caroline Richards, also pointing to the polarity harmony-disharmony, is speaking of the evolution of her consciousness, of the individual consciousness. Bohm writes of the interaction between theory and hypothesis. Richards writes of the polarity of contraries within herself, as a play between inner forces, a dialogue between conflicting impulses. But it is conflict that is a generative, transforming force, for Richards, the "fire of life." If Bohm's essay could be described as an exposition of the polarity of contraries, Richards' contribution could be considered a celebration of polarity — polarically opposite modes of the "one nature." Both papers indicate the underlying transforming process of polarity, the generative power of the opposition of the forces. "One wind, two directions," as Richards writes, evoking in one image what polarity is.

Considering the evolution of consciousness also from the perspective of science, and like Bohm, contending with scientific orthodoxy, R. H. Barfield, brother of Owen Barfield, breaks the taboo of our positivist culture against "turning the world upside down." He asks us to question the assumptions on which the Darwinian theory of evolution is based: the principles of natural selection and survival of the fittest. For they rule out consideration of the evolution of human consciousness. In conjunction with this, he asks for the scientific recognition of the validity of the subjective side of experience and of secondary qualities, necessary for the imaginative grasp of the process of the evolution of consciousness. But fear of turning the world "inside out" makes us cling to the old view that survival value alone accounts for life. The voices of science here, Bohm and Barfield, seem most concerned with the fixity of tradition, with orthodox scientific views. Bohm speaks of the need for creative response; Barfield emphasizes the weight of tradition in particular, positivist thought and its effect on our contemporary consciousness. The penalty for continuing to accept without question the orthodox Darwinian doctrine, of not awakening out of our "single vision" — the one-sidedness of objectivity — Barfield fears, may mean the destruction of our civilization.

On the other hand, we find concern for the disintegration of tradition and its effect on contemporary consciousness among the literary voices. The essay by Richard Hocks parallels, in the literary sphere, David Bohm's paper. Hocks analyzes the process of polarity in works of Coleridge and Eliot in a way similar to what Bohm has done in relation to scientific theory. Hocks points out that in the polar relation between "novelty and admitted truths," newness and tradition interpenetrate: only by way of the tradition is newness engendered and only when that happens is the tradition validated. His thesis is that, in this relationship of true polarity, the tradition suffers modification with the introduction of the new which, in turn, enlivens the tradition. The dynamic relation between newness and tradition is grounded in the process of polarity, in which "extremes meet" and undergo mutual transformation.

But the tradition fails to support the contemporary consciousness, according to Robert Preyer. His paper considers the effect of the loss of tradition, the crumbling of the paradigms, which afflicts the modern consciousness. Contemporary poets suffer from the inability to mediate between the transmitted symbols and modern conditions. The death of culture, the loss of a "providential order" which mediated the tradition, to which R. H. Barfield also referred, leaves a void in the modern consciousness and has, as its outcome, the failure of tone of the poets. The dialectic of literature is such, Preyer says, that when the tradition fails, poets turn to "fact" not "value," concurring in Barfield's view that "value" has been ignored in favor of "fact." Preyer tells us, however, that a tensive polarity between the two, between value-laden mediated experience or tradition and bare facts, the direct experience of the poets, is what keeps them "alive."

R. K. Meiners agrees that poets suffer in this situation of loss. He addresses himself to the subjective emptiness, the sickness of spirit that poets suffer as a result of the disintegration of tradition and says that this suffering is the modern problem and central subject of literature. He is primarily concerned with the isolation of the individual consciousness, which he describes as having become constricted and detached from tradition to the point of madness. In the polarity attachment/separation, the pole of separation predominates in respect to the individual consciousness. He fears, as does R. H. Barfield, that this detachment endangers man's survival. The metaphor of the flame, which serves for Richards to evoke the shaping and transforming process in the vessel, becomes for Meiners the metaphor of the devouring flame, which represents the isolated individual consciousness consuming itself. The penalty of consciousness is madness, he says, when the possibility that the individual consciousness participates a "prior world of consciousness" is denied. To realize this requires that we turn the world "inside out," as we heard before.

In his essay on Milton, Paul Piehler also writes of the cleavage in modern consciousness, as he describes the modification of the character of consciousness between 1500 and 1700 that is manifested in Milton's writings. Noting the importance of having a sense of the relativity of consciousness, he traces the shift from the "bondage of original participation" to the "bondage of materiality," from unity to division, and from value to fact, the last of which Preyer and Barfield have also noted. Piehler describes the change from a "visionary landscape" — that is, sacred landscape — to one which has become literal, ordinary — Paradise lost. In this landscape, bound to materiality, spirit is endangered, as Meiners, Preyer, and Barfield have warned. Reality is divided into interior and exterior, whereas what is required truly to regain Paradise is a dynamic relation between those two aspects of reality. What is required is double vision.

The landscape of the Underworld of Homer and Vergil is the subject of Colin Hardie's paper. Implicit here is the polarity of the contraries of upper and lower worlds. It is not seen in terms of turning the world "inside out," but rather there is the implication of turning it downside up, of revealing its underside. Hardie distinguishes between evocation of that landscape and descent into it, pointing out that the *Odyssey* is essentially an evocation of the Underworld, emphasizing the terrors of the descent, whereas Vergil's Underworld is decidedly a descent, enhanced with psychological depth. Underlying the paper is the idea of the crossing of the threshold and the correlative possibility of the transformation of consciousness.

The polarity enjoyment/contemplation is considered by Lionel Adey in his paper on *Hamlet*. Hamlet's dilemma, as Adey puts it, was that he could see but not feel, contemplate but not enjoy, the beauty he contemplates. Contemplation alone, an "observer's non-participation," breeds superficial judgment and drains the world of meaning. Yet enjoyment alone would lead to self-preoccupation. Either mode by itself is insufficient; both modes are mutually dependent polarities. The subjective pole of enjoyment — "that which one experiences from within" — requires also the objective pole of contemplation — "whatever one observes from without."

In his paper on etymology and meaning, G. B. Tennyson parallels and illustrates the evolution of consciousness with that of etymology. He discusses the relation of meaning to the history of consciousness and points to Owen Barfield's central thesis: the correlative change in language and in human consciousness. The polarity inner-outer concerns him as it has Paul Piehler and R. H. Barfield. But in this instance, it is examined in the context of changes in meanings of words. In the evolution of etymology itself in echoed the evolution of consciousness as it shifted from original participation — "true meaning" — to separation — "accurate account." But now, what Tennyson refers to as Owen Barfield's "redemption of etymology" propels us toward the possibility of final participation, in which there would be conscious participation in "true meaning." There is a similarity in this paper with Bohm's understanding of the birth of new images, as reflecting a new way of perceiving the world — the "re-birth of meaning."

As Owen Barfield has redeemed etymology for G. B. Tennyson, so he has redeemed romanticism for R. J. Reilly. Reilly holds that the Romantic impulse failed to come to maturity in the nineteenth century because it was caught up in a worldview uninterested in time and uncommitted to Christianity. Time was seen as unreal, but, he writes that Owen Barfield corrects this with his understanding, and it is Coleridge's as well, that time is not only not illusion, it is holy history. Although each essay recognizes it implicitly, if not explicitly, it is this aspect of Barfield's thought — his view of time in its polar relationship to history — that Reilly, in particular, emphasizes. It is in the Incarnation that there is a meeting of the polar opposites, God-history, timeless-temporal. Barfield's work, Reilly tells us, has brought this double vision to Romanticism and has accommodated Christianity and history to that movement. Full consciousness of the polarity man-God would be the goal of the process in time that is the evolution of consciousness. It would be final participation.

When the Romantic impulse is so propelled, then, according to the view put forth in Shirley Sugerman's essay on Coleridge, man himself will, in the evolution of consciousness, come to maturity. Imagination is the faculty, according to this analysis of Coleridge's philosophy, that makes possible the access of human consciousness to the process of polarity, the interpenetration of the two contrary forces of the one nature — the "seminal principle" of Coleridge's, as well as Owen Barfield's thought. Man will come into his own when the Romantic movement is propelled to the point at which man will speak from "the Kingdom" within, when he will, by virtue of a self-willed effort of imagination, be in a "directionally creator relation to the appearances."

This, however, raises the moral issue that has concerned Owen Barfield and is, as well, the subject of Clyde Kilby's paper: man's responsibility, in his use of the faculty of imagination, for the kind of world he creates. Kilby writes that ugliness is nature deformed, its very being changed. Evil and ugliness are not merely negative states, states of lack, but states in which there is positive destruction of form. When ugliness is considered analogous to evil, art is not dissociated from life; metaphysics and morality are related. For it is ontological deformity that constitutes ugliness: a thing *ought* to be what it *is*. In this correlation of the ugly and the evil, Kilby echoes Barfield's concern for the deformation of nature, unless man makes himself responsible for it. At the same time, he echoes the sense of several of the papers that the modern mode of consciousness is dangerous — a common madness-single vision.

Concluding with Kilby's paper on *aesthetic perception* in relation to the *integrity* of being and Richards' understanding of the *art* of transformation through conflict to *wholeness*, we have come full circle. Extremes meet — if we look back to Bohm's view that the *art* of intelligent *perception*, in response to disharmony, might make possible the revelation of a deep harmony — a *unity* underlying diversity. At the same time, we find in this volume an underlying unity: the voice of Owen Barfield, in its various tones, can clearly be heard through the diverse essays.

S. S.

Drew University
November 1975

I

Owen Barfield

"polarity . . . is not only a form of thought,
but also the form of life."

Owen Barfield: *Speaker's Meaning*

A CONVERSATION WITH OWEN BARFIELD

by

SHIRLEY SUGERMAN

The place of the following conversations was Owen Barfield's study in his home at Orchard View, South Darenth, Kent, England. They extended over several days during April of 1974, at which time Owen Barfield was in his seventy-sixth year. The sun was shining in the west window onto walls lined with books; the only sound was the steady ticking of the clock. An extraordinary sense of serenity and orderliness pervaded the study. We were sitting not far from his desk, before the mantle shelf, and directly in front of a picture of his father. He chose to refer to what we were doing as psychography, rather than strictly biography, because it emphasized the unity of the personal and intellectual or spiritual aspects of his life.

SS: Perhaps we might begin with where you are — as far as I know always have been — that is, in England. Do you have any particular feelings about England as a climate for writing?

OB: I have the feeling I am very English, although I am not like a large number of English people you see and hear about on the BBC and so forth.

SS: How would that be different?

OB: Well, I think it goes deeper.

SS: I would like to hear about that. Do you feel you need any particular environment or does a particular environment make a difference, in influencing a person's work? Or is it just happenstance, whether it's England, or India, or China? Does it matter?

OB: Yes, it certainly matters. It's so closely linked up with one's whole individuality and whatever created it — the parents you had, the upbringing you had, marriage, the friends you meet. It's very difficult to isolate the element called Englishness.

SS: That's pretty much what you were saying last night when you said that the situations in which you find yourself are very important, so that the country in which you find yourself, as your situation, would be extremely important.

OB: I think the close affinity that I feel with German, the German language and the way in which the German language can express philosophical ideas and thoughts more easily and accurately sometimes than English, together with the fact that I am nevertheless English, and tend to bring things down to earth, has been important. To that extent there is some resemblance, I think, to Coleridge — to compare small things with great. He anglicized the German philosophical inspiration at the time of the Romantic movement. Nobody else understood that or tried to at all. His whole task, as he felt it, was to bring that to English people. Now in the course of bringing it, it changes somewhat. The way in which it is expressed in English means that different aspects of it are emphasized. There is a certain element of bringing down to earth.

SS: In the light of your emphasis on the importance of the particular environment, it would be good to know something about your early life.

OB: How much am I to say about it? I was born in a London suburb at a time when London suburbs were not nearly so urban as they are now. I was the youngest of four children who had a very happy family life together. My father was a solicitor; my mother was an ardent feminist and she was also very musical. My father also was a lot more musical than I, and I became acquainted at a very early age with quite a number of pieces of classical music played as pianoforte duets. I realized afterwards that it had meant a tremendous lot to me, being always surrounded with music.

SS: Is that your father's picture I see behind you on the mantle?

OB: That's right. He used to play only the bass. He wasn't educated to the piano from childhood, as my mother was. He learned what he knew after they were married.

SS: Would you want to elaborate further on the significance of music in your life?

OB: I remember once I put it this way to myself: supposing (a wildly hypothetical question) you were offered the choice of doing without any poetry for the rest of your life or doing without any music. Well — I would give up the poetry.

SS: What about your religious background? It is my impression that you said at one time that you were brought up without religious beliefs —

OB: Yes. I was brought up definitely without religious beliefs and there was in fact something of a bias against them. There was certainly an anti-clerical atmosphere. My mother and father were both brought up in rather narrow, nonconformist circles and they both broke away from it. At the same time my father particularly had a tremendous feeling, something like reverence, for the moral teachings in the gospels — especially through Tolstoy. If one was encouraged by something that had been said to be a bit flippant, for instance, about Christianity or the gospels, one was ticked off for it definitely. And a curious survival was that in the house where I spent most of my boyhood we had a tennis court and we weren't allowed to play tennis on Sunday morning, but we could play on Sunday afternoon!

SS: Well, that's an interesting definition of the Sabbath Day!

OB: Yes. Anyway, I think the relevance of this is that, when I first began to think about such things as literature and art and religion, I had no background to speak of and my mind was a kind of *tabula rasa*. There was nothing particular to hold fast to.

SS: I wouldn't have guessed that. I would have guessed that you had a more traditional religious upbringing.

OB: But you'll see it was rather important that it wasn't there, when it comes to the early books I wrote. It's awfully difficult to distinguish when you go back to your early life between a retrospect that you are making of it from your present point of view, looking at it from outside and saying "this and this was happening to me," from what you actually experienced and thought was happening at the time. You didn't think of it in those terms at all at the time.

SS: That's your view of history in general, isn't it?

OB: Perhaps it is really. If I now go on to say that this business of being brought up without any religious belief created a kind of vacuum in me, and I think it did, that doesn't mean I was aware of it at the time. I didn't say to myself: "there is a vacuum in me, what shall I do about it?"

SS: But retrospectively —

OB: Retrospectively I can see that it was so and you can put it if you like that I felt one wanted to know if there was any meaning in life. I should add, perhaps, that the atmosphere in my family was predominantly critical and skeptical. Not only in the matter of religion, but about, for instance, the kind of people one met. One was apt to suspect any kind of enthusiasm as being a bit humbugging and an affectation. In fact it was a very common word in my family, that someone was "affected." I was led to see myself too in those terms and I suspected anything in the nature of what seemed like powerful emotional experience, in terms of such things as poetry, as being a kind of self-deception. I had to justify it to myself, so to speak, before I could feel confident that I wasn't being an affected ass.

SS: Yes. You had to justify something which you later developed a whole theory to justify.

OB: Yes, quite. That's the essence I think.

SS: I was also thinking of your use of the word "enthusiasm," which you used when writing, in *Saving the Appearances,* of man re-speaking what was once spoken by God. Now you speak of enthusiasm being considered, perhaps, an affectation. It seems to me that those terms represent two extremes. It's almost as if you had to achieve some kind of balance there to justify what you really wanted to feel.

OB: Yes, but not only what I wanted to feel — what I really did feel. I suspected myself of not *genuinely* feeling these things. This is where it begins to link on with my books. At about the age of twenty, I suppose — I had been reading some poetry before and liked poetry fairly well — there was a sudden rapid increase in my appreciation, particularly of lyric poetry. I was fond of poetry, but it was about that age that it became a much more powerful, immediate experience, together with the impulse to try to write poetry myself. Well now, that was the only thing I had, so to speak, to fill the vacuum — the strong experience that poetry gave me. And on that I tried to convict myself of believing it because I wanted to believe it, I mean of believing that it meant more than just my subjective feelings and that there was something behind it, more to it. And I was conditioned strongly to think that any theory of that kind was simply a self-deception. So one went ahead and tried to state exactly what was happening and what could be deduced from it. That really was the origin of the book *Poetic Diction.* If you read it as a whole, as I said in the Introduction to the 2nd Edition, it isn't really the right name for it; it's much more than a book about poetic diction; it is a theory of poetry as a form of knowledge.

SS: If it is a theory of poetry as a form of knowledge, and if, as one learns in your succeeding books, knowledge is the equivalent of being, then poetic diction would be a theory of being, finally.

OB: Yes, because that is the kind of knowledge that it is. If it's knowledge at all, it's as much being as knowledge. It's immediate experience and not just head work.

SS: Not just intellectual.

OB: But you see, again this is looking back on it, when one puts it that way. Even at the time when I began to write *Poetic Diction* I couldn't have put it that way.

SS: So this is again a retrospective point of view.

OB: Yes. Well, what particularly impressed me, from this point of view of the powerful experience one could get from hearing lyric poetry, was the way in which a particular word, in a particular passage, in a particular context, produces a kind of magic which alters the meaning of the word, gives the word an entirely new meaning. I wrote an article on the word "ruin" and the various poetic contexts in which it had been used and how its own meaning had developed poetically and so forth. It may have been to some extent rather dilettantish, but anyhow I did it. And it was really out of that article that the whole book, *Poetic Diction,* grew.

SS: It strikes me that what you said earlier about the individual and the environment you are now saying about the word in its context.

OB: Yes. The word in its context, which context had been carefully selected by the poet. The poet has given new meaning to the word by the particular context and the way he uses it.

SS: I was thinking of that in relation to the individual, as you said before, in the context of the country in which he lives, the individual and his environment. There seems to be an analogy there between the two worlds, the world of the word in its context and the world of the individual in the context in which he finds himself.

OB: Yes. I suppose there is. I don't think I had thought of that before. It's a new one on me.

The other thing that came from this rather sudden growth of intensity in this period with poetry was a vivid awareness of the way in which one's experience in poetry reacted on one's experience of the world outside, especially the world of nature. The obvious example is Wordsworth's nature poetry. It isn't just the poetry you enjoy. When you go back to the mountains or the woods afterwards they are something different.

SS: Isn't that what a great artist does? — Creates new worlds for us.

OB: Yes. As I say this was a very vivid experience and of course it was a support to any theory I was feeling my way toward, without knowing it, that poetry is a form of knowledge, because you felt you knew more about the things you see, about what you were looking at. It wasn't just that you *thought* that you knew more. You *knew* more.

SS: Then we could say that poetry is a way of knowledge as much as the sciences or mathematics or what have you.

OB: Yes, that is how it came to me. I wouldn't now limit it to poetry or even art in general, but at the time that was the way I found it. Perhaps if I were to read these two sentences from the Introduction to *Romanticism Comes of Age,* it might help. "Thus, without any particular exertion or theorizing on my part, I had had two things strongly impressed on me, firstly that the poetic or imaginative use of words enhances their meanings and secondly that those enhanced meanings may reveal hitherto unapprehended parts or aspects of reality. All this seemed to promise a way out of the vacuum and I began to pursue my investigations more systematically." That is a fair summing up of what we've been saying.

SS: Yes, and it's a good way for me to understand your impulse to write.

OB: Yes, the impulse was to write the kind of stuff that would have the kind of effect on others that we've just been speaking about. You could put it that I wanted to contribute to the evolution of consciousness.

SS: Right — a good reason!

OB: Yes, although I was also quite ambitious and anxious to have a reputation and be talked about.

SS: Well, I'd be very suspicious if you hadn't had that also. . . . You once suggested that I stop to see your old Oxford College, Wadham, and I have wondered, perhaps others have also, how it is that you chose Wadham.

OB: Wadham is a famous law college. A good many great lawyers were trained there, Sir John Simon and others, and when people hear that I was at Wadham College and was for most of my life a solicitor, they're apt to jump to the conclusion that I went to the university with the intention of becoming a lawyer.

SS: Isn't that why you chose Wadham?

OB: No, the reason I chose Wadham was a very simple one. I'd seen Wadham. I liked the building and the gardens very much and it had to do with my anxiety to get a scholarship if possible, which I'm glad to say I did. It had nothing whatever to do with my subsequently going into the law. At that time I never dreamed of going into the law.

SS: Have you accounted for the intense increase in appreciation of poetry of which we also spoke earlier?

OB: No, I don't think so. You are a certain kind of person when you are born. I don't believe this nonsense about everybody being the same and only being changed by their environment. You bring something with you, whatever it is.

SS: You sound like a geneticist. It's the same line of argument, even though their basic philosophy may be different. But in both it is understood that you do bring something very definite with you.

OB: Well, yes. You might call me one. If you like, my interest has been in genetic psychology.

SS: It's a whole field of study now.

OB: I suppose it is. I don't suppose it means what I do. It's mixed up with genes, isn't it?

SS: Yes. It's mixed up with genes, but then, genes are metaphors also.

OB: Yes, but they don't know that!

SS: Isn't that what makes the difference between the way you view genetic psychology and they do? . . . I'd like to get back to what you said earlier — that you had never dreamed of going into the law.

OB: Well now we've come on to removing the misunderstanding which a good many people seem to be under who are interested in my literary career, and that is the connection between the literary part of my activities and the legal period.

SS: Yes, I know that people are often quite astonished when they learn that your vocation was that of a solicitor and that you haven't spent all of your time writing.

OB: What happened was this. I was already about thirty-three years old before I even thought of going into the law. I had already written and published three books, *History in English Words, Poetic Diction,* and *The Silver Trumpet.* I should put it this way: I can't say that I'd established a reputation because I certainly hadn't, but I'd laid the foundations of my literary output so to speak, because *Poetic Diction* in particular, was and still is what you might call a fundamental Barfield work. And I could never have written it if I'd gone straight into law from Oxford.

SS: This refers back to our conversation of yesterday when we were talking about the earlier and the later Barfield. There isn't any such, is there?

OB: No. Very definitely not, no. I have always been saying the same thing. Only the literary impulse, activity, whatever you call it, was largely under eclipse during quite a long period — about twenty-five years or more, when I was engaged in being a solicitor.

SS: So for those twenty-five years, really, from the early thirties until the early fifties, your literary career was extremely limited.

OB: I kept up a contact with things like literature and philosophy, partly through my friendship with C. S. Lewis. I used to go to stay with him regularly. And partly through a few people who knew about *Poetic Diction* or my other books, for instance, *History in English Words,* and who would — at rare intervals — write and ask me to read a paper. An example of that was somewhere in the late thirties or early forties, when I did a paper for St. Catherine's Hall, Oxford, "Poetic Diction and Legal Fiction." A good many years after that, when Lewis was doing a kind of *Festschrift* for Charles Williams, he asked if I had anything and I sent him this. It was first published in *Essays Presented to Charles Williams.* That was the article that long afterwards led to my original invitation to lecture in America. So although I was under eclipse, I wasn't quite. I did occasionally manage to do something literary. It maintained my contact with the literary life. The other contact was that I was by that time very much committed to and engrossed in the anthroposophical movement of Rudolf Steiner. They were very glad of anything I could write, in their periodicals and so forth, and I did quite a lot of that. A good many of them were reprinted in the book *Romanticism Comes of Age.*

SS: Was this the time of your acquaintance with the Inklings, or was that later?

OB: I was well acquainted with the Inklings but not quite so closely as is sometimes assumed. Or not so frequently. Lewis and I became friends when we were both undergraduates, but we didn't develop a really close association until after our time as undergraduates had finished. We were both very keen on writing good poetry, if we could. That was our main connection. But we soon came to talk, while going for walks and so forth, about philosophical matters as well, which in any case are closely connected with what is good poetry and what is not. The Inklings were, simply, a group of individuals, friends of Lewis who acquired the habit of dropping into his rooms on one evening a week. There was no formal society or statutes or rules or by-laws. And they didn't always all come. Sometimes a very few, sometimes more. It didn't begin until some years after we'd both finished as undergraduates, when he was well established as a tutor and fellow at Magdalen. It may be that I was already by that time living in town and only going down there for an occasional weekend. Certainly during most of the time during which the Inklings were meeting, I was only really on the fringe of them because I could very rarely attend. They consisted of Lewis himself; later on his brother Warren Lewis; J. R. R. Tolkien; Charles Williams, who was in Oxford during the later part of the war, but of course remained in close association and close friendship with Lewis after he went back to London; Nevill Coghill; Lewis's doctor, Humphry Havard; J. R. R. Tolkein's son, Christopher, rather later; Lord David Cecil occasionally, and one or two others. Hugo Dyson, originally of Reading University, was a very regular attendant.

SS: The Inklings are sometimes called a romantic religious movement. I'd appreciate your comments on the question as to whether your books are primarily philological or basically religious or — aren't these two, by virtue of your understanding of the nature of language, really inseparable?

OB: I would have thought that the point of my books was to reveal them as ultimately inseparable.

SS: Would you say a little more about that?

OB: Philology in the sense of the history of language, especially the etymological and semantic history of language, is itself a symptom or function if you like of the evolution of consciousness. And you can take it either way, you can either approach the evolution of consciousness through language, particularly the history of language, which is what I did in my earliest book, *History in English Words*. That was at the time when I was getting at the evolution of consciousness through the changes in words, and in the meanings of words. Or you could take it the other way and could start off by finding out things, reading things, knowing things about the evolution of consciousness, and you could see how that affects itself in the changes of meanings and changes of forms of words.

SS: Then the "Word," or Logos, would clearly be a fundamental religious category or a concept, as well as being the foundation of language.

OB: That is almost self-evident. When you use the word "Logos," you are laying your finger on the link or the oneness between whatever language is and whatever Christianity or religion is. And that might perhaps lead us back for a moment to what I said when I was talking about *Poetic Diction*. I mentioned that *Poetic Diction* grew out of that article on the word "ruin." In the original form the article finished up by quoting verse 1, chapter 1 of St. John's Gospel, which is where "the Word" is mentioned. I had the feeling that it was somehow right — "this is along my line" — without properly knowing why. I didn't know anything about Neo-Platonism or what happened to the doctrine of the Logos in the course of the history of philosophy or of religion at that time. I just liked the sound of it.

SS: Well we might say then that you knew, but you didn't know that you knew.

You have spoken of your debt to both Steiner and Coleridge and I was wondering how they influenced you.

OB: It would be best if I started off with Steiner, probably, although I'd heard of Coleridge and read some of Coleridge long before I'd ever heard of Steiner. I think I'd better go back a little to my earlier years, to the time when I left Oxford and was not engaged in any regular occupation. For six or seven years I was a gentleman of leisure, much of which I spent in writing *History in English Words* and *Poetic Diction.* I also did quite a lot of reading and studying and at that time I renewed such acquaintance as I had from school with the Greek and Latin languages, in which I'd got very rusty. I also learned Italian in order to read Dante and, during that period, I read the late Platonic *Dialogues,* which are not so much about ethics but more about the nature of perception, as well as Aristotle's psychology, *De Anima* — with great excitement. A special reason for the excitement was because at the same time I had begun to grasp Steiner's teaching. It was half that and half the way in which I had been approaching the question of philology, the history of words, the way words change their meanings. I became very much aware of the ineffectiveness of any current English translation of these *Dialogues* of Plato, dealing with the nature of perception, because they used words — words which perhaps were even derived from the Greek words in the text or if not derived from the Greek, were derived from the Latin translation of that Greek word — but which had come to mean something entirely different. They were talking about abstractions. Plato wasn't.

SS: The translator would be looking back on another kind of world, another stage of consciousness.

OB: Yes, and without knowing it, he'd be converting it all into a replica of his own. He would be misreading what he was finding in Plato because he was rephrasing it in a terminology which had only come into existence later, in his own time.

SS: And instead of *recreating* a consciousness of the fifth century, he would be translating out of the twentieth-century consciousness.

OB: That's right. He would be reflecting back his twentieth-century consciousness onto the text.

SS: And with that light he was distorting the language of the fifth and fourth centuries.

OB: That is to some extent dealt with in my book *Poetic Diction,* where I call it "logomorphism." On this aspect, and this connection, particularly with Steiner, the chapter in *Romanticism Comes of Age* called "Thinking and Thought" is, I think, relevant. I had this conviction about the evolution of consciousness as displayed in the history of the changes in meaning of words. I don't think that would have been enough by itself to produce the kind of almost revelatory quality which I seem to find in these old books, like the late Platonic *Dialogues*. I was becoming more and more familiar with Rudolf Steiner, who — and you see here it's very difficult to put it without reading or explaining Steiner.

SS: Well, try it and I'll ask you questions where I don't understand.

OB: A great deal of anthroposophy and its teaching is concerned with principles of the human being other than purely intellectual or purely physical, something between the two; for example what he calls the etheric body and there's also an etheric earth, which is neither exclusively mental nor yet physical. It is neither really.

SS: It wouldn't be equated with spirit, either?

OB: Yes, equated with it but only at a later stage — only in something the same way as the physical world is also related to the spirit, not equated with it. No, it is sharply distinguishable from spirit, pure spirit so to speak, but all the same, you are getting nearer the spirit if you are dealing with and experiencing the etheric than you are if you are stuck in the exclusively physical.

SS: This is a realm then between the spirit and the physical.

OB: Yes, and he made it clear to me that the Greeks in particular really lived in an experience of this etheric. Our thoughts, by comparison with the thoughts the Greeks could have, are really a kind of shadow of the real living thoughts cast by the impact of these living thoughts on the physical brain. We get a sort of after-echo or shadow back from the physical brain of what the real thoughts are.

SS: Don't you think this was what Plato was picturing in his description of the cave?

OB: Yes, certainly. And it also comes out in what the Greeks were able to do with their sculpture. They didn't have to measure the length from the elbow to the shoulder and so forth; they actually experienced in the formative force that was creating the body. That was what enabled them to produce those marvelous statues.

SS: This was something that they "knew," rather than a reflexive awareness.

OB: This was something that they experienced, rather than knew. That was made clear to me by Steiner and it seemed to me to be obviously true. I suppose what we want to get at here is the connection between what can be called my own thinking and Steiner's. That's why I'm going into all this, to try to make clear how it looks to me when I look back. Another thing, on which the light that Steiner threw is very important and is closely related to what I've been saying, is his placing of the history of natural science as an integral part of the evolution of consciousness. That was something which I'd been feeling toward myself in a dim and groping way but which he set out in crystal clearness to me. That you'll find, in my own language, put most clearly in *Saving the Appearances*.

SS: As part of the separative process.

OB: Yes, the separative process as positively seen — "positively," because it is what makes union possible; you can't have union without separation.

SS: In order to have relation you need distance, as Martin Buber has said.

I wanted to ask you about what seemed to me to be one of your favorite phrases or at least one that you've often used in your lectures and conversations. That is "residue of unresolved positivism," which you've often referred to as "RUP" and I wonder if you'd say again now what it means and how unresolved positivism gets to be resolved, if it does.

OB: This is of course something quite different from the sense in which I have just been using the word "positively." Awareness of RUP is in itself a kind of overcoming of positivism. Positivism is the philosophical statement of the position that there is an unbridgeable gulf between mental experience or the mental world on the one hand and the objective world, the outside world of nature on the other. That position was formulated finally and most clearly by Descartes. Of course, it was coming about in the course of the evolution of consciousness long before Descartes was born.

SS: But it became epitomized by him.

OB: He formulated it.

SS: And this is what we refer to as the mind/body dichotomy.

OB: Yes. Well, *unresolved* positivism occurs when that conviction, that imagination, that way of looking at mind and body remains in fact in a man's mind even though he may have in philosophical theory rejected or resolved it. For instance, someone like — well any of the subjective idealist philosophers of the nineteenth century. They wrote books which showed that that unbridgeable gulf was not really unbridgeable because it wasn't really there. Nevertheless in other things they said, when they were referring to science or any particular subject matter other than philosophy, they would still assume it was there.

SS: You're speaking about something that I recall in Coleridge. I'm thinking of Coleridge's distinction between an idea one has and an actual experience of that idea.

OB: Yes, many people have the idea, but very few have experienced the connection. That is the primary difference then between them and Steiner or Coleridge. That's unresolved positivism. Then there's the *residue* of unresolved positivism, which is what you get in people who think they've realized that there's such a thing as unresolved positivism. People like Jung, I'm referring to, I think, here. Who nevertheless themselves, when it comes to the crunch as it were, when the chips are down, you find are thinking of things like mind, or the unconscious mind, as something that is enclosed in a specific physical body. They're not thinking of it as something which transcends the separateness of an individual human being's physical body.

SS: Even when Jung speaks of the collective unconscious?

OB: Jung is very ambiguous. There are passages in Jung where he very definitely does show that he has this residue of unresolved positivism. He calls the unconscious "collective," and he says also that it is a residuum of innumerable racial memories or something like that. He's thinking of the whole historical series of individual human beings as collecting up the collective unconscious.

SS: So it is a collectivity?

OB: Yes.

SS: Rather than a matrix in which one lives — that understanding of collective unconscious.

OB: The collective unconscious is really understood only if you see it not as something which arose out of the aggregation of a number of experiences had by individual human beings but as something out of which the human individual and his physical body originally arose. There are other passages in Jung where he does speak of archetypes as if he meant it that way. But I accuse him of RUP because more often he speaks in the other way.

SS: Is there an example other than Jung?

OB: Yes. A. N. Whitehead in his book *Science and the Modern World*. He traces the way in which the history of science arose out of this dichotomy between body and mind, and in a way shows that it can't be maintained philosophically. And then — for practical purposes — he is prepared to throw it all away. I was struck by something I found in Berdyaev's which showed he'd overcome even the residue, I thought. It seems to me I found that all of these people who were writing idealistically or Jungian-ly about the relation between mind and body, although they were ostensibly overcoming the gulf, were really thinking in terms of it at the bottoms of their imaginations.

SS: If one has no residue of unresolved positivism, one understands experientially that mankind has arisen in mind and body out of an unconscious matrix.

OB: Yes. One experientially understands it, and therefore one doesn't forget it when one starts to talk about other things.

SS: It's a living experience.

OB: You'll find this in the last chapter of the book *Speaker's Meaning*. I think that it is largely due to the tremendous, the deep incision made by Darwinism in contemporary thought.

SS: You mean the dichotomy has been deepened by Darwinism?

OB: The inability to really imaginatively bridge the dichotomy. People like Jung who seem to be bridging it, the gulf between subject and object and so forth, you find them nevertheless imaginatively thinking in terms of Darwinian evolution; which you can't do if you really are convinced that there is this origin from what you just now called a matrix of consciousness. You have got to give up the ordinary view of Darwin but somehow they can't give that up.

SS: Harry's article (Dr. Harry Barfield) will be on this. If one does have a residue of unresolved positivism, then would you tell me something of how it could be resolved? I think most of us are caught in what you call that residue.

OB: Well, it is a very big problem of course. Because it is one thing to overcome it as theory and another to overcome it as experience. What you called "understanding experientially" comes somewhere between the two. To overcome it as ordinary daily experience would mean you would have to become a different kind of human being. As it is, we can live responsible controlled self-conscious lives, self-conscious because we are separated, isolated in our individual bodies; and it is out of that separation that we envisage the positivist separation between mind and matter. If you begin to drop that experience, the danger of course is that you lose your self-consciousness, you sort of dissolve into a mushily "selfless" condition — which is what quite a lot of young people seem to be trying for now in the world, by way of drugs or some kind of meditation without tears.

SS: What you're saying, really, is that one must experience first a kind of death in order to come to that kind of life.

OB: Yes, and you've also got to get the strength somehow to do for yourself what the physical body itself does for you as long as you have unresolved positivism.

SS: I can understand, then, our tremendous resistance to giving up that residue.

OB: Yes, I think that is the root of it, that fear and it is a well justified fear.

SS: Perhaps it is a well justified defense against the dissolution of ourselves as persons, if we have the feeling that that might happen.

OB: Yes, exactly.

SS: But now it sounds as though you're talking about a tension one must live in, between a sense of being separate and a sense of being attached — the polarity of separation and attachment.

OB: Very much so. It was because of that, because I thought he appreciated that, that I was attracted by Laing's first book.

SS: You felt that Ronald Laing appreciated that?

OB: Yes. His first book — I wasn't so sure about *The Politics of Ex-*

FINAL PARTICIPATION

perience. Of course this is also connected very strongly, not only with your relation with nature, whether you feel yourself isolated or separated, but with other human beings as well.

SS: Yes. Laing wonders where the line is between self and others, especially in his second book.

OB: It's a line but also a kind of life-line in a way, because you can't have a self unless you are prepared to merge yourself in others, in a sympathetic way as well as being separate from them. It's all very complicated.

SS: It sounds very complicated, but what it seems that you are saying is that it is necessary to maintain a precarious balance between separation of self from *not-self* and attachment of self to *not-self*. It is a very delicate balance between self-encapsulation and self-loss or fusion. In that balance there is a tension and one lives in that tension between the two extremes.

OB: Yes, that of course is also where polarity comes in. That kind of tension is what polarity means.

SS: Right. But the people who are trying to lose themselves or immerse themselves, in something other than or beyond themselves, by way of drugs, or various counter-culture methods, it seems to me, may have the right goal in mind, but they have a method that's not so good.

OB: I wouldn't say the right goal, I would have thought they are swinging away to the other end of the pendulum in a way — because there's too much isolation, too much separation, their only idea is to get rid of the separation and to get rid of isolation. Actually, if you got rid of it altogether you'd be as badly off or worse, although in a different way than you are with it, because you'd cease to exist.

SS: All Eros, as once we were saying, is Thanatos. Either extreme is death.

OB: Yes.

SS: Would you like to continue with Steiner now?

OB: I emphasized that the way he dealt with any subject in terms of the etheric was a kind of remedy for unresolved positivism, but Steiner also wrote two or three books in which he justified his position philosophically. The best known of these is called the *Philosophy of Freedom*. It used to be called the *Philosophy of Spiritual Activity* in an earlier edition. That book, more than any other, enabled me to overcome my own unresolved positivism intellectually; and also to see that Coleridge had done the same, and how he did it. There's a very close connection there I think between what Steiner meant to me and what Coleridge did.

SS: I am interested to understand the difference between what Steiner meant to you and what Coleridge did.

OB: A main difference — apart from his immeasurably greater stature — is Steiner's understanding of the etheric. What Coleridge was concerned to do for his generation, if he could, was to refute positivism intellectually and logically. I find it very difficult to recall the stages by which I became really well acquainted with Coleridge as a thinker.

SS: When do you think you first came to understand Coleridge?

OB: That's what I can't make out. I find it very hard to specify. I really only got right into Coleridge when I began to teach at Drew University in 1964.

SS: Aside from the historical record would you say that your understanding of polarity is mainly due to your work with Coleridge?

OB: Well now what do you mean by understanding? My *experience* of polarity I owed to Steiner largely, because everything he writes is in terms of polarity — he doesn't philosophize about polarity in his philosophical books, but in his nonphilosophical, scientific, or spiritual-scientific writings everything is presented in terms of polarity. It's taken for granted so to speak. What you get there is the imaginative experience of it, as a matter of course. And heaps of his followers think in terms of polarity without ever having read any Coleridge or ever feeling a need to justify it philosophically.

SS: I am thinking of your articulation of the notion, when you quote, for instance, Coleridge's statement "grant me a nature having two contrary forces."

OB: Yes, the articulation of polarity or the philosophizing of it and the making polarity itself a basis of a philosophical system or structure is Coleridge, very much so. Steiner doesn't make it the basis of a philosophy, but it is in fact the basis of his whole way of interpreting the world.

SS: Would you say that the difference then is that Steiner is thinking and writing *out of* a clear, experiential kind of understanding of polarity, whereas Coleridge is philosophizing *about* polarity?

OB: Yes, that I would say in general — but not of course that Coleridge had *no* such experience. But when Steiner philosophizes, which he did in his earlier books, he doesn't in a sense get as far as polarity. He leaves that for his nonphilosophical works. His philosophical books are concerned with justifying the possibility of another form of knowledge than the positivist one. Looking back it seems, there has always been some sort of affinity in me for Coleridge. It's all very mysterious. I can't get much further than that. When it came to writing a book on Coleridge, I was finding out more and more of the things he had said that exemplify his concept of polarity and the way in which he saw polarity as basic to all objective knowledge of the world; but I already knew that was so; I was only finding all the various places where it could be shown.

SS: You know we talked about polarity a good bit, but we haven't talked about what it is, or what polarity means. You once said to me that you would describe your philosophy as objective idealism, and I was wondering if you would relate this to the idea of polarity — polarity of the subject-object, conscious-unconscious, man-nature. Yes?

OB: Very definitely I should because the primary polarity, as I have always seen it, and as I think Coleridge saw it, is a polarity between subject-object, which can also be characterized, though the two don't exactly coincide, as a polarity between man and nature. Now if one asks what one means by objective idealism, perhaps the best way to approach it is to ask what is meant by *subjective* idealism. I think the general position of subjective idealism is that there are two kinds of idealism, one being a Platonic idealism where the Ideas are conceived as having a kind of independent, separate existence of their own, whereas subjective idealism treats ideas as a subjective process in individual human minds but nevertheless, in the development of this philosophy, it presents them as being more real than the objective world. I must say here that all this has to be very superficially expressed, in an attempt to give a short answer to your question. You can say, then, that the subjective idealists see the two disjunctively: either you believe in Platonic Ideas or you believe in ideas more in the modern sense, but nevertheless also conceive of those ideas as being in some way as real, or more real, than the objective world. Objective idealism contends that that disjunction is itself an unreal one, and that reality, individual being, however you think of it, consists in the polarity between the subjectivity of the individual mind and the objective world which it perceives. They are not two things, but they are one and the same thing and what you call the objective world is merely one pole of what is a unitary process and what we call subjective experience is the other pole, but they are not really divided from each other. I don't think I can put it shortly any more clearly than that.

SS: I think you've put it more fully in *Saving the Appearances*.

OB: Yes, that's true. I tried to put it in *Saving the Appearances,* treating it there especially from an historical point of view. I would say that the attempt to express it philosophically was more fully worked out in *Worlds Apart,* which could be characterized possibly as almost a presentation in dialogue form of objective idealism.

SS: I would like it if you could clarify for me your understanding of polarity in relation to the evolution of consciousness.

OB: It's awfully difficult to try and put it shortly and not superficially. Polarity, I think, can be conceived in two ways: one timelessly, outside of time, and the other as a process in time.

SS: Within history?

OB: Or any process in time including organic growth, vegetables, animals and so forth, biological growth. But in the timeless aspect, it is what Coleridge called "Two forces of one Power." Looked at either way it's equally true to say you're talking about one thing as it is to say that you're talking about two things; the opposition between the two is essential, on the other hand it is an opposition which itself characterizes or forms true unity, true identity. It's really hard to put.

SS: Yes and yet I would like to ask another question which occurs to me now. Do you image or conceive this as a *tension* between those two opposites or as a *coincidence* of those opposites, or perhaps I might even say as a *fusion* of those opposites? I would appreciate it if you could clarify that aspect of it.

OB: If you have one Power consisting of two forces, then, if you say they have been "fused," you may mean they are no longer two, but are one. So I think your first suggestion, that tension is an essential feature of polarity, is nearer the truth. This is all getting very abstract.

SS: Yes, it is abstract, and I know that you favored Coleridge's suggestion that we must raise the idea to the experiential level. But I am trying, now, verbally to sort this out a little bit. I know we spoke earlier of the tendency nowadays for people to run away from separation, from the isolation of the individual and of the individual ego into "fusion." I think that's why I was trying to get clear about the "two forces," that is, whether they are a tensive kind of polarity or whether there is the same sort of fusion that some of the young people seem to be seeking.

OB: Definitely not the same kind of fusion that you have attributed to the young people — the oriental type of complete fusion which, in effect, means disappearance of the individual pole altogether. Certainly not that. The whole point of polarity is that the more opposition there is, the greater the unity. That is the mystery of it, and therefore you can't, as I see it (and of course as some others see it as well, I'm not talking just about Barfield's thought) — the point is that you can't, as a human being, really become universal, except by way of polarity. You may disappear, cease to exist altogether, but you can't really *acquire* anything that could reasonably be called universal consciousness except by becoming still more individual than you are now. The more individual you become, if it is really individual and not just simply self-centeredness, the more universal you are.

SS: Well, that's really very helpful. I wanted to bring that out because there seems to be a good bit of confusion on just this matter and I felt, several years ago, when you and Norman O. Brown were talking, that this was the essential difference between your view of things and his. I think that he saw fusion of opposites as the desirable goal and I felt then that you were talking of the tension of opposites.

OB: Yes, I think that's quite a fair way of putting it. He saw fusion of opposites as involving the disappearance of the opposition and of the tension, or so I felt.

SS: Right. And you see the opposition as persisting and even intensifying.

OB: Yes, and at the same time, being more and more of a unity. And it's a mystery, you can't get away from that.

SS: It's a paradox?

OB: It's a paradox, yes, in terms of abstract thought. It's a mystery as it begins to be experienced.

SS: Now you're beginning to sound like Gabriel Marcel.

OB: Well, Gabriel Marcel thought very highly of *Saving the Appearances*. He had a scheme for having it translated into French, but in the end nothing came of it.

SS: I think that the way you have distinguished between tension in polarity and fusion of opposites is very useful.

OB: It's essential. If one is going to think in terms of polarity at all, then one must think in that way. I began by saying I would first of all consider polarity in its timeless aspect. I think what you have just said, in the contrast made for instance between Norman O. Brown and myself, has already really entered into the concept of polarity as a process in time. Now I don't think there should be any difficulty about being able to consider it *either* timelessly *or* as a process in time, because as I see it, the whole relation between time and eternity is that eternity appears in time as process. Or as Plato put it many years ago, "time is a moving image of eternity."

Perhaps it's best now to go back to Coleridge's language. When he is writing or thinking about polarity as a process in time, he tends to use other phrases, not so much the word "polarity," as either "productive unity" or, at least on one occasion, "separative projection." Conceived as a process in time, you can say that the unity comes before the separation of tension and opposition and is restored afterwards. But, seen from eternity, so to speak, the unity is there all the time and the tension or separation is there all the time.

SS: Doesn't Coleridge also speak of "detachment so as to reproduce attachment"? That would clearly be a process in time. In order for there to be attachment, there must, prior to that, be separation.

OB: And then again at the highest level of all you can see it as trinitarianism, either theology or cosmology. The Father, from his unity, projects the Son, the Logos, and then ultimately there's a unity on another plane, another level, the Holy Spirit.

SS: Would you elaborate on that a little?

OB: I said "trinitarianism," but that doesn't mean of course that the concept or imagination, whatever you call it, is limited to Christian theology. You find this three-fold conception of the nature of being and of human being itself going through the great religions of the world, and the great myths of the world prior to Christianity.

SS: Yes. I find in the gods in the Oriental religions the tripartite model. I was thinking of Shiva as the creator, preserver, and destroyer, just for one example.

I think it would be good if we could go on now to take a retrospective look at the manifestation of polarity in your own life.

OB: I can't say that during much of my life I've been aware of myself as living in polarity, or that I thought formally in those terms. Looking back, it's quite true that there does seem to have been a rather marked element of it. It may be that there is in most human beings. It does come out, I think, very strongly, in the fact that I went into the law, law being almost by definition the very opposite of the poetic. It's abstract, and so forth, and the poetic is living and organic, or however you like to put it. And my being instinctively in the one and being compelled to live with my mind and activity very much in the other did lead, over a great part of my life, I suppose, to a kind of polarity as tension, very much as tension. And the tension at one stage became so violent that, together with other pressures, it very nearly resulted in a nervous breakdown; and I think I've always thought, looking back, that I avoided a nervous breakdown largely by writing that little book *This Ever Diverse Pair* and really in a way I did it more out of that impulse, out of desperation, rather than having any hope of ever publishing it as a book. The characters Burden and Burgeon are embodiments or symbols, or whatever, of a very real experience of polarity and tension in my own life.

SS: When I think of them — please correct me if I'm wrong — I think of them as representing not only two opposite poles or two opposite forces operating or functioning in your own being, but I also think of them as representing microcosmic aspects of the larger polarity of Poetic and Prosaic. Neither one is favored over the other but both are necessary, the Poetic being the more formal source of one's being and the Prosaic being the ordering and the making of distinctions in one's own being.

OB: Yes, and thereby transforming what was unconscious unity into conscious unity — in the first place only conscious tension, then ultimately conscious unity also, one hopes.

SS: Well now, you have perhaps helped to answer the second part of the question, when I asked you to relate polarity to conscious/unconscious and to subjective/objective.

OB: Well, the polarity between subject and object in its most characteristic form, polarity between mental or inner experience and the world outside of us, can be seen, I think must be seen, if you are an objective idealist, as the same thing in a slightly other aspect as the polarity between conscious and unconscious. You can talk about "the unconscious" and think of it as the unconscious mind and then you are concentrating on the subjective pole, or you can talk about nature and the world we experience through the senses which is also "the unconscious," so that the relation between the two polarities is very close and immediate.

SS: It is very difficult.

OB: I know it is. That's the difficulty of polarity. It is an imagination, not just an idea. You can't really put it into strictly logical terms, without using contradiction, without using paradox. But continuing with the accident of polarity as a part of my experience of life, my biography — again retrospectively (and I think hardly until after his death) I have felt that there was a relation definitely in the nature of polarity between myself and C. S. Lewis. That I think has become more and more of a reality to me the more I have reflected on it.

SS: You are reminding me of your inscription to him on the dedication page of *Poetic Diction* — that "opposition is true friendship."

OB: Yes, but I wasn't thinking then in terms of polarity, I was thinking in terms of good old knockdown argumentative opposition.

SS: Here again you were knowing something that you didn't at the time know.

OB: Yes, it went much deeper than I knew. It was also very subtle. I don't think I could enlarge on it without being forced into a degree of crudity that would amount to actual misrepresentation.

SS: Would you say Lewis himself thought in terms of polarity?

OB: Emphatically not. I tried once or twice to interest him in it and he always turned it off quickly with a joke.

SS: How did he understand then the fundamental forces operating in life if he didn't understand them in terms of polarity?

OB: After his conversion in terms of an arbitrary act of creation by God. Human beings were created by God and they were entirely other than God. I mean there was no real unity between them and you'll find emphasized over and over again in his theological writings this complete dichotomy between the creature and the creator. That's why he didn't like — he hated — anything like occultism and moreover became shy about the sort of conclusions people come to through romantic philosophy.

SS: Then he took the more traditional Christian viewpoint of the disjunction between man and God and the complete transcendence of God. Yes?

OB: He did after his conversion. Earlier, when he was a subjective idealist, it was quite otherwise. He had a big hand in transforming a mere theory into something like an experience for me. I mean what you called "fusion," that is to say, the merger of the individual consciousness into the Absolute, so that there is ultimately no individual self. The only self is the self of the whole of the universe; and that's how he resolved the contradiction between free will and predestination.

SS: By way of the fusion of the one and the All — by their unity.

OB: Before his conversion he himself was trying to make it a real experience and in argument I learned a tremendous lot from him from that point of view. I take it as a very real point of view, not just nonsense because one thinks of it oneself in another way. Well he taught me that really, and then abandoned it all after his conversion. He wouldn't combine the two, which is the only possible true concept of polarity.

SS: Are you saying that there is really no one ultimate truth and that his was a very real point of view and therefore just as true, so to speak, as yours?

OB: No, I'm not saying that, but I'm saying that there's not much good seeing intellectually how to reconcile one position with another, or seeing that one is more correct than the other. It may be much less important to be able to do that than that either or both of them shall be an actual experience and not just an abstract theory which doesn't mean anything to you. This position of subjective idealism, merger in the Absolute, experience of oneself as the Absolute, was very real to him. It comes out in some of his early writings, poems and so forth, and he made it real for me. Just as, much later, reading the *Bhagavad Gita* made it real.

SS: What I hear you saying is that the important thing, in a point of view, is the actual experience of that point of view and not just an abstract description of it.

OB: Yes. And when I use the word "real," if one is thinking in terms of polarity each extreme is a reality conceived in itself and without the other extreme — it's a reality in the sense of being an important experience.

SS: I think perhaps we've been saying all along that you have known so much at each stage of your life, but you didn't know that you knew. Would that knowing that one knows describe the state of final participation?

OB: Yes. I think that that's certainly one quite good description of it, too.

SS: Do you think the fact that you are read more widely than you were twenty or thirty years ago means that perhaps the intellectual and spiritual climate is changing? Or do you think perhaps there's still the same resistance on the part of most of us to understanding and accepting other than a materialistic view of the world?

OB: I do see some signs of change. The taboo on acceptance of any other than a positivist or materialist outlook, which I stressed in *Speaker's Meaning*, seems to be weakening a little. I think it probably is also the case that such recognition as has come, has come more slowly and has not come as fully as it might have done because I have made so clear, in, I think, most of my books, the very big debt I owe to Steiner; and Rudolf Steiner is a kind of taboo as well, largely because of his association with occultism. We won't go into the true meaning of the word "occult," because I don't think it is very relevant.

SS: But it would be interesting.

OB: Well, you'll find that clearly stated in my Introduction to the little book called *The Case for Anthroposophy*. It consists mainly of the translation of part of a book by Steiner but with a full introduction by myself. There I suggested the proper reference of the word "occult," is to the whole *qualitative* aspect of nature, the investigation of which is ruled out from contemporary science because of its exclusive basis in passive sense experience. Modern science began by ruling out what it called "occult qualities," and I have argued there that in effect *all* qualities are occult, inasmuch as they are not accessible to passive sensation alone. There has to be an element of feeling in the perception, which is ruled out by the presuppositions of the scientific method. That is why science has become all quantities.

SS: Well, perhaps I gravely misunderstood something. It seems to me that the modern theoretical physicist doesn't depend on his senses at all for his understanding of reality, "out there," but depends tremendously on mathematics and instruments which can be understood, I guess, as an extension of the senses; but he simply doesn't depend on sense perception to explore the physical world.

OB: He depends on passive sense perception for the objective element in what he is thinking about. It is quite true that there is very little, a very small element indeed, of actual perception left, but that is what he argues and mathematicizes about and experiments with.

SS: In what category would you put the atom or the quasar?

OB: Well, from the point of view we are now talking from, I don't think it matters what category we put them in. What's talked about, and mathematicized about, is some form or other of sense perception. It may be the sense perception of a spot on a screen, of a cloud chamber or something of that sort, but the fundamental method is that you perceive certain things irrespective of any activity you may exert in the perception. Perception is clearly passive, and then you form theories about it.

SS: The occult would then refer to an imperceivable process going on. Is that what you mean?

OB: Yes, imperceivable without our mental or spiritual cooperation. That's what they meant by occult qualities. I think it is generally accepted. It really applies to all qualities as such, because the perception of quality is not a purely physical process. It has the element of feeling in it.

SS: Then you do feel generally that the intellectual and spiritual climate has been changing and that there is beginning to be a loss of confidence in the old positivist materialist framework?

OB: Yes, and I also hope that my books — in a very modest way — may have contributed somewhat to the change. As a matter of fact I'm inclined to think that materialism is going to break up one way or another anyhow and it's showing signs of doing so now. The crucial question is what is going to be put in its place? My answer is that we can't be sure — but it's up to us.

SS: I would like to talk about that a little more, but before we talk about it, I was anxious to stay with the question as to how, suddenly, we are moving out of an age that we could call an age of loss of feeling or of anesthesia, or which has been described as an age in which the traditional structures and symbolic systems have been disintegrating. I'm wondering if there is some way of accounting for this shift. You know in psychology, just to be concrete, at the time of Freud, he found in his patients primarily cases of hysteria, whereas today, instead of that, we find primarily the incidence of schizophrenia. It is a curious thing to account for these really striking cultural shifts.

OB: Yes. As I see it, and here I base very much on Steiner, that *is* a symptom of the evolution of consciousness. Evolution of consciousness doesn't simply depend on the progress of ideas, the impact of one idea on another and so forth. Intellectual development. There's an underlying evolution of unconscious mind going on as well as of conscious mind. I use the term "unconscious mind," because that is the term that will be used in such studies as psychoanalysis. But in terms of anthroposophy, Rudolf Steiner, it is the evolution of human consciousness being mediated by spiritual beings, beings in the spiritual world, and that of course you find elaborated in detail, if you go into the literature of anthroposophy. I obviously can't go into it in detail, but I do see this definitely as a process of evolution and there is going to be a violent change of some sort fairly soon, I think.

SS: You say you think it is going to be a violent change.

OB: Violent in the sense of abrupt, extreme change, very quick change. And possibly no doubt also in the other sense.

SS: Yes, your article for the *Denver Quarterly* referred to this as a traumatic demise. What would you see as the result of this, or as a next step, so to speak, in the evolution of consciousness.

OB: I think what I said was, one would hope it would take the form of a step further in the direction of what in *Saving the Appearances* I call "final participation." But, I'm not optimistic enough to see civilization or humanity as a whole quickly taking that step. Indeed, practically none of them might, if things went wrong so to speak; this is all tentative prophecy, speculation I suppose. I think I see an increasing division between almost two different kinds of humanity, one part of them having passed beyond materialism and the other having sunk further and further into it. I think there are beginnings of that showing now.

SS: Would you say that it's the task of the Poetic to enable a new participating consciousness and that this metamorphosis, if it were to come about, would come about by way of the interpenetration of polar opposites?

OB: Rather by an increased apprehension of the already existing interpenetration of opposites. This is how I really see imagination — a becoming aware of it *as* interpenetration.

SS: Imagination?

OB: Yes, in the widest sense of the word.

SS: Would you say that it's the function of imagination, and language also, to materialize spirit? — that meaning is the materialization of spirit and that language, so to speak, brings the world into being and if language does bring

the world into being and into consciousness, it does so by making unindividu-
ated meaning into distinct meanings?

OB: I think I see what you mean. The function of imagination is to materialize spirit, using imagination in the sense that has mostly been given to
the word since the Romantic movement or a little earlier. But if you look at
it in terms of the evolution of consciousness, you would more accurately say
that only the first stage, the first half if I may put it so crudely, of evolution
can be characterized as the materialization of spirit; but the second part —
that is, the progress in the direction of final participation — is really the
opposite. It's the spiritualizing of matter. Does that answer? That is the function of imagination in the wide way in which I tend to use it.

SS: If I understand you correctly, the spiritualization of matter would refer
to what we were just talking about, the awareness that you would call the
participating consciousness.

OB: Yes. You see, if you manage to discard "RUP," Residue of Unresolved Positivism, then participating consciousness is not something which
affects consciousness only, leaving matter to carry on by itself, so to speak,
it *is* the spiritualization of matter.

SS: Well that makes it quite clear. Very little is said of the role of the will
these days, and I recall that you hold that role to be an important one, in
respect to final participation, especially the role of unconscious will.

OB: I inevitably see this in terms of the polarity of three-fold man as
Rudolf Steiner presents it. We have spoken of it before. You have the pole
of the visceral man so to speak, at the opposite extreme to the head or nerves-
and-senses man; and if you remember, the correlation is between the head,
nerves, and senses on the one hand with thinking, and on the other hand the
visceral is related to willing. I think it is more than related. I would feel that
the body, considering it now as the visceral body, really *is* unconscious will
and the task, function, of attaining final participation would be the transformation of unconscious will into conscious will; which would also involve spiritualization of the material body itself. You would have something like a body
consisting of will instead of gristle!

SS: How can we assure ourselves that the will will will participation in this
fashion? — what sort of participation it will will. It could opt for the kind of
fusion which we agreed would be death. It could opt for further separation,
as you said. One perhaps whole segment of the population might do just that.
Or it might opt for a miserably distorted reality and make us even more
"mad" than we already are.

OB: It's true all those things could happen and there are very, very disturbing symptoms that they're trying to happen. I suppose, looking at it from
the point of view of the will willing toward final participation or failing to do
so, the alternatives are as follows: either the unconscious will becomes more

conscious, instead of being merely a physical structure that embodies and enables willing — or the whole body would become really head, nerves, and senses and there would be no "body of will" at all. That could very well have physical consequences, so that you would have human beings going about almost as all head and nerves and no viscera.

SS: You are describing pretty much what's been happening in recent years. We've become all heads, over-intellectualized, over-rationalized, as some have called it, and many people have said that this is one of the reasons for the appearance of a discipline such as psychoanalysis, because psychoanalysis begins with a failure of the will.

OB: Yes, I think so, yes.

SS: Then what would you say our responsibility is in this? I know that Coleridge speaks of the equation of consciousness and conscience and I would ask, then, what our conscience is telling us to do. Presumably, it has to do with increasing the consciousness of our present unconscious intention or will.

OB: The answer to that is, yes. You have to bear in mind that, as you yourself have pointed out, the unconscious will is not all good will. There are elements working in the opposite direction from the true evolution of consciousness, and really, the dictates of conscience are to enhance the one, become aware of the one, use the one, however you put it, and not the other.

SS: Could you clarify that any further? Would you say that final participation is a *willed* consciousness of participation?

OB: Yes. But what I wanted to get at was that you've got to see it in terms of a tri-une interpenetration of thinking and feeling and willing. In thinking there is already an element of feeling and willing. Willing has an element of thinking in it, and there's an element of both in feeling. Well now, if you think amaginatively, using the word in that wide sense, you are already increasing the element of willing in the thinking and, as a consequence of that, you'll find that the element of thinking, truthfulness, truth-seeking or whatever it is, in the world, is also enhanced. So that by increasing the interpenetration of your willing and your thinking, interpenetration in the deepest sense, you are pursuing a path in the direction of what I call final participation. Is that fairly clear?

SS: Yes, it's clear. I was hoping that you might say more about what the state of final participation would mean or would be. Would it be not only a state we would refer to as materialized spirit as well as spiritualized matter, but also what some refer to as a "cosmic consciousness"?

OB: Yes. Final participation would no doubt amount to what some people call "cosmic consciousness"; as long as that does not imply abolishing individual consciousness. As we said, the mystery or paradox is, how can you have a number of separate individuals, all of whom are at the same time the whole? You can only *envisage* that in terms of rather crude imagery. I tend to think of it as something like this: if you take a circle or a sphere you can have that sphere colored in all shades of color and all degrees of shading of a particular color. In the physical world as we know it, you can't have them all together, because one color washes out another one. But it isn't so very difficult to imagine that all the colorings of the whole sphere could coexist at the same time, in which case each one would in a sense be the whole, but would also be itself. Something in that way. Of course it's a crude picture, but it's the only way I can envisage final participation in a form that is expressible in words.

II

To Owen Barfield

"no passive vehicle of inspiration
possessed by the spirit, not
possessing it."

Coleridge: *Biographia Literaria*

OWEN BARFIELD

by

CECIL HARWOOD

This book of essays in honour of Owen Barfield is essentially a tribute from his academic friends and admirers. I would like on behalf of his extramural friends, of whom he has very many, to salute with gratitude the honour that it does him in so worthy and appropriate a fashion.

It has always been a matter of astonishment to us all that amid the cares of an arduous professional life — undertaken for the most altruistic reasons — Owen has been able to master the complicated field of linguistic studies and produce therein so many books of high scholarship and great originality, opening up new approaches to the study of words and meaning.

His friends were much distressed that one with so gifted and original a mind should be caught up in the mundane affairs of a solicitor's office. Many people, however, are deeply indebted to his brilliance as a lawyer, and I believe that this association with the ordinary run of life has added weight and judgment to his writings. His book *This Ever Diverse Pair,* published anonymously, is a profound, faithful, and humorous record of his experiences as a lawyer.

I think that from the time when I first knew Owen I dimly recognised that he possessed an exceptionally original and creative mind. His family held advanced views and admired modern writers and philosophers who were regarded with dark suspicion in my own orthodox home. His father, a remarkable man of an acute intelligence, who had won his own way in life, used to alarm me by shooting questions at me as to why I believed this or that, when I had no valid reason except that I had been brought up to believe it. At Highgate School, where we sat next to each other for many years, Owen made no attempt to win favour with the Establishment (we did not then know the word) in the ordinary way, but he was always regarded as an exceptional person. His contributions to the school magazine were sometimes critical and caustic to a high degree, but they were printed all the same. Our classical Sixth Form Master, a former Fellow of his College and a Scholar of the old school, amused himself by writing a Latin hexameter poem on his pupils, whose names he Latinised. The verse on Owen ran as follows:

CLAUSTRAGER AETATIS SPES NON INFIDA FUTURAE
Barfield no faithless hope of later years.

(My own verse was much less complimentary, though perhaps equally prophetic.) I will not reveal his nickname in case he should retaliate by revealing
mine.

War service separated us, but we met again at Oxford, and though in
different colleges, we belonged to the same circle of friends. Here began his
long and fruitful association with C. S. Lewis, on whom he had a profound
influence, and who later characterised him as the "wisest of my unofficial
advisers." At Oxford again his originality impressed everyone. Vivian (afterwards, Professor) de Sola Pinto, a member of my college to whom I introduced him, wrote of him in his autobiography, "I liked and admired him
immediately, and very soon formed the opinion that he had the most original
and interesting mind of any of my contemporaries in Oxford. This opinion
has been amply justified by his subsequent publications." (Much of Pinto's
other information is incorrect.) We crowned our association in Oxford by an
idyllic year in a thatched cottage in the (then) purely rural village of Beckley,
to which our friends used to bicycle out for long walks and long discussions.
In the winter we lived with the rigours of an open Tudor fireplace, but the
Spring — surely we felt, the most glorious ever known — brought all the
beauties of a still uncontaminated English countryside. Owen was an eager
collector of flowers, and a great lover of the stars. At this time also, as well
as preparing a thesis for a B.Litt., he was writing a good deal of poetry.
A moving sonnet sequence was published in the *London Mercury,* but he
has never sought publication for later works. Perhaps they may yet see the
light of day.

Many of Owen's later friends may be unaware of the variety of his capacities. At school he had been an excellent gymnast, and through an interest in
folk dancing, first he, and then I, became part of a Song and Dance Company
organised by the remarkable Radford Sisters to tour the villages of Cornwall
and Devon — in the days before radio. In this company Owen met his wife,
Maud Douie, a professional dancer who had worked with Gordon Craig. He
was himself so gifted in the sphere of movement that at one time there was
a serious question of his making a career in dancing.

But words claimed him. They led him for a time to a fruitful association
with Logan Pearsall Smith, and then to the production of his first books,
History in English Words and *Poetic Diction,* perhaps still the most popular
of all his writings. They are the foundation of all his subsequent work on
words and meaning and the development of consciousness.

It was at this time that — through a member of the Cornish concert party
— we both were introduced to the works of Rudolf Steiner and came to
regard him as the — still unrecognised — genius of the modern age. Those
of Owen's friends who share his devotion to Steiner cannot sufficiently admire him for openly acknowledging his debt to a philosopher whose approach

to life and knowledge is based on faculties then and perhaps still highly suspect. But for Owen, Steiner's ideas were seminal, as indeed the latter would have wished, and in his own sphere he has brought them to his own rich harvest.

The present volume is a tribute to that harvest, for which his friends are happy to find an increasing recognition. But all who have known him personally will wish to record also their profound admiration and love for him as a man.

For Owen Barfield   from Norman O. Brown

I Corinthians XIV, 13: Wherefore let him that speaketh
in tongues pray that he may interpret.
For edification.
There is a house to be built.
There is a community to be made.
Besides poetry there is interpretation.

On Interpretation
The title of Paul Ricoeur's beautiful book on Freud
Which takes its title from the title of Freud's epoch-making
                                                        book

The Interpretation of Dreams.
Not the science of dreams.
Freud wrote first, but did not publish, A Project for a
                                    Scientific Psychology.
After discarding it, Freud turned to The Interpretation of Dreams
                            the interpretation of symptoms
                            the interpretation of culture.

The Interpretation of Dreams is the discovery of meaning
                                                    in dreams
Discovering intentionality
              unconscious ideas
              meaning in the meaningless
              forces become meanings
              instincts express themselves symbolically
              symptoms are a mysterious language
                        signs needing interpretation.
Symptoms speak
The "body" is an utterance
Man is a Logos, a word, to be interpreted
              a code to be deciphered
                  not a machine to be manipulated.
Libido speaks, desire speaks, love speaks,
It is the unspoken meaning
Like the Delphic oracle
οὐ τι λεγει ἀλλα σημαινει
It does not say but signifies.
Recovering the original meaning of semantics:
A theory of signs and wonders
Oh wonder of wonders!
The dumb things speak.

Interpretation is translation.
Every sentence is bilingual, or allegorical; saying one
thing and meaning another.
Every sentence is translation.

Translation, or hermeneutics.
Hermeneutics, the form of philosophy today,
                the form of theology today
                the search for meaning.

Hermeneutics from Hermes, the god, Mercury --
Hermes the Thief, the original trickster, shape-shifter --
Hermes Trismegistus, Thrice Greatest Hermes, the greatest magician--
Translation is metamorphosis
"Bless thee, Bottom, how thou art translated!"
A secret art, a hermetic language
There is always hiding as well as seeking
And we never say what we mean.
Even psychoanalysis is a hermetic language
                          not to be taken literally.

Hermes the interpreter
interpres divum, interpreter of the gods,
inter : he is the go-between
He is psycho-pomp, conductor of souls,
Between two worlds
                    as above, so below,
Interpreter between macrocosm and microcosm
            between our own thoughts and our own bodies
            between Consciousness and the Unconscious.
And on the battlefield
Hermes is the herald that comes between the combatants
            the mediator
            the herald, or angel, or messenger,
The herald voices say Peace on earth, good will to men.

Interpretation mediates between languages
         undoing the consequences of the Fall
                                the Tower of Babel
         re-membering the unity of human language
         restoring communication.
A language that makes peace not war
A language that makes love not war
And therefore it does not argue.
                    argumentation is the logic of contention
                    based on separate identities
                              fixed definition
                              single meaning
                              self-assertion.
Interpretation seeks a class-less consciousness; it does not classify.
And does not criticize.
Susan Sontag didn't say what she meant
                        (she needs to be interpreted)
The new sensibility is not against interpretation but against
                                             criticism
It says, Judge not
And it says, Forgive us
For we ~~know~~ know not what we do or say.
And we are all in the same boat or body.
     Here Comes Everybody.

Going beyond the I-Thou relationship
The interpreter is the third person, the mediator.
Instead of the representative who fights on our behalf
The mediator who unifies the whole scene.
It is a synthesis.
It is the third person who makes it a crowd
Of us
A community of interpretation.
We Three.
A Trinity in Unity; neither confounding the Persons, nor
dividing the Substance.
Josiah Royce, forgotten voice of American idealism, says:
Interpretation seeks a city out of sight, the homeland where,
perchance, we learn to understand one another.

Interpretation seeks consent rather than conviction
            discovering what you meant all along.
A language of listening, rather than assertion
            discovering another meaning
            (there is always another meaning)
            discovering another's meaning
Just being an ~~an~~ interpreter.
Surrendering a bit of the asserting ego
Listening to the voice of the other
                            obedient — —
This listening is in the philosophy of Husserl the epoché:
A suspension, or pause,
A suspension of hostilities,
Which is also an epoch, the beginning of a new era.
Stop, look, and listen.
Waiting.
            waiting for — —
Thinking is waiting
            exexpectation
The psalmist says exspectans exspectavi
            I have waited waitingly.
Heidegger says ~~that~~ Thinking is in every instance a letting
be said of that which shows itself, and accordingly an answer
to that which shows itself.
Let it speak, let it show itself
The Freud id instead of the Freudian ego
The impersonal id
The collective unconscious
The over-soul
The language: let it speak to us.

Thinking is not a statement but an answer
                         an interpretation
                         saying it again another way
                         an echo; amen, even --

A response
Poetry calls us to respond
              or correspond
Till all the woods do answer and their echo ring.
The chorus
           or choir
                invisible
O may I join the choir invisible.

EXCEPTIONS & RULES

by

HOWARD NEMEROV

To Owen Barfield

I

A simple-minded proverb, much heard of in my youth, said: the exception proves the rule. At least, it certainly looked simple-minded until I began to turn it over and around and take it apart, when I had to realize there were at least three ways of understanding it.

Some people read the word 'proves' as having the sense of 'tests' or 'tries out,' and if you read it that way (which I suspect was the original intention) the statement is plainly a scientific one. But I noticed in earlier days (back when there used to be proverbs) that people who used this statement in daily life commonly meant something quite different, even contrary; by a change in the meaning of 'proves' the proverb had come to mean to those people that an exception showed the rule to be right. In that sense the statement is nonscientific, or even anti-scientific, for to the scientist the exception would show either that the rule was not inclusive enough or that the rule was just wrong, or wrongly applied.* In that sense, too, the statement is antipoetic, because the poet has still a third meaning for 'proves,' and would say, as a fair statement of his belief. The exception turns out to be, or proves to be, the rule. I shall return to both the scientist's and the poet's reading of the proverb after a bit, but first I want to describe a little more carefully what I have taken to be the common acceptation of the proverb in daily life, where the exception shows that the rule is right, and in that way is said to prove the rule.

Proverbs, which have a way of being antiscientific and antipoetic at the same time, nevertheless have a certain practical shrewdness to them, which we need not dignify with the name of wisdom, but which we ought to pay some attention to anyhow. My sense of this proverb is that it speaks with the voice of authority, as from olders to youngers, from parent, say, who

* Though in the world of microphysical phenomena, in transactions covered by the law of large numbers, 'exceptions' are assumed into rule, or cause, considered as statistical aggregate.

knows that life is not always explicable, to a child who still hopes it is always explicable. For instance, in autumn a father and son are standing under a tree. The son says, "Daddy, what are all these leaves?" Daddy says, correctly enough, that they are oak leaves. The son picks up a ginkgo leaf and says," Why is this oak leaf shaped so funny?" At some nearby point in the ensuing discussion Daddy may say, rather heavily, that it is the exception that proves the rule. And indeed there is no disputing the rule that all those leaves came from the oak, except the one ginkgo leaf, which a passerby happened to have been looking at while out walking and carelessly dropped there when he tired of it, not knowing, or not caring, that he had deranged the order of the universe. You would not say, either scientifically or poetically, that the one ginkgo leaf proved the rest to be oak leaves; but as a way of getting around and through the complications of life in this vale of tears the proverb seems to have been a help.

As the proverb speaks with the voice of authority, so the sense of its somewhat complacent morality is that it is a ruling-class proverb, much concerned with keeping the status quo; no trifling discrepancy, it seems to say, is going to change MY idea of the world. And the authority assumed is so well established that there is even a little humor to its assertion, as though to allow that you can't spend your life accounting for every last little item in the universe, you've got to stop somewhere, and so on. Its variously elaborated applications in politics and morality might concern us, though, in such forms as "the sinner testifies to the divine mercy," "by his crime the criminal attests the majesty of the law," or, drawing on Blake, the magnificent assertion: "To be an Error & to be Cast out is a part of God's design."

An interlude. Just for the sake of the amusement of bewilderment it may be worth following to the end, which is not far away, the formal implications of the proverb. The exception proves the rule. But that statement is itself a rule, stating that the exception proves the rule; has that rule also an exception? Let us assume that there exists a rule without exception. That rule without exception would be an exception to the rule that the exception proves the rule, and, as such, by being an exception, proves the rule that the exception proves the rule. But, on the contrary, a rule without an exception cannot be proved, and if it cannot be proved it cannot be admitted to be an exception to the rule that the exception proves the rule, and if it is not an exception to that rule then it cannot be the exception that proves the rule that the exception proves the rule, and that rule in turn cannot be proved.

So much for that. The head, in testimony of its living in a round world, slowly begins to spin. But I put in that piece of logical parody, or parodied logic, as a humbling reminder that all that we think we think depends upon language, language that already exists before we think, and in which we inherit, in the measure that we are capable, human wisdom and human folly

at the same time. You can see something of this, something of what language
does for us and to us, from the circumstance that the one word 'proves', in
what looked to be a simple enough statement, turned out on inspection to
have three different meanings making possible three quite different statements of the proposition that the exception proves the rule; but that through
these transformations of meaning, which I have divided up as common sensi-
cal, poetic, and scientific, the sentence itself remains formally coherent and
grammatically the same.

II

The poetic form of the proverb asserts that the exception proves (to be) the
rule. I found this out as a sort of inexpensive revelation that came to me
when I was nearly run over by an ambulance; picking myself up out of the
snow I said: "Metaphor is an exception caught becoming a rule." For to be
even nearly run over by an ambulance is a strikingly exceptional occurrence
(though becoming less so), and yet it may be applied accurately enough to
the dual nature of civilization, always ready with the instruments of com-
passion once the victim has been made helpless. Alternatively, the figure may
be applied to the situation of the accused, who under our law has the right
to be deemed innocent until he is proved guilty; but this right has no actual
existence until someone has deemed him guilty by arresting him. Blake again
sums it up:

> Pity would be no more
> If we did not make somebody poor;
> And mercy no more could be
> If all were as happy as we.

To elaborate a little on this theme. I think many writers would agree with
what I have experienced, that very often you are afraid or embarrassed to
put down something because it comes directly from your own life, and
hence appears to you as too intimate, too idiosyncratic, too aesthetically
inert, ever to illustrate any general nature in things. But if you overcome
your timidity or shame and put it down anyhow, you will very likely find that
it puts out many filiations with the experience of others, the nature of life;
it grows, in addition to its being, a meaning, or several meanings.

This is a mysterious business: how does the particular, in the course of
being examined most particularly and for itself alone, as a unique fact existing in the world, become meaningful, become illustrative of general or even
universal propositions? It is so mysterious, indeed, that nobody knows the
answer, any more than any one knows how it is that things become thoughts
and thoughts things. But I may illustrate it as it happened by a curtal sonnet

of Gerard Manly Hopkins, which illustrates the happening itself and at the same time asserts a theory about it.

> Glory be to God for dappled things —
> For skies of couple-colour as a brinded cow;
> For rose-moles all in stipple upon trout that swim;
> Fresh-firecoal chestnut falls; finches' wings;
> Landscape plotted and pieced — fold, fallow, and plough;
> And all trades, their gear and tackle and trim.
> All things counter, original, spare, strange;
> Whatever is fickle, freckled (who knows how?)
> With swift, slow; sweet, sour; adazzle, dim;
> He fathers forth whose beauty is past change:
> Praise him.

The assertion of that poem is that only a religious guarantee is sufficient for the holding together of fact and meaning, unique and universal. But observe too that if you try to do it without the religious guarantee you don't at all dispose of the problem; the relation itself doesn't even become less mysterious: how can a finch's wing convince you that there exists an All, an Everything, which is somehow the same (the "Nature") in all things? A scientific guarantee, as for instance that number is the nature of all things, or that the elementary constituents of the universe perceived by the senses are invisible particles, is also not an overcoming of the same mystery, but a different way of asserting it.

For one more illustration, here are some lines in which my definition of metaphor is applied to some drawings by Saul Steinberg:

> The enchanted line, defying gravity and death,
> Brings into being and destroys its world
> Of marvelous exceptions that proves rules,
> Where a hand is taken drawing its own hand,
> A man with a pen laboriously sketches
> Himself into existence; world of the lost
> Characters amazed in their own images:
> The woman elided with her rocking-chair,
> The person trapped behind his signature,
> The man who has just crossed himself out.

All these instances, taken directly from the work of that marvelously ingenious artist, are exceptions, that is, strikingly unique phenomena — which yet express to us something of what we acknowledge to apply shrewdly to the conditions of our life in this world: with a man laboriously sketching himself into existence, for example, we might compare the saying of Ortega y Gasset: "Man is the novelist of himself," where what Steinberg gives as a unique image is asserted as a general rule about the relation between imagination and reality. So the poet would assert our proverb in the form: the exception turns out to be, or proves to be, the rule.

III

The third interpretation of the proverb is pre-eminently the scientist's, and for him the word proves means 'tries out' or 'tests'; if the exception cannot be brought under the rule, so much the worse for the rule. And yet the scientist in formulating his hypothesis is not behaving so very differently from the poet in making his metaphor, though the rules and procedures for 'proving' are very different indeed. Here is a somewhat elaborated expression of our proverb, by Teilhard de Chardin, who says:

An irregularity in nature is only the sharp exacerbation, to the point of perceptible disclosure, of a property of things diffused throughout the universe, in a state which eludes our recognition of its presence.

That statement about exceptions and rules was made by a scientist who was also a priest. Hard to be certain whether he says this, in the course of his brilliant and speculative prophetic book about evolution, in his character as scientist or in his character as priest. If he said it as a priest, he might well have been defending the occurrence of miracle, which is defined in the great dictionary as follows: a miracle is 'an event or effect in the physical world beyond or out of the original course of things, deviating from the known laws of nature, or transcending our knowledge of these laws. . . .' But do notice that although the priest will indeed break with the scientist in any argument flowing from this statement, he has not broken yet, for the immensely rapid development of science has had a great deal to do with its concentration on "irregularities in nature," events "deviating from the known laws of nature, or transcending our knowledge of these laws," and the boldest revisions of hypothesis have been necessary (and are still going on) simply in order to bring "miracle" once again under the dominion of "law." And if Teilhard de Chardin made the statement as a scientist, the position is not vastly different, for attention to "irregularities in nature," or to what I am calling 'exceptions', has brought forth upon the world a good many phenomena that might well have been called miraculous in earlier states of 'the known laws of nature'. For example: electricity, in the eighteenth century, was just such an exception, such an irregularity, good for such parlor amusements as picking up bits of paper on a comb statically charged. Consider the immense and immensely poetic power of the imagination, though belonging not to one man alone but to many, that could play with this oddity, speculate about it, devise situations in which it might yield up more information of its ways, until now it is no longer an exception but something close to the principle of existence, as well as the source of practical powers unthinkably great, which have utterly transformed the world. For another example: slips of the tongue, dreams, jokes — these had been around since the beginning; dreams had always been interpreted, too, whether in a systematic or an ad hoc manner, while the other two had been less regarded. But now, because one man took with the most literal seriousness some form equivalent to Teilhard de Chardin's statement, these exceptional, curious, or trivial phenomena have revealed the existence of a huge realm of the world which before had been suspected only in the passing speculations of poets, the strange stories of tradition and religion, the sinister or grotesque images shaped by painters; and it is not too much to say that the world has been as thoroughly transformed by the investigations of Freud as by the development of electricity.

To sum up. Commonsense tells you to neglect the exceptional and live within the known world. But art and science are for a moment one in the injunction, even the commandment, to look first, only, always, at the exception, at what doesn't fit: because, one says, it will turn into the universal while you look; because, says the other, it 'will show you the way to a universal not yet known. There is probably a moral in there somewhere, but I am in favor of leaving it in there where I found it. I never saw that people got better for being moralized at, especially by one of the wicked.

III

Studies in Polarity

"And twofold Always. May
    God us keep
From Single vision and Newton's
    Sleep!"

William Blake, in a letter to Thomas Butts,
November 22, 1802

IMAGINATION, FANCY, INSIGHT, AND REASON
IN THE PROCESS OF THOUGHT

by

DAVID BOHM

ON IMAGINATION AND FANCY

The power to imagine things that have not been actually experienced has, on the one hand, commonly been regarded as a key aspect of creative and intelligent thought. On the other hand, this power of imagination has equally commonly been regarded as a rather passive and mechanical capacity to arrange and order the images of thought arising associatively out of memory, with the aid of which the mind may at best make routine sorts of adjustments and at worst contrive to deceive itself in such a way as may be conducive to its own pleasure, comfort, and superficial satisfaction.

As Owen Barfield has brought out so well in his book *What Coleridge Thought,** such a distinction between two extreme forms of imagination was taken by Coleridge as being of fundamental importance for the understanding of the nature of thought as a whole. Coleridge gave the name "primary imagination" to the one extreme and the name "fancy" to the other. *Primary imagination* is, for Coleridge, an act of creative perception through the mind, in which the images are generally fresh and original rather than derived from memory, and on which all the differences and manifold features arise naturally and harmoniously as aspects or sides of a single undivided whole. At the other extreme, *fancy* (which is actually derived from the word "fantasy") is mainly a construction involving the putting together of basically separate and distinct images already available from the memory. Coleridge meant it to include not only the routine, passive, and often self-deceptive evocation of images by association, but also a wide range of more active and intelligent modes of thinking, starting from simple everyday arrangements first planned out in the mind, and going on to composition, design, and possibly invention, in fields such as literature, art, and science.

---

* *See,* for example, reference 1 on page 68, for a discussion of Coleridge's views on the subject. For Hegel's views, *see* reference 2.

Between these two extremes of primary imagination and fancy is a whole range of possibilities through which Coleridge suggested that thought actually moves. He did not regard the two extremes as entirely separate and distinct. Rather, in his terms, they are the two basic poles of thought. That is to say, the energy and ordering action underlying thought as a whole arises through a kind of tension between the two poles. (As in physics, the action of electrical forces on charged particles can be looked at as arising in a field that expresses a sort of tension in the space between positive and negative charges.)

However, as Owen Barfield has brought out in some detail, Coleridge was ambiguous as to the nature of the relationship between primary imagination and fancy. The very term "primary imagination" would tend to suggest that in some sense fancy should be taken as a sort of "secondary imagination" so that the two differ mainly in being different degrees or orders of what is basically the same quality. He frequently suggests in his writings that this is indeed his point of view. On the other hand, he also implies in other parts of his writings that primary imagination and fancy differ in kind or in quality. So ultimately the meaning of this basic distinction is not clear.

IMAGINATIVE INSIGHT AND IMAGINATIVE FANCY IN SCIENTIFIC RESEARCH

In the present article, I should like to go further into the implications of this question, from a point of view in which one regards imagination universally as the power to display the activity of the mind as a whole through mental images. What Coleridge considers as primary imagination will then be considered as the display through such images of creative and original *insight*, while what he regards as fancy will be taken to be the corresponding display of the more mechanical and routine aspects of thought. Thus, the one activity, indicated by the word "imagination," is to be distinguished mainly according to the order of its *content*, which moves between the extremes of imaginative insight and imaginative fancy.

It has to be kept in mind, however, that this way of looking at the subject is not meant as a definite conclusion, but rather, as an inquiry or exploration into what can be learned by seeing the polarity pointed out by Coleridge in a different way. In carrying out this inquiry, I shall begin by giving some emphasis to the field of science, with which I am relatively familiar, though later, I shall go on to consider the implications of this work for more general fields.

The most creative and original aspect of scientific work has generally been in the development of *theories*, especially those having such a broad and deep significance that they are felt to be universally relevant. We may obtain a significant hint or clue to what is involved here, by noting that the word "theory" derives from the Greek "theoria," which has the same root as "theatre," in a verb meaning "to view" or "to make a spectacle." This suggests that theory is to be regarded primarily as a way of looking at the world through the mind, so that it is a form of insight (and not a form of knowledge of what the world is). Thus, in the field of science, the extreme of imaginative insight can best be studied by giving attention to the origin and development of fundamental theories, which aim at some universal sort of significance.

For example, in ancient times, men had the fundamental theory that celestial matter was different in kind from earthly matter, so that it was natural for earthly objects to fall, and for celestial objects, such as the moon, to remain up in the sky. With the coming of the modern era, however, scientists began to develop the point of view that there is no essential difference between earthly matter and celestial matter. This implied, of course, that heavenly objects, such as the moon ought to fall. But for a long time, men did not notice this implication. In a sudden flash of mental perception, Newton *saw* that as the apple falls, so does the moon, and so indeed do all objects. The fact that the moon never reaches the surface of the earth, while the apple does, was explained by the tangential motion, possessed by the moon, but not by the apple. This tangential motion continually accelerates the moon away from the center of the earth, at a rate which balances the falling motion so that the orbit remains approximately a circle, at a very nearly constant distance from the earth.

By considering the behaviour of matter more generally, Newton was led to the theory of universal gravitation, in which all objects were seen as falling toward various centers (e.g., the earth, the sun, the planets, etc.). This constituted a new way of *looking* at the heavens, in which the movements of the planets were no longer regarded in terms of the ancient notion of an essential difference between heavenly matter and earthly matter. Rather, one considered these movements in terms of different rates of fall of all matter, heavenly and earthly, toward various centers. And when something was seen not to be accounted for in this way, we often discovered new and as yet unseen planets, toward which celestial objects were falling. In this way, the new concept of universal gravitation demonstrated its fruitfulness, by showing itself to be capable, not only of explaining already known facts, but also, or helping direct our minds and our physical observations to hitherto unknown facts and even to hitherto unknown kinds of facts.

The moment of insight, in which Newton suddenly realised that the moon *is* falling, even though it never reaches the earth, was evidently quite different from the ordinary process of discursive thought, in which one step follows another more or less logically, over a period of time. Rather, it was an extreme example of something that everybody experiences when he is thinking about a problem containing a number of contradictory or confused factors. Suddenly, in a flash of understanding, involving in essence no time at all, a new totality appears in the mind, in which this contradiction and confusion have vanished. This new totality is at first only *implicit* (i.e., enfolded). The first step in making it explicit is its display (i.e., unfolding) through some mental image which, as it were, contains the main features of the new perception spread out before our "mental vision." Perception involving this display, which is inseparable from the act of primary perception itself, is what may be called *imaginative insight* (or creative imagination). Such a display plays a necessary part, because with its aid, the mind can apprehend the meaning of what has been created in the flash of understanding. From this apprehension, the mind can go on to think and to reason out more and more of the consequences implied by the new insight.

It is in this latter process that imaginative fancy (or constructive imagination) begins to play an important part. For example, in Newton's case, it was necessary to have a relatively precise notion as to just how fast an object will fall. In developing such a notion, we may generally begin by putting forth a *hypothesis* (i.e., a supposition), which has to be tested by experiments and observations. If a given hypothesis "passes" such a test, it is accepted as a particular realisation of the primary insight. If not, it is necessary to seek further hypotheses, until one is found that fits in with the available experimental facts and observations. However, even after such a hypothesis has been found to be acceptable in this way, it may be shown in later tests to be incorrect or of limited validity. It is then necessary, of course, to go on with the search for yet further hypotheses, until one is found that will fit the new facts. And so, a deep insight of universal significance, such as that of Newton, may in principle lead to an indefinite development of more and more detailed hypotheses.

In this process of development, hypotheses may often be suggested by images already available in other contexts, the relevance of which may be indicated by a detailed consideration of available facts. Thus, from the data known to him, Newton was able to show that the moon falls considerably more slowly than an object at the surface of the earth. This meant that the force of gravitation must decrease in some way with the distance. But the question was, "Just how fast does it decrease?" It is quite possible that the precise form of the hypothesis adopted by Newton may have been suggested by calling to mind some already available image, such as that of the light intensity from a radiant object, which was already known to fall off as the inverse square of the distance. So then, the thought would arise naturally: "As with light, so perhaps with gravitation." Even if in actual fact, it may not have been this image but perhaps some other one, that suggested the inverse square law, the essential point remains that hypotheses generally involve new forms, arrangements, connections, and meanings of images already available in the mind. So, a hypothesis is primarily a form of fancy, or of constructive thought, the validity of which has to be continually tested by further appeals to observed fact.

It has to be kept in mind, however, that the distinction between insight and hypothesis is not a hard and fast one. Thus, even to notice that the rate of fall of intensity of light from an object that is a light source may be relevant to the rate of decrease of gravitational force from such an object requires a certain imaginative insight. However, what is crucial here is that this involves the perception of a relationship between two already known sorts of images (i.e., the light intensity from an object and the force exerted by an object), while Newton's primary insight involved a fresh and original total perception displayed through a single new *kind* of image (i.e., an object that is falling, but that never reaches the earth in its fall).

On the other hand, it must also be kept in mind that even Newton's insight was not *totally* free of known types of images (e.g., his thought still contained certain familiar images, such as those of material objects in motion through space). So the full description of what is happening here is rather more complex than we have thus far indicated. Insight and fancy are in fact never separated. They are both present in every step (e.g., even at the level of experiment and observation, a considerable degree of insight is needed to see what the fact actually means). However, in any particular case, there is a different degree of emphasis in each of the two extremes. Thus, in Newton's perception of the primary notion of universal gravitation, the side of insight was much more heavily emphasised than in the action involved in the proposal of the hypothesis of the inverse square law.

Insight and fancy are, in the first instance, two qualitatively different modes of operation of the mind as a whole. So, in this sense, Coleridge was right to say that they are different in kind. However, as has been pointed out above, each act of discovery always contains both sides, inseparably connected and related. Indeed, a content that was first perceived as an insight passes over into the domain of fancy, and a content first seen in the domain of fancy may be the key clue to a new insight. Through such a process of continual transition, insight and fancy come to reflect each other. But more deeply, they interpenetrate and ultimately, they are seen to be only two views of what is one undivided and whole mental movement. However, as indicated before, at any moment this movement may emphasise one side or the other. And thus, Coleridge was right to say that the difference is also one of degree. But perhaps through this inquiry we may have come to a more clear view of this situation, which, in Coleridge's language, could be called "a polarity between kind and degree" (or in Hegel's language "the unity of quality and quantity").

A full understanding of the relationship between insight and fancy requires us to note, however, that no form of insight remains relevant and fruitful indefinitely. Thus, after several centuries of working very well, the Newtonian form of insight, when extended into new domains, eventually led to unclear results. In these new domains, new forms of insight were developed (the theory of relativity and quantum theory). These gave a radically different picture of the world from that of Newton (though the latter was, of course, found to be still valid in a limited domain). If we supposed that theories gave true knowledge, corresponding to "reality as it is," then we would have to conclude that Newtonian theory was true until around 1900, after which it suddenly became false, while relativity and quantum theory suddenly became the truth. Such an absurd conclusion does not arise, however, if we say that theories are ways of looking, which are neither true nor false, but rather clear and fruitful in certain domains, and unclear and unfruitful when extended beyond these domains.

This means, of course, that there is no way to prove or disprove a theory (especially if it aims at a universal sort of significance). For even if a particular realisation of the theory is disproved, it is generally possible to find an alternative hypothesis, allowing the theory to be maintained. Ultimately, we have to decide between such an attempt to save the old theory and the attempt to create a radically new kind of theory. This has to be done with the aid of more general judgments, such as that of whether the net result is clear, simple, beautiful, generally adequate and fruitful, etc. These involve a kind of aesthetic perception of harmony or disharmony within the overall structure of the theory, as well as between theory and the total body of fact available, similar to that needed in the visual arts and in music.

On the other hand, when a hypothesis is tested, the judgment of its validity is usually based on the simple fact of whether there is a *correspondence* between some of the inferences drawn from it (e.g., numerical predictions) and appropriate features of the observed fact. So we have to be careful not to confuse the testing of hypotheses with the (basically aesthetic) judgment as to whether or not one regards it as worthwhile to go on with a given general line of theory. The ability to make this judgment properly is perhaps one of the key qualities, which are required for a creative and original step, rather than a continuation or development of an insight that is already available.

The interplay of theory and hypothesis indicated in this discussion can be brought out by considering some of the lines of thinking that helped lead Einstein to the special theory of relativity.

Toward the end of the nineteenth century, there had developed a great deal of confused evidence concerning the properties of light. On the one hand, from the electromagnetic theory, which had explained the then known properties of light very well, one concluded that light was a form of wave motion, consisting of oscillations of the electromagnetic field. The speed of these waves was calculated from the theory and found to be in agreement with that observed experimentally. The theory implied, however, that the speed of light, as measured relative to an observer moving in the direction of a light wave, should be less than that measured by an observer who is not moving in this way. We can see why this follows by considering a sound wave, which moves through air at a certain speed. An observer on an airplane moving in the direction of a sound wave would find that the speed of this wave relative to him was less than that relative to that of an observer fixed on the ground. Indeed, if the airplane speeds up, it can catch up with the sound wave, and eventually overtake it by going faster than sound. When this happens, the observer on the airplane does not hear any of the sound produced by the airplane, because this latter is "left behind" as a "shock wave."

On the other hand, actual measurements with light did not show this sort of behaviour at all. Rather, they showed that all observers obtained the *same* speed of light, regardless of their speed relative to each other. These experiments implied, for example, that if a rocket ship accelerated to nine-tenths of the speed of light relative to the earth, an observer inside the ship would still obtain the same measured speed of light as would be obtained by an observer at rest on the earth. This was of course very puzzling. Many attempts were made by means of various *hypotheses* to explain the fact, while retaining the general lines of Newton's theory. But such explanations of a given feature led only to a paradox or puzzle in some other feature.

Einstein's thinking on this question did not center, however, on explaining the detailed experimental facts with the aid of hypotheses. Rather, like Newton, he gave his main attention to broad and deep questions, relating to general concepts that had previously been largely implicit and taken for granted in a rather habitual way. Thus, at the age of fifteen, he asked himself the question, "What would happen if one moved at the speed of a light ray and looked in a mirror?" The light from one's face would never reach the mirror. Evidently, there is something strange about an object supposed to move at the speed of light.

From our more modern vantage point, we can bring out this strangeness even more by considering the atomic constitution of all matter. According to the generally accepted theory, the atoms that make up any object are held in a certain relatively fixed structure, by the balance of the attractive and repulsive electrical forces, between the charged particles (electrons and protons) out of which the atoms are in turn constituted. And according to the electromagnetic theory, when such an object reached and overtook the speed of light, each atom would leave its electromagnetic force field behind it, as a "shock wave," similar to that which arises when an airplane exceeds the speed of sound. Because there are no longer any forces holding them together, the atoms would drift apart. Any attempt to make a material object exceed the speed of light would therefore lead to its disintegration.

It seems clear that there is a fundamental difference between the theoretical significance of the speed of light and that of any other speed (such as that of sound waves). For it seems that insoluble difficulties and paradoxes arise from supposing that a material object can exceed the speed of light. Einstein already had a premonition of these difficulties, when he asked what would happen if one could move with a light ray. So, as Newton answered the question, "Why doesn't the moon fall?" in a surprising way by saying that it *does* fall, so Einstein answered his own question in a correspondingly surprising way by saying, "No material object can actually reach the speed of light." In other words, the speed of light has a new quality. It is not something that can be overtaken, but rather, it is more like a horizon. No matter how far we go, the horizon remains the same distance from us. And no matter how fast we go, the velocity of light remains the same, relative to us.

Einstein's new insight fitted in with the experimental facts that we have cited here. But much more than this, with the aid of some further discussion (which we need not go into here), he was able to show that it implied a new notion of the measure of time and space. Whereas, in the Newtonian theory, this measure had been taken as absolute and independent of all observers, Einstein's insight led to the conclusion that this measure has to be regarded as relative to the speed of the observer. Of course, this implied a radical change in many of the most fundamental concepts of physics. And as is now very well known, from these new concepts with the aid of certain simple and reasonable further hypotheses, he was able to draw a wide range of inferences, many of a highly novel character, which have thus far withstood the test of experiment and observation.

It is important to point out, in this connection, that the older form of Newtonian insight, has never been definitively disproved. Thus, working more or less at the same time as Einstein did, Lorentz proposed certain hypotheses about a material medium called "the ether," which was supposed to fill all space and to carry electromagnetic waves. In this way, using Newtonian conceptions of time and space, he was able to arrive at essentially the same mathematical predictions as those following from Einstein's theory. Nevertheless, Lorentz's theory was dropped, mainly because it was felt (evidently on grounds that are essentially aesthetic in nature) that the full set of hypotheses needed for such an ether theory were complicated, arbitrary, unnatural, ugly, etc. So we see once again that simple correspondence or noncorrespondence with experimental facts can test hypotheses but not theories.

RATIONAL INSIGHT AND RATIONAL FANCY

It is clear from the preceding discussion that creative and original insight in science is intimately bound up, not only with the formation of new kinds of mental images, but also, with new sorts of *rational insight*. For, evidently, discoveries of fundamentally new ways of looking at the whole world, such as those arising in the work of Newton and of Einstein, depend very strongly on the perception of the relevance of certain key questions, which help point to some contradictory or confused features of previously accepted general ways of thinking. The fresh insight into the general nature of things taking place in the "moment of understanding" is then unfolded or displayed both in the imagination (new mental images) and in the appearance of new lines of discursive reasoning, which are free of the contradiction and confusion that was previously present.

It is evident, then that we have to consider the relationship between imagination and reason, if we wish to obtain an adequate account of the operation of the process of thought. Since we have here departed somewhat from the lines of Coleridge in our inquiry into imagination, it will now be necessary to do so again, in our inquiry into rationality. So we should not expect to arrive at exactly the same role for reason as that suggested by Coleridge (though, of course, there will still be some rough parallel between our notion of rational insight and Coleridge's notion of reason).

A relevant indication of how we may understand what is to be meant by reason or rationality, can be obtained by considering the origin of these words in the Latin "ratio." This would suggest that when we see the reason for something, we are aware of a totality of interrelated ratios or proportions, which imply the necessity of the main essential qualities and properties of that thing. But, of course, the sense of the word "ratio" is not restricted to relationships of numerical proportions (e.g., $\frac{A}{B} = \frac{C}{D}$). Rather, it also includes "qualitative proportions" such as "A is to B as C is to D" (to be expressed more succinctly as A : B :: C : D).

For example, the ancient Greeks had the view that heavenly matter is more perfect than earthly matter, and that it expressed the perfection of its nature by movement in a circle, which was regarded as the most perfect of all possible forms. This reasoning is implicitly based on the analogical ratio or proportion. "Heavenly matter is to earthly matter as the ideal of aesthetic and moral perfection of human behaviour is to ordinary, everyday, imperfect human behaviour."

Through such a "ratio," one was able to obtain an explanation of the whole cosmic order. But, of course, it is now well known that this sort of explanation did not work very well. And, as has already been indicated, modern science ultimately came to a radically different mechanical type of explanation, in the development of which Newton's insight of universal gravitation played a key part. But now we can see that this insight had to be displayed not only *imaginatively* (through the image of an object that falls and yet never reaches the earth), but also *discursively*. The discursive display was, in this case, essentially an expression of a "ratio" that was implicitly present in the original flash of perception. Put in an ordinary verbal form, this was: as the successive positions of the falling apple are related, so are those of the falling moon, and so also are those of any falling material object. Or, to state it more precisely, if A, B are the successive positions of the apple, C, D, those of the Moon, E, F, those of any other object, then:

$$A : B :: C : D :: E : F.$$

Because this ratio applies both to all actual objects, and to all possible objects, it is *universal* and *necessary* (in the sense that it could not be otherwise). It is thus a *law*, which expresses rational harmony that is expected to prevail in all aspects of natural process.

More generally, all our concepts and explanations (whether of universal and necessary character or not) have at their core the perception of a totality of ratios or proportions, certain essential aspects of which may be displayed discursively in the way described above. Thus, to perceive such a simple thing as the straightness of a line is to see that each segment of it is related to the next segment, as the next is in turn related to the one that follows it. Or, in more concise terms, if S_1, S_2, S_3, denote any three successive segments, then $S_1 : S_2 :: S_2 : S_3$. If, however, the line should suddenly change its direction, at a certain point, then we would see that the segment that precedes this point is not related to the one that follows in the same way as prevails among the rest of the segments. If we could introduce the symbol $\times$ to mean 'is not to' then, for this case, we could write $S_1 \times S_2 :: S_2 : S_3$ (i.e., S_1 is not to S_2, as S_2 is to S_3).

When we are perceiving one line meeting another, we are immediately aware of a totality of such similarities and differences of ratio. And, of course, as our attention goes to more complex structures of lines and surfaces forming a geometrical figure, we begin to be aware of a whole hierarchy of such ratios and their relationships. This hierarchy can develop indefinitely in its complexity and subtlety, as our perception extends into every phase of life. No matter what we perceive, however, the essential meaning or content of this perception involves a totality of ratio, in the most general sense of this word.

It cannot be emphasized too strongly that the apprehension of this totality of ratio takes place in an act of insight, within which the whole content is implicit or enfolded. As has already been pointed out, the first unfolding or display of this insight is in the form of an image. Within this image, the precise specification of the various ratios or proportions is evidently still mainly implicit (as relationships of various features of the form). But then, a bit later, through discursive thought and language, certain essential features of the totality of ratio are displayed explicitly as well. It is only when this has happened that the mind is fully ready for the content of an insight to pass into the domain of fancy or constructive thought.

In such fancy or constructive thought, a qualitatively different process takes place. Here, we begin, not only with already available images in the manner indicated earlier, but also with already available concepts, consisting of structures of ratio or proportion logically arranged in ways that come mainly from memory. And so, we are led to distinguish between *imaginative and rational insight*, which is the primary act of perception through the mind, along with its immediate display, and *imaginative and rational fancy*, which is the construction or putting together of known concepts and images in a logical order.

An extreme case of rational fancy arises when a theory is *axiomatized*. In axiomatizing a theory, we select a certain set of basic concepts along with their relationships as expressed verbally or mathematically; and from these, we aim to derive all the significant consequences of the theory in question, through a process of logical inference. Of course, as has been indicated earlier, every mental process must contain the two sides of insight and fancy together, though in each particular step there may be more emphasis on one side or on the other. Thus, in axiomatizing a theory, we need a certain insight to select suitable axioms and to draw certain inferences from them, but evidently this insight does not generally extend to novel and original perceptions, such as those of Newton and Einstein, in which new kinds of images and new ways of thinking about the world as a whole first emerged into view.

The process of axiomatization is often very useful in facilitating certain lines of application of a theory. In addition, it can play a key role in making new discoveries possible. For example, geometrical insight was first axiomatized in the work of Euclid. This led to further work, which ultimately demonstrated certain arbitrary features of Euclidean geometry. This demonstration ultimately proved to be the key clue pointing to the possibility of new non-Euclidean forms of geometry. These latter generally had features not fitting in with the ordinary intuition of space as derived from general experience and sense perception. So the axiomatization of geometry helped lead to new insights. And it was able to do this, mainly because the extreme precision of expression of the axioms make possible the detection of certain contradictory, confused, and arbitrary features of common and ordinary ideas about space.

In more modern approaches to mathematics, the meanings of the basic axiomatic concepts are often left fairly free, so that they are often determined mainly by the way in which the axioms are related. This is evidently a move toward emphasizing the side of creative and original insight. It corresponds to the possibility, envisaged by Coleridge, of permitting the basic images of imaginative fancy to be considerably altered, so as to allow the total construction to reach a greater degree of harmony. But of course, such a mode of thought is still primarily a development of rational and imaginative fancy, rather than an act of creative insight, in which a new totality of images and ratios are perceived as a single, harmonious whole, first implicit and enfolded, and then explicit and unfolded.

The axiomatization of theories has, however, also had some negative effects, in the development of modern science. What has happened is that when a theory has been given a more or less axiomatic form, the resulting appearance of precision, fixity, and perfect logical order has often given rise to the impression that knowledge has finally arrived at a kind of ultimate truth. And so, the axiomatic form can act as a set of "blinkers" preventing people from looking in new directions, rather than as a set of hints and clues, pointing to contradictions and inadequacies in existing lines of thought.

Indeed, the emphasis on the axiomatic mode of thinking tends to lead modern physicists to look on the development of precise mathematical formulations of law, along with detailed mathematical predictions of experimental results, as the main end of research in physics, while insight and perception through the mind are regarded as little more than incidental means of achieving such an end.

The whole matter is thus turned upside down. Rational and imaginative fancy are taken as the base, or the deep foundation and substructure of our knowledge, while rational and imaginative insight are, at least tacitly and often explicitly as well, taken as a relatively superficial structure, which works from this base. And so, it is not seen that the deep origin of our general lines of thinking is in creative and original acts of insight, the content of which is then further unfolded and developed in the domain of fancy, ultimately to serve as hints or clues which help to indicate or point to new acts of insight, and thus to complete the cycle of the process of knowledge.

THE PARALLELISM BETWEEN INTELLIGENCE AND THE PROCESS OF THOUGHT

As has already been indicated earlier, terms such as imagination, reason, and thought are being used in a somewhat different sense in this article from that in which they were used by other authors such as Coleridge and Hegel. Such a difference is, perhaps, inevitable. For in the nature of the case, this sort of term cannot be given a precise denotation, so that if we look at the subject in a different way, we will have to use words differently, to indicate the meaning that we have in mind.

In my view, the clearest way of considering the overall operation of the mind is through the inquiry into the distinction between intelligence and thought. I propose that the word 'intelligence' commonly signifies a kind of mental alertness, which is in essence a sort of perception. In the primary act of insight, which, for example, takes place in a flash of understanding, we *see* (though evidently, not through the senses) a whole range of differences, similarities, connections, disconnections, totalities of universal, and particular ratio or proportion, etc. This insight, which is of the essential quality of intelligence, cannot ultimately be a mere product of memory and training, because in each case it has to be seen anew. Rather, it is an act of *perception through the mind* (essentially what was called "nous" by the ancient Greeks). As such, it is a particular case of perception as a whole. This latter includes, not only perception through the mind, but also sense perception, aesthetic perception, and emotional perception (i.e., perception through feelings).

It seems clear that the totality of perception cannot appropriately be analysed further, or traced back to some yet more fundamental faculty. Rather, this perception is itself a primary act. Of course, we can analyse certain details concerning how the organs of perception (e.g., the eye) work, and how the nerves connect these organs to various functions in the brain. But this is in no sense an analysis of *perception itself*. Rather, before we can even make such an analysis, we have to take for granted the operation of intelligence or perception through the mind. Without this, such an analysis would have no meaning. For how can the intelligence needed to perceive the meaning of this analysis be itself perceived and compared with what is implied by the analysis?

Nor is it appropriate to try to identify perception in its totality with some particular faculty, such as imagination or reason. For, after all, the meaning of the word "imagination" must ultimately be restricted in some way by its implicit reference to the power to make mental images. And the meaning of the word "reason" is similarly restricted in some way by its reference to the power to develop discursive displays of "ratio" or rational thought. In my view, both Coleridge and Hegel tend to put something rather limited in its implications, such as imagination or reason, into the place for the primary source of creation and origination in the human being as a whole. I would rather suggest that the act of perception, considered as a totality which is not yet differentiated, is closer to this source. For the origin of this act must evidently be intrinsically unknown and undefinable, not capable of being attributed to some particular faculty, that may be involved in perception. (This means, of course, that perception in its totality could not ultimately be explained or accounted for in terms of any theory, scientific or otherwise, because each theory is itself a form of insight, and therefore merely a particular and special kind of perception.)

The other side of the operation of mind is indicated by the word "thought." Considering that this word now refers to what in Coleridge's terms would be called "the pole of mental process opposite to intelligence," we note that in thought, the aspect of recurrence, repetition, identity, and stability, is what is given a primary emphasis. The roots of thought are indeed indicated by all the uses of the prefix "re," which means "to turn around" and "to come back again." Thus, the eternal recurrence of day and night, or of the seasons, must make a deep impression on the mind of man. Long before he could consciously think of the subject, the whole operation of the mind must have become stably attuned to this recurrence, so that, for example, the expectation of the following of day and night on each other became a fixed feature of his mental processes. Similarly, when men continually repeated certain operations, conscious or otherwise, these became fixed in their minds as habitual reactions. Indeed, even the most abstract operations carried out today, such as those used in mathematics, soon result in similar reactions so that a skilled mathematician has a great deal of his knowledge 'at his fingertips' in a form that requires little or no conscious attention. So in all these ways, man's thinking process slowly came into being and formed itself into what may be called *reactive thought*.

Reactive thought works quite well as long as experience does not go too far outside the context in which such thought developed. But sooner or later, something is bound to happen, with which the existing pattern of reactive thought cannot deal adequately. A very elementary example can be obtained by considering a young child who finds bright objects pleasing and develops a reaction of reaching for them. This is evidently an elementary type of reactive thought, in the sense that the reaction includes a kind of knowledge from experience that bright objects are pleasing objects. But now suppose that the child reaches for a fire and burns himself. Immediately the reaction is powerfully inhibited. The next time the child sees a bright object, he may react toward it, but this reaction will now be associated to an inhibiting movement, based on the memory of the painful feeling. So the outgoing energy is held back and directed inward. It is such a reversal of energy direction that is the beginning of a process of *reflective thought*. This moves mainly within the nervous system, seeking a solution of the problem which is, in this case, to enjoy bright objects without being burned by them.

Now every outgoing impulse has a structure that corresponds at least in some rough way to the object toward which it is directed. When this impulse is reflected or turned back, it will stimulate the sensory nerves, in ways similar to how they would be stimulated by the object itself (though, of course, different as well). Thus, some kind of *image* is created in the nervous system, which can be perceived along with the object, or even when the object is not immediately in the field of perception. Such an image is not merely some idle fancy, arising passively out of memory in the stream of consciousness. Rather, it is actively produced by reflection of the outgoing impulses, and is therefore systematically related to the problem or difficulty that led to the reflection in the first place. So, in the internal process thus set in movement, it is possible to seek a combination of thoughts that resolves the difficulty, first in relation to the image (i.e., in the imagination) and later, in relation to the actual fact.

Evidently, then, reflection is in the first instance a way of meeting some difficulty, by constantly changing the pattern of reactive thought, to adapt it better to the actual fact. The primary function of such reflective thought is thus to try to reestablish a state of stability and equilibrium, in which reactive thought is once again adequate to meet the situation in which we find ourselves. Indeed, once reflection encounters a pattern that gives a solution, then sooner or later as this pattern is repeated, it is absorbed into the whole body of reactive thought. We shall thus say that thought of this kind is to be characterised as *reactive-reflective* (indicating that reaction is what is primary in this polarity, in the sense that reflection is mainly a means of adjusting or adapting a basically reactive pattern).

From the above it is clear that as we approach the extreme in which reactive thought is the principal factor in mental operation, the process will tend to become mainly mechanical. What characterizes a mechanical process is a certain kind of repetitiveness. That is to say, its essential feature is that when left to itself, it moves according to a law of inertia (i.e., of the necessity for a certain property of the motion to continue to repeat indefinitely until the system is disturbed from outside). Reactive thought evidently moves with such an inertia, which arises largely through associative links that are established in a habitual pattern by repetition of a series of similar mental and physical operations. This sort of pattern tends to change mainly when external circumstances alter, and force thought to react in a different way. It is thus clear that reactive thought is in essence a mechanical process.

Reactive thought is, of course, necessary because without it, we would have to reflect on every step. Very often this would be much too slow (e.g., when driving a motor car). And besides, the totality of steps is generally so great that we could not reflect on all of them at once. So even though it is basically mechanical, reactive thought is an essential side or aspect of the process of thought as a whole. Nevertheless, unless there is an opportunity for reflective thought to respond beyond the framework of such a mechanical mode of operation, thought as a whole will inevitably entangle itself in a growing mass of problems and difficulties that it cannot resolve.

We can see, however, that as ordinarily carried out, even the response of reflective thought tends rather easily to fall under the domination of a mechanical pattern. Thus, the attempt to solve a problem often does not go beyond the mere search of memory patterns, to try to discover one that will provide a solution. In the long run, this will result in a little more than a repetition of memory patterns on a new level. That is, instead of having an *immediate reaction* dominated by a memory pattern, we will have a reflection, leading to a *delayed reaction* dominated by a memory pattern. The delayed pattern may be richer and subtler than the original pattern, but it is nonetheless basically mechanical.

The next higher stage of thought arises when there is a problem for the solution of which it is seen that no memory pattern is available. What happens then is that the mind tries to "figure out" what to do. Generally, this process tends mainly to involve imaginative and rational fancy. That is, by ordering and arranging available images and concepts in new ways, as well as by adapting or modifying such images and concepts, the mind may arrive at a solution. As pointed out earlier, a certain insight is involved in such a process. Yet it is clear that in the long run what can be done in this way is rather strictly limited by the total set of basic images and concepts that may happen to be available. Thus, ultimately this sort of process must at best remain within frontiers determined in a basically mechanical way.

In a wide range of contexts, however, the response of rational and imaginative fancy is limited much more seriously than would be implied by the mere fixing of certain frontiers, beyond which it cannot go. What happens further is that reflective thought allows its basic mode of operation to be dominated by the apparent need to provide a solution that would fit in with the vast background of already existent reactive thought patterns. Now what is characteristic of such reactive thought patterns is a certain grossness and crudeness (i.e., an inability to respond sensitively and freely in new ways, to subtle indications of significant changes in the observed fact). For after all, a reaction is such that either it works in its general accustomed way or else it doesn't work at all. So when reflective thought is dominated by the attempt to find a solution that would fit in with the background of already existent reactive thought, it inevitably commits itself to imitating these crude and gross patterns of response. The main way in which it does this is by overemphasising the hard and fast definition of logical categories.

For example, a child may suffer a violent adverse reaction to a certain kind of food. When he reflects on this, he may incorporate this reaction into his conscious thought by thinking: "*All* food of this nature is bad." By implication, this constitutes a precise and fixed distinction between all food similar to that which disturbed him and all food different from that which disturbed him. Behind this implication is the general notion: "Either a particular item of food is in the 'disturbing' category or it is not, and that is *all* that is possible." Such a lumping of things into opposing and sharply defined and fixed categories evidently corresponds very well with the reactions that give rise to this line of reflective thought. This fit between reflection and reaction then permits a solution of the problem, in the form of the development of a fixed response of keeping away from foods of a "disturbing" nature.

It must be pointed out, however, that man's discovery of the rules of formal logic (e.g., a thing is either A or not A) constituted an important step forward. Such rules were necessary, in a wide range of contexts, in which they were appropriate (i.e., those in which simple and sharp distinctions can consistently be made). Nevertheless, this very same development also led man into a dangerous and destructive trap. Thus, for example, while it might be appropriate to divide all objects of a certain kind as being either inside or outside a certain region of space, it is generally inappropriate and even harmful to divide all types of food in this simple way, between "disturbing" and "nondisturbing." For the reasons why food may cause a disturbance are quite complex and may have to do with all sorts of factors, going outside the question of whether the food is of one type or another.

Yet, as long as the mind is dominated by the background of reactive thought patterns, reflective thought will tend automatically and mechanically to respond in all cases indiscriminately with some sharp and unalterably fixed formal logical distinction in the manner described above. (An extreme case of this arises in a hostile reaction to people of another race, to which reflective thought responds with prejudicial judgments, such as: "People are divided into mutually exclusive races, and all people of this particular race are bad.")

How then can thought respond to a problem or a difficulty without being dominated by an irrelevant, confusing, and generally destructive mechanical pattern of reaction? Evidently, what is needed for this is a quality of insight, going beyond any particular fixed form of reaction and associated reflective thought. This insight must be free of conditioning to previously existing patterns, or otherwise it will, of course, ultimately be just an extension of mechanical reaction. Rather, it has to be fresh and new, creative and original.

As indicated earlier, insight of this kind is a form of perception through the mind, which is the essence of what is most deeply meant by the word "intelligence." When such intelligence operates, then in each case there is a perception of where the everchanging dividing line between a given pair of opposing categories properly falls, and of whether a given pair of such categories is relevant. So the mind is no longer dominated by its mechanical tendency to hold unalterably to such fixed and limited sets of categories, nor by the automatic reactions that have ultimately given rise to the tendency to hold unalterably to such fixed and limited sets of categories. And thus, whenever there is a difficult problem, the mind is able if necessary to drop the old categories and to create new forms of rational and imaginative insight, which now serve to guide thought along the new lines that may be necessary for resolving the problem.

It is implicitly accepted in a large part of our common notions on the subject, however, that intelligence is an extension or development from thought. That is, thought is regarded as providing a sort of base or ground, from which intelligence arises, and on which in turn it operates. It cannot be too strongly emphasised that what is being suggested here is that intelligence does not thus arise primarily out of thought. Rather, as pointed out earlier, the deep source of intelligence is the unknown and undefinable totality, from which all perception originates.

Clearly then, intelligence is not to be regarded as a result of accumulated knowledge, which could be learned, for example, as a science or as a technique. Rather, it can perhaps best be regarded as an *art* — the art of perception through the mind. Such an art requires great insight and skill. When these are absent, thought quickly gets lost in confusion.

There can be no system or specifiable method for avoiding the tendency for thought to fall into such confusion. Rather, what is required is a general alertness, which makes us aware, from moment to moment, of how the process of thought is getting caught in fixed sets of categories. However, even such alertness does not provide for perfect harmony in this unceasing movement. Nevertheless, with the right quality of mental energy, insight and skill, the art of intelligent perception will enable us sooner or later to meet whatever difficulties may arise, without getting lost in the fixity of categories that leads to unresolvable confusion. And so it may perhaps be said that it is just in such creative perception of disharmony in the process of thought that man may come upon the deepest harmony that is open to him.

REFERENCES

1. Barfield, O. *What Coleridge Thought*. Middletown, Conn: Wesleyan University Press, 1971, (a) 76; (b) 128.
2. Wallace, W. *The Logic of Hegel*. London: Oxford University Press, 1904, (a) 92; (b) 379.

DARWINISM

by

R. H. BARFIELD

I

In his introduction to a recent edition of the *Origin of Species*, Sir Julian Huxley[10] says: "The universal principle of Natural Selection is now firmly and finally established as the sole agency of major evolutionary change." This must surely be one of the most unscientific pronouncements ever made by a scientist (and Sir Julian is preeminently one who bases his whole life, beliefs, and theories on proclaiming himself as a scientist). Indeed, to find it refuted, one has only to read the introduction to the latest "Everyman" (1969) edition, in which Professor W. R. Thompson[16] concludes by saying of the *Origin of Species*: "To establish the continuity required by theory, historical arguments are invoked even though historical evidence is lacking. Thus are engendered those fragile towers of hypothesis based on hypotheses where fact and fiction intermingle in an inextricable confusion." Moreover, practically the whole of this introduction is in effect one long contradiction of Sir Julian's dogmatic assertion. The issue thus raised is by no means an academic one — of interest only to experts and specialists — but is of vital importance to mankind at the present critical stage of its evolution. It has a decisive bearing on the question that every man must, at times, either consciously or unconsciously, ask himself, "For what purpose, if any, do I find myself alive and in this world?"

The theory referred to by Sir Julian is a simple one. It is a pronouncement on life itself and, in some way, at least, an answer to the question posed above: namely, that the origin and development of life arises from the chance motions of elementary particles, irreducible entities, so to speak. These particles are governed by forces by which they are condensed into stable groups of atoms. The atoms, by the same agencies, are formed into molecules of ever-increasing complexity. These molecules, under the influence of a favourable and very special environment, form still more complicated structures having the property of *reproducing* themselves indefinitely, but with occasional slight modifications of a random nature. The modifications result in a process of selection and rejection: the most favourable ones flourishing and the unfavourable ones dying out.

In this way there comes into being the simple living cell. It is these cells that form the basis of all living organisms. In the course of ages, more and more complicated organisms arise, all due to this selection, or principle of "survival of the fittest." The different cells in an organism have different functions, subservient to the needs of the creature as a whole. Slight variations in each generation of such organisms result in a population of slightly varying types of individuals, some of which have better chances of surviving than others, and this enables a higher and ever higher form of life to arise, which culminates in man himself. The principles of natural selection and survival of the fittest are here recognisable, and the assertion is made that the rest of the multiform complicity of creation which constitutes the living world around us is the result of these two principles. Granted the initial stage of this process (that is, the formation by accident of molecular activity capable of reproduction), we note that to go any further the units reproduced must not be exact copies of the parents. These slight differences enable the second agency to come into action; that is, the variations that are more favourable than others survive and replace the less favoured ones, and thus the beginning of an evolutionary process is established. Thus survival of the fittest and natural selection are brought about by the struggle for existence.

The serious objection that nearly proved fatal to the simple idea was that a single favourable change in one organism would, after several generations, become swamped or deleted by the inheritance of the unchanged characteristics from all the other ancestors.

The discoveries of Mendel, which prove the stability of any particular modification throughout successive generations, rescued it however and it was still further made secure by the discovery of genes and complex molecules able to reproduce themselves. Then came molecular biology with its incredibly ingenious experimental techniques. This field of research has discovered complete molecules actually able to reproduce themselves. The genes derived from these molecules have fantastically complex structures that contain a kind of code of instruction, so that, when they become incorporated in the embryo of the developing organism, they constitute a pattern that this embryo must copy as it develops. Thus "reductionism," relentlessly pursued, appears to enthusiastic Darwinians to uncover facts that "explain" life and evolution.

II

The evidence for the general acquiescence in the above-quoted pronouncement of Sir Julian Huxley is not hard to find. Conversations with those of one's friends, relations, and acquaintances, who have thought at all about the subject, almost invariably produce, in my experience, the impression that they have been aware of the doctrine of natural selection since their schooldays and have accepted it without question as being true. Elementary biological textbooks either explicitly or implicitly regard it as almost axiomatic. Thus T. Dobzhansky,[5] the eminent biologist, says, "Every student taking an introductory Biological course accepts that Mechanism is right and Vitalism is wrong, thus supporting the fundamental assumption of Darwinism and Neo-Darwinism." In his brilliant and fascinating study of the robin, David Lack[12] repeatedly takes it for granted that each special feature of the bird, and most of his actions (including his song!) possess what is known as "survival value," which alone accounts for it.

The general impression gained is, in fact, that people today are, so to say, soaked in the presupposition that natural phenomena of all kinds — the colour and beauty of flowers, the habits of insects and of animals with all their variety and peculiarities — can be accounted for by the free play of chance variations coming under the influence of the natural selection of the most favourable variations surviving in the struggle for existence or making the most of the advantages offered by their environment. The assumption is, indeed, so common, so subconscious, and its acceptance so universal in almost all popular scientific and psuedoscientific writings (not excepting many, though by no means all, those of eminent biologists) that it is difficult to specify explicit examples any more than it would be easy to find explicit evidence of belief in Newton's theory of gravitation.

Broadcast talks, however, provide one convenient source. A cursory survey of a recent issue of *Listener's* (a publication of the BBC) provides many examples of this all but universal acceptance.

An article entitled "The End of the World"[15] begins, "The evolution of the Universe is determined by that of its parts (the galaxies) and by that of their constituents the stars," and so on down to the particles and sub-particles, that is, to the ultimate "reduction" of the world by physicists. In the review by H. Millar[14] of the *Mind of Man* by Nigel Calder, an "engineering" approach to brain research is described. The characteristics of an individual such as laziness, lassitude, etc., are determined by chemical factors; for example, drugs can remove depression and can radically alter personality. In other words, we are really only machines. The consequences of this belief, if applied with conviction to every day affairs, would merely be to affirm that no one could really be responsible for any of his actions or inaction since it is all a matter of being supplied with the right chemicals.

In a debate between Medawar and Bamburgh[13] the discussion turns to the theme of "reductionism," that is to say, to the present ingrained habit of all sciences, particularly that of pure physics, of explaining all macrophenomena by their microconstituents. Physics, for example, explains material bodies by their molecules; the molecules by their atoms; and the atoms themselves by the lesser atomic nuclei with their protons and electrons; and, still smaller, down to the whole galaxy of particles, which seem at the same time to be waves in a mysterious something called a "field" of force. This field, it should be noted, is completely immaterial.

This principle again applies to biology where the constituents are now the microorganism the cell, the protein molecule, the chromosome, and the gene, which are themselves a series of very complex molecules. This has been said, by one skeptical commentator to imply that everything living can be explained by "little causative thingummies."[6] In a review by M. Warnock[17] of Jacques Monod's book *Chance and Necessity*, she quotes the passage: "Life itself, the very existence of life has been shown to be the result of chance mutations which could not have been predicted." What she does not point out is that the introduction of the word "predict" lets in an activity that is of the mind and therefore something that is of another world from that of the presumed preexisting material substance from which the author builds up his structure of life. The review proceeds: "A Nobel prizewinning chemist gives the latest and most up to date official view of the Biochemists on evolution — an exposition of Neo-Darwinism with an altruistic presupposition." These scientific conclusions form the main content of the book, which is philosophical, having a definite doctrine — to preach of man's salvation from his present predicament or, as he calls it, from the "Horrible Soup" in which he now finds himself and which lies at the root of our modern sickness of spirit. The crux of this salvation is the strict adherence to the principle that scientific *objective* knowledge is the highest good. "Values" as such of whatever kind are entirely irrelevant and their study has no part to play in this supreme task, a task only to be accomplished by the strenuous pursuit of this kind of scientific knowledge.

"This sickness of the spirit," says Monod, "witnessed by the conglomeration of muddled ideologies and isms, is a very profound and deadly one and threatens mankind with death." It is perhaps rather remarkable that he completely ignores the modern vigorous growth of opposition — referred to later — to the claims of Neo-Darwinism to have discovered the key to evolution.

The *Encyclopaedia Britannica* (1970 edition) forms a very good comprehensive storehouse from which the modern attitude to Darwinism may be garnered. Notable among the many articles bearing on the subject are those on "Biology," "Evolution," "Genetics," "Instinct," and the "*Cell*." The article on "Biology" concludes that "Natural Selection remains the keystone to modern evolutionary theory and can now be rigorously applied to the treatment of populations containing given proportions of individuals carrying Mendelian genes that alone, or in combination, promote or diminish the chances of survival of the individual bearing them." This somewhat bald statement seems to be considered as containing a complete explanation of the whole of the great emergence into being of all natural life with all its astonishing variety and complexity, which we now find around us. In a concluding passage the article affirms that no really serious objections to the hypothesis of evolution have ever been advanced and that the occurrence of evolution is now accepted as a matter of course. This last statement is somewhat ambiguous as it leaves it doubtful whether it refers simply to the fact of evolution, which hardly any one would now question, or also to the Darwinian or Neo-Darwinian mechanism that causes it to take place. In fact at the beginning of the next paragraph the author himself actually says that "Evidence for Evolution tells us nothing about its mechanism." In the article on "Evolution," statistical genetics is the magic formula or phrase that accounts for the whole phenomenon of evolution and the infinite variety of life. Owing to the absence of any but the scantiest evidence of this process taking place or having taken place, the whole of his intricate and ingenious account of what has happened is *almost* purely conjectural, and one can only marvel at the naïve faith with which the so-called mechanism is accepted as truth, by its exponents. For example, in a *Dictionary of Genetics*[11] we find the following definition of *Courtship Ritual*: "A characteristic, genetically determined behavioural pattern involving the production and reception of an elaborate sequence of visual, auditory and chemical stimuli by the male and female prior to mating. Such rituals are interpreted as insuring that mating will occur only between individuals of opposite sex and the same species." Hence, it would appear to follow, the behaviour of Romeo and Juliet. Indeed, we have only to let our imagination rove over the vast phenomenon of zoology as a whole to see at once how inadequate and fragile is the foundation on which the mechanistic hypothesis is built. Everything is accounted for by "gene adaptation." One of the pillars of the argument is that each generation is observed to produce such immense numbers of offspring (e.g., trees, other plants, fish, etc.), that only a few can survive. Surely, however, this fact cuts both ways. The very plentifulness of the supply would ensure that some would survive despite competition. The fact that the supply in numbers is unlimited means that there is no need to bother about improving adaptability since there is so much available material to draw on. Nature herself has here provided a guarantee of survival of *existing* types without the need for any modification.

III

The case against Darwinism and its later development, Neo-Darwinism, is simply that there is really no case *for* it. It is a wonderful idea but nothing more. It is nearly all surmise. In her recent book *Darwin and the Darwinian Revolution* Dr. Himmelfarb[9] concludes her chapter on the arguments of the *Origin* with the words "Posing as a massive deduction from the evidence, it ends up as an ingenious argument from ignorance." This judgment is equally applicable to the arguments of the Neo-Darwinists. Their engagingly simple hypothesis of the means by which life or nature came into its present state of being is, and always has been, unacceptable to anyone with intelligence and diligence enough to call up by his imagination the nature and succession of the minute changes that would be required to produce even the very simplest creature. Such an exercise of thought, of which a very large majority of human beings must be capable, will indeed result in the discovery that the Darwinian idea is nothing but, in a colloquial idiom, a "hunch" and not even a plausible "hunch." Nothing but the most overwhelming evidence of the process actually working could avail to make it worth considering for a moment, and there is, in fact, practically no evidence of this kind. This is not to say that there is no evidence for *evolution*; this no one would deny who has studied the fossil record in its chronological aspect as determined geologically. There are also some rather trivial and obvious observationally established instances of changes brought about by environmental alterations. Thus there is the case of moths (quoted ad nauseam) that have changed from white to black as the trees on which they settled grew blacker with the process of smoky industrial development in their neighbourhood. This amounts to little more than saying that if a cat were turned loose in the dark in a field containing an equal number of black and white mice, there would afterwards be mostly black mice surviving. It is just obvious.

We can divide the total process that this materialistic, mechanistic hypothesis involves into several stages:

(1) origin of life itself from mere matter;
(2) development up to the simple cell;
(3) evolution of the cell into complicated living organisms;
(4) development of organism into plants, fish, animals, birds, and finally to man himself.

It is the intermediate steps in these changes that are always missing. That is to say, the minute jumps by which the various persistent stages are reached are not observable. In fact they are conspicuous by their absence.

The "Everyman" edition of the *Origin of Species*[16] has an introduction already referred to which strongly criticises and in fact totally rejects the claims of the mechanistic explanation of evolution. This introduction is written by Professor W. R. Thompson FRS, director of the Commonwealth Institute of Biological Control, Ottawa. The gravamen of Thompson's attack amounts to the assertion that the proposition that chance and natural selection are the causes of evolution is not a scientific theory at all as it cannot be verified. It cannot be proved by an appeal to the facts and is therefore without scientific value. Thus palaeontological evidence today, as in Darwin's time, does not produce evidence in support of the hypothesis. Such observational facts as emerge require numbers of subsidiary and unverifiable hypotheses to bring them into line with the main postulate.

Darwinism fails to explain the division of the animal world into some ten great groups of phyla. This clear-cut division applies equally to insects. Everywhere we are faced with gaps in the process that is the very basis of the Darwinian hypothesis. *FLIGHT IN ① INSECTS ② MAMMALS ③ AVES*

The argument or surmise that these gaps would have been eliminated by natural selection is an unproved supposition that cannot be accepted as an argument for Darwinism.

"There is a great divergence among biologists about the causes and processes of evolution which arises out of the lack of adequate evidence and this should be made known to the non-scientific world." But Thompson says that Darwinian evolutionists think otherwise. He actually hints at suppression of criticism in defence of a doctrine they are unable to demonstrate or, in fact, to *define* scientifically.

Thompson then touches on the relation of evolutionary hypothesis to religion and rationalist philosophy and shows how the new theory came as a blessing those foremost in the new trends of thought (e.g., rationalists at war with the last vestiges of superstition, opponents of narrow orthodoxy and literal interpretation of biblical writing). The *Origin* effectively dissipated the evidence of providential control. "There is much to be said for the view," he says, "that the decline of Christianity was largely due to the influence of Darwin." Though this is a tenable supposition, it appears more probable that the decline of Christianity and belief in the supernatural provided a background for the eager and uncritical acceptance of the Darwinian conceptions. In fact, as Thompson says further on, "there existed and still exists a 'natural' appetite for materialistic or mechanistic explanations of what have formerly been regarded as containing spiritual or supernatural or supersensible ingredients."

A few years ago there were two important conferences[4] of biologists, physicists, and other scientists: one at Alpbach in Austria under the initiative of Arthur Koestler, and the other at the Villa Serbelloni on Lake Como, organised by C. H. Waddington. These assemblies, which lasted for several days and at which many original papers were read and discussed, centered round the phenomenon of evolution and may be said to have arisen out of the general dissatisfaction among active research workers with the oversimplification of and lack of satisfactory objective evidence for the orthodox Neo-Darwinian theory.

It is difficult to summarize the general outcome of these conferences. One of the most interesting among the papers was that by Professor Bohm, a distinguished physicist, who was mainly interested in the part played by chance in the Darwinian view. Professor Bohm has evolved some revolutionary ideas out of this aspect of modern nuclear and atomic physics, putting forward the view that chance may be only an apparent phenomenon, reflecting order at another level. When applied to biology he suggests that instead of attempting to employ reductionism to the final explanations (that is, seeking to *explain* the whole in terms of its parts), it seems more probable that it is more in accordance with the facts of evolution to assume that the whole *determines* the parts.

Much attention was directed to the importance of introducing the dimension of time into the matter. Organisms have, so to speak, a "built in" time factor as they are, in fact, dynamic not static, and this is a factor that is not predicted by reductionist explanations based on molecules and genes. Professor Waddington went so far as to compare organisms to musical compositions.

The general impression emerging from these conferences was of life coming into material being and giving rise to forms predetermined in a nonmaterial world, the genetic and molecular structure being, so to speak, directed so as to conform with the final pattern. It may be remarked that a nonmaterial world is now accepted by physicists as constituting the true nature of particles.

Marjorie Grene[8] in her book *The Knower and the Known* says, "In the modern 'orthodox' conception of the world 'what is real' is by definition, the non-living," and "Darwinism is the extension of the machine image to life itself." She sees Darwinism as a religion, the religion of the late nineteenth century bestowing the final triumph on rationalism — that doctrine which has no place for superstitious beliefs or any form of mystery, including the doctrine of Christianity itself.

The Neo-Darwinian logic, in fact, accounts for everything happening by the two great principles "chance" and "necessity." "Nature," she says, "is like a vast computing machine, set up in binary digits." Moreover it is self-programming. With this accepted — as it surely is now almost subconsciously by the educated population of the world — there is no longer need to invoke "providential guidance" or even any purpose in nature or, in fact, in the world in general.

She has many weighty criticisms against this oversimplified but extremely ingenious thesis.

The "Origin of Species" is not *about* the *origin* of species at all but rather a reasoned explanation of how minute and specialised adaptations come to occur. There is no evidence to account for the "massive novelties" of evolution, the sudden appearance of startling new ideas of living. There is just the one simple formula and the rest is conjecture, surmise and hypothesis piled on hypothesis.

More than once she refers to the fact that a comprehensive and imaginative survey of the whole phenomenon of evolution is significantly analogous to the ontological development of a seed or an embryo in animal and plants. Philogenesis, in this view, is the ontogenetic process of the whole earth.

"On re-reading the 'Origin of Species,' " writes Professor M. Grene, "we find that it simply is not about the origin of species at all. It deals with minute specialised adaptations which lead, unless to extinction, to nowhere and the same is true of the whole immense and infinitely ingenious mountain of work by present-day Darwinians."

Dr. Jung, in a conversation with Grant-Watson,[7] dismissed summarily the Darwinian chance and selection hypotheses as being too simple to account for all the phenomena of life.

IV

So we have arrived at a position from which we see Darwinism and Neo-Darwinism as an almost desperate attempt to reconcile our experience of life and living things with our Cartesian presuppositions of the world system of observer and observed, an attempt which has failed to bring any satisfaction to an imaginative intellect. Thus we are forced to ask the question "Why do men still cling to it?" The answer is a very simple one. It is because the whole drift or trend of men's thinking since the theories of Copernicus, Galileo, Kepler, Newton, and many others has been in the direction of the elimination from natural phenomena of all qualities relating to the soul or spirit.

Galileo revealed that, in scientific objective observations based on measurable or calculable properties of substances, it was necessary to distinguish between what he called "primary" and "secondary" qualities. Thus number, size, weight or mass, motion, and time were *primary* qualities and colour, sound, smell, taste (and anything involving sensation) were *secondary* qualities in as much as they had no objectivity since they were bound up with feelings and were, therefore, subjective and unreal. This, in one form or another, is the fundamental presupposition underlying all pure science and, to a large extent, demonstrates the approach to, and content of, all quasi-sciences, among which biology must be included.

Modern physics has gone even further and excluded from primary qualities everything but number, motion, and force; thus even solidity and shape are ruled out and placed with the other secondary qualities on the subjective, and, therefore, unreal, side of the Cartesian dividing line.

Thus a search for objective truth and scientific reality virtually only amounts to asking questions of nature that can be answered in terms of primary qualities. But science has established itself as being the only satisfactory means of establishing universally acceptable truths so that all other kinds of assertion or belief are subjective, that is, dependent on the peculiar state of mind or feeling of the man or men from whom they emanate, and are, therefore, a priori, unreliable, and suspect.

Thus in such subjects as anthropology, biology, psychology, and sociology

— all sciences in fact except physics, mathematics, and chemistry — we are obliged, by hypothesis, to eliminate all aesthetic or ethical considerations from our field of enquiry; with the result that there is a tendency to *reduce* the fundamental subject matter of these disciplines to the smallest possible entities, the interaction of which microphenomena determine the characteristics of the macrophenomena being investigated — these particles or molecules, genes, etc., being themselves the seat of only primary qualities.

There is, perhaps, irony in the fact that the almost fanatical adherence of these Darwinians to their hypothesis arises out of the almost indisputable fact of evolution, though indeed a much wider interpretation of that word than they themselves imply is here required.

Evolution, to make sense, must cover the whole evolution of the world including, and most important of all, that of man's own consciousness, or his inner world of thought and feeling with all the secondary qualities which these supply to the apparent outer world to which the term evolution is normally applied.

To appreciate this we require an imaginative grasp of all that has happened in this subjective side of the dividing line between the observer and the observed.

Descartes, who is the prophet of the scientific age, is responsible for insisting on this sharp line as the only means of obtaining scientific detachment by which alone the truth can be isolated from illusion. In postulating this duality he was not aware of the consequences that it would have, on the one hand, in the incredible advance and success of technology, which largely constitutes the scientific revolution, and, on the other, in its metaphysical and philosophic aspect and indeed in its profound effect on religion. In the first of these, the assumption he made set free energies and methods that have proved outstandingly, almost miraculously, successful in producing working results. This itself constitutes a fact that seems to imply the absolute establishment of his postulate as the sole and sufficient philosophical truth. In the second of them, however, the Cartesian duality has had a somewhat less satisfactory, perhaps almost disastrous, effect on man's view of the world.

At this point, I only wish to draw attention to the relation of the Cartesian philosophy to the whole movement of thought and feeling in the Western world before and after the time at which it emerged. If we survey the history of the world of thought and of man's mind over the previous centuries or millennia, we become aware of man's experiencing a gradual withdrawal from participating in nature, while, at the same time, he becomes more and more conscious of himself as standing self-aware and detached from his surroundings. Thus if we go back far enough, man took for granted that gods and supernatural beings are at work in nature and in his own life; though it is true he did not do so with his intellect. We are in the period of the great myths and legends. As time proceeds he became more and more detached from these experiences, which however are transferred, so to speak, to the subjective side of the Cartesian line. Since the Cartesian philosophy is now firmly established in his mind as the only possible approach to generally acceptable truth, man is obliged, as I have pointed out, to ask questions with respect to the nature of the world in which he finds himself that can be answered in terms of primary qualities. Thus when he enquires into the nature of life he can only get a reply that assumes all other kinds of qualities, such as social, ethical or religious, are ruled out, or, at least, ignored "ex-hypothesi Cartesian." Even if doubt is thrown on the satisfactoriness or adequacy of this reply he is bound to adhere to it since any worldview that lets in the secondary qualities would make the Cartesian position untenable and that would turn his whole world upside down. It is, in fact, the subconscious dread of this that makes men accept and cling to any plausible suggestion that may avoid it. Hence they cling to Darwinism in face of all its absurdities.

V

Looking out into the world of human thought today — or to the way in which the world is seen by the great majority of thinking human beings — we are aware of great areas of conflicting ideologies, philosophies, metaphysics, and religion. But there is an area in which there is little or no conflict. That is the area covered by the scientific method of approach or what may be loosely called the realm of science.

Scientific authority — its reputation gained from tested theories in physics, chemistry, astronomy, medicine, and many other fields — gives a kind of stability to the world. It brings under its sway the most extreme areas of world conflicts. It is not divided by the iron curtain nor influenced by the otherwise estranged Far Eastern, Communist republics. In some ways it may be looked upon as the modern equivalent of a universal church.

The faith accorded to science and to scientists has even established a truce — perhaps an uneasy one — in the military field of the arms race between East and West today. The great powers pause before letting loose the super-weapon. This is because scientific authority declares the universal doom that must inevitably result from so doing.

Scientific orthodoxy, therefore, commands universal respect, and like other religions, this orthodoxy has established its dogmas and taboos, although it perhaps should be said that many people, if not the majority, are unaware of this having happened. The world is, in fact, united by scientific orthodoxy as it never has been by any one religion. Many books have been written on comparative religions; there are none on comparative sciences.

The importance of Darwinism in this context is that it occupies a key position in the kingdom of Cartesian science. Starting with physics, this system has worked its way upwards and outwards until it embraces all fields of knowledge and in fact claims that there is no field to which it does not apply.

To justify this claim it must show that biology — or the whole field of living things — can be also brought under its sway. That is to say it must be able to account for the origin of life and evolution subsequent to this origin, up to and including man himself, with all his special attributes. Failure in any part of this vast field will throw doubt on the whole of the realms over which it has established itself with such marked success, and this is the reason why Darwinism has been so welcomed by scientists and the world in general.

In fact in the attempt to eliminate the idea of the "creation" in its religious sense — a word that nineteenth-century materialism could not stomach, and that today has become almost a "dirty" word in the collective psyche of our age — wishful thinking pounced on Darwin's *Origin of Species* as a veritable windfall; it became, we might almost say, the bible of the negation of God or spirit in nature.

It is, however, the object of this section of my essay to draw attention to the bad or even evil effects of this situation. In this Cartesian world man is conscious of himself as an observer who, as regards his purpose of existence, finds himself, so to speak, in the air. He conceives himself as the product of evolution from a natural universe, as a result of chance and natural selection. He is the summit of this process; there is no need for anything higher to "explain" him or to which he is responsible. There is an obvious danger here of arrogance, on the one hand, and irresponsibility, on the other.

When he contemplates nature man cannot forget that it is a machine and, therefore, not worthy of reverence or awe. It is kept going by mechanical urges and chance variations. Its most fascinating and beautiful features exist merely because they have "survival value." Any reverence is reserved for great discoveries or the men of genius who have established its laws and unfolded its technological or therapeutic possibilities or for clever research workers. Though why this reverence and respect should be forthcoming at all is rather hard to say, since, according to their own presuppositions, it is all a result of chance and mechanistic forces.

As it has already been said, all *values* in the Cartesian world outlook are subjective and, therefore, presumably to be taken seriously if they have survival value. The seven virtues as well as the seven deadly sins have no foundation in observable reality. And yet, of course, it is true to say that most of us, the overwhelming majority in fact, still *act* as if these secondary qualities still existed as realities. We bow to the wisdom inherited from the past. This has sunk into our subconscious. We feel that life is good and kindness and hope and the urge to work to keep things going are natural phenomena even though they cannot be measured or weighed. We value our civilisation and the freedom we have won or inherited. But without some recognition or perception of cosmic purpose these things may not survive. That is the peril in which we now live. Our instincts are sound, but without some metaphysical backing, better than that obtained from Darwinism or Neo-Darwinism, it is even probable that our civilisation cannot long survive.

Perhaps even, the violence, sex aberration, and despair, the underlying sense of nothingness or rather of nothing to look forward to but death which ends everything, are the results of this lack of anything better.

VI

In what goes before I have drawn attention to the nature of the Darwinian and Neo-Darwinian theory and shown how it has been largely accepted by the majority of men and women at the present day as a true explanation of the living world. I have then revealed the strength of the case against it which might well be thought to be overwhelming. I have gone on to show why this somewhat astonishing acceptance of Darwinism has persisted despite its naïveté. I have traced this to the key position it occupies in a mechanistic or nonvitalistic view of the world as a whole, in accordance with the prevailing spirit of our age, or with the process of the evolution of consciousness. This is characterised by the application of the Cartesian philosophy (without perceiving its inherent limitations) to the world of appearances.

I have finally tried to show the danger to the world resulting from this outlook and have suggested that some of the physical unrest and other unpleasant phenomena of the modern world may be a result of this outlook.

What then is the alternative? If a mechanistic, chance-grounded explanation has failed the world is indeed "turned upside down." Life must come from the periphery not from, or as well as from, the centre. We are, in a sense, back to Genesis but not, of course, in a literal sense. The observer and the observed are part of one world and theories or explanations of evolution must embrace both. Our priorities must be reversed. The material world is precipitated from a nonmaterial world; from a world of *thought*, which is an ultimate reality; a world with which we are so familiar that we pass over its existence as we pass over the existence of the air that we breathe. We must examine a past in which things and thought are combined. We must, in short, include both sides of the Cartesian dividing line in the scope of our enquiry, both the primary and the secondary qualities. In this way we shall unite both measurable quantities — mathematical theories and physically observable phenomena with the subjective qualities, such as colour, harmony, and the aesthetic, moral, and religious feelings. Nothing can be left out of our enquiry into evolution.

It will therefore be clear that this much wider enquiry cannot be carried out by the measurements, the mathematical theories, and the techniques of advanced physics and chemistry, which have hitherto been employed, but that other methods of approach must be adopted.

The fundamental subject matter of physics, passing downwards through the stages of atoms, electrons, and particles has now been dissolved into a nonmaterial world of fields having dynamic properties of change in space and time. Since it appears that matter itself thus originates, it is fairly obvious that the wider phenomena that must now be included in an evolutionary investigation must also have its origin in a nonmaterial or supersensible world.

It is beyond the scope of this essay to develop this theme. It has already been developed and indeed perhaps in its most lucid and easily assimilable form by Owen Barfield[1,2,3] to whom this book is dedicated. Evolution can only be comprehended as the evolution of the whole world of our inner experiences and outer perceptions. To limit it to a fragment — an attempt to limit it to those things that we mistakenly conceive to exist by themselves — can lead only to confusion or a meaningless result.

REFERENCES

1. Barfield, O. *Saving the Appearances*. London: Faber & Faber, 1957.
2. ———. *World's Apart*. London: Faber & Faber, 1962.
3. ———. *Unancestral Voice*. London: Faber & Faber, 1965.
4. Davy, J. *Observer (Supplement)* London. 8 and 15, February 1970.
5. Dobzhansky, T. *The Biology of Ultimate Concern*. New York: W. W. Norton & Co., 1969, p. 18.
6. Esperazin, P. G. "The Concept of the Gene." Paper read to the British Society for the Philosophy of Science, 1959.
7. Grant Watson, E. L. *Mystery of Physical Life*. London: Abelard Schuman, 1964, p. 18.
8. Grene, M. *The Knower and the Known*. London: Faber & Faber, 1969.
9. Himmelfarb, G. *Darwin and the Darwinian Revolution*. London: Chatto & Windus, 1959.
10. Darwin, C. *Origin of Species*. Introduction by J. Huxley. London: New English Library, 1958.
11. King, R. C. *Dictionary of Genetics*. London: Oxford University Press, 1968.
12. Lack, D. *The Life of the Robin*. London: Wetherby, 1948.
13. Medawar, P. B. *The Listener*. 86, 2206 (July 8, 1971), p. 33.
14. Millar, H. *The Listener*. 85, 2190 (March 18, 1971), p. 334.
15. Taylor, J. *The Listener*. 86, 2215 (September 9, 1971), p. 321.
16. Darwin, C. *Origin of Species*. Introduction by W. R. Thompson. London: Everyman's Library, no. 811, 1967.
17. Warnock, M. *The Listener*. 86, 2228 (December 9, 1971), p. 788.

"NOVELTY" IN POLARITY TO "THE MOST ADMITTED TRUTHS": TRADITION AND THE INDIVIDUAL TALENT IN S. T. COLERIDGE AND T. S. ELIOT

by

RICHARD A. HOCKS

> In poems, equally as in philosophic disquisitions, genius produces the strongest impressions of novelty, while it rescues the most admitted truths from the impotence caused by the very circumstance of their universal admission.
>
> — Coleridge, *Biographia Literaria* (chapter 4)

> What happens when a new work of art is created is something that happens simultaneously to all the works of art which preceded it. The existing monuments form an ideal order among themselves, which is modified by the introduction of the new (the really new) work of art among them.
>
> — Eliot, "Tradition and the Individual Talent"

I

These two statements, by perhaps the most influential literary critics in the English-speaking world of the preceding and present centuries respectively, and found in what are probably the most influential of their critical documents, convey aesthetic proposals unexpectedly similar. Coleridge's assertion, to be sure, seems to account philosophic and poetic genius as virtually interchangeable, whereas Eliot clearly refers only to the product of the artist. Furthermore, Coleridge's conception of genius implies, among other matters, that we distinguish it from mere talent;* but Eliot's conception demands a far more positive response to the idea of artistic talent (as seen by the title of his essay), and even that we distinguish *it* from the sort of vague, undisciplined, self-oriented, and isolated individuality frequently connoted by the word "genius." There are in fact a host of differences one could cite and develop from these two brief passages. And most of those differences would in turn derive ultimately from Coleridge's ties with the "romantic temper" and Eliot's with the "classical temper."

---

* The distinction between genius and talent is for Coleridge, as for Emerson and several others in the nineteenth-century romantic tradition, essentially the same as that between imagination and fancy.

Nevertheless, the similarity to which I refer resides in the basic perspective both take on a most knotty and important issue, that of originality in the work of a person of genius and/or genuine artistic talent. Particularly, both Coleridge and Eliot seek to express the actual relationship between what is the inevitable novelty of freshness present in each successive work of art and the equally inevitable fact that what is "really new" in each such instance is, precisely, what is already received and transmitted through its predecessors; moreover, that it is only by virtue of those predecessors that such newness is engendered, and only because the newness *is* engendered each time that the received tradition is thereby validated and manifested *as* tradition, i.e., as living and dynamic. In short, the relationship is that of genuine polarity, the life-endowing one through opposition. Leaving aside for the moment the consideration of Eliot and polarity, it may not greatly surprise us to discover that Coleridge, seven years before writing the *Biographia*, had already composed virtually the same statement for *The Friend* and had immediately glossed it by referring explicitly to polar opposition:

In Philosophy equally as in Poetry, Genius produces the strongest impressions of novelty, while it rescues the stalest and most admitted Truths from the Impotence caused by the very circumstance of their universal admission. Extremes meet — a proverb, by the by, to collect and explain all the instances and exemplifications of which, would employ a life.[5]

Polarity, as distinct from mere dichotomy or juxtaposition, is necessarily a most difficult relationship to discuss and apply. Owen Barfield, at once the most penetrating examiner to date of Coleridge's philosophy and himself a philosopher of well-nigh Coleridgean dimensions, has defined the law of polarity as follows:

A polarity of contraries is not quite the same as the *coincidentia oppositorum*, which has been stressed by some philosophers, or as the "paradox" which (whether for the purposes of irony or for other reasons) is beloved by some contemporary writers and critics. A paradox is the violent union of two opposites that simply contradict each other, so that reason assures us we can have one *or* the other but not both at the same time. Whereas polar contraries (as is illustrated by the use of the term in electricity) exist by virtue of each other *as well as* at each other's expense. For that very reason the concept of polarity cannot be subsumed under the logical principle of identity; in fact, it is not really a logical concept at all, but one which requires an act of imagination to grasp it. . . . Unlike the logical principles of identity and contradiction, it is not only a form of thought but also the form of life. It could perhaps be called the principle of seminal identity.[2]

If Barfield's definition here is at all adequate to the polar relationship (and there is none better in so brief a space), small wonder, then, that we have just before heard Coleridge maintain it "would employ a life" to explain fully the simple proverb, "Extremes meet." Nor can there be much question, particularly since the appearance of Barfield's landmark study of the poet-philosopher, *What Coleridge Thought*, that polarity not only accounts for Coleridge's famous "reconciliation of opposites" but also constitutes the essential, permeating conception for his entire thought. Regarding the specific question of originality, Barfield, in *What Coleridge Thought*, points out that "[Coleridge] was not interested in 'originality,' if the word is taken to mean novelty. For the principles advanced in his Essays on Method he claimed 'no other merit, than that of having drawn them from the purest sources of Philosophy, ancient and modern.' "[3a]

Coleridge's disclaimer might appear at first to contradict his "impressions of novelty" passage. That it does not do so is owing ultimately to the law of polarity operative in the dominion of originality vis-à-vis "sources . . . ancient and modern." Coleridge may have felt personally — or at least publicly — that the genius he perceived and espoused "in poems, equally as in philosophic disquisitions," did not apply so much to himself as to Wordsworth, or to Shakespeare, or Bacon. But the two proposals as such and the generic issue they signify are expressly not contradictory, because the law of polarity, which underlies and defines the relationship they attach to, cannot, as Barfield has already told us in his book *Speaker's Meaning*, itself be "subsumed under the logical principles of identity and contradiction." Coleridge himself expressed much the same understanding, when, just before the same "impressions of novelty" passage, he wrote in *Biographia*: "To find no contradiction in the union of old and new; to contemplate the ANCIENT of days and all his works with feelings as fresh, as if all had then sprang forth at the first creative fiat; characterizes the mind that feels the riddle of the world, and may help to unravel it."[4a] Perhaps the entire issue may be restated thus: Barfield has maintained that Coleridge "was not interested in 'originality,' if the word is taken to mean novelty." But suppose instead we take the word to mean what it does mean — at once the beginning of things (i.e., origin, originate, original sin) *as well as* that which is most recent, most "novel" (i.e., original, originality). Such opposed meanings relate — or interrelate — through polarity, and that relationship cannot be subsumed under the principle of contradiction. Coleridge's grasp of the nature and activity of genius, his sense of the relationship between tradition and the individual talent, thus recapitulates the very etymological history of the word "originality" itself.

I should now like to suggest something that would, I suspect, have been either too perplexing or too facile to state sooner without at least some preliminary discussion. And that is, that the "romantic temper" and the "classical temper" are themselves contraries that define each other in polarity; and that strong expressions by gifted and imaginative men such as Coleridge and Eliot that seem at times to assert one "temper" at the expense of the other amount, really, to a condition of genuine polar-concentration or polar-predominance. This, however, does *not* mean, "there is something to be said on both sides," or, "each position contains a part of the truth" — and the like. Such locutions do not get at polarity, but express the thinking of dichotomy or, at best, dialectic. In either case they bespeak juxtaposition, far less likely interpenetration, and certainly not "seminal identity" — as opposed to the logical principle of identity (opposed in dichotomy, not polarity!).

Polar-concentration means that the predominating pole never ceases to require its opposite pole to *be* predominating; in fact, the very reason it is predominating in any given instance is that the energies of the nonpredominating pole are concentrated at their opposite! That is actually what polar-concentration is, the energy of the nonpredominating pole concentrated at the predominating pole. Consequently it is, really, not too much to say that the essential test of whether we are grasping polarity in the first place, are resisting, that is, the many "look-alikes" of dichotomy, is whether we can grasp the relationship of polar-concentration. Polarity, after all, is the only relationship involving opposition in which the contraries can and do transform *into each other*, back and forth, in predominance or polar-concentration. Perhaps it is this fact, finally, that can drive home to us the point that the selfsame contraries must, if they transform into each other, also transform each other more fundamentally through their given polarity *to* each other. Otherwise there would simply be no way for the relationship in question not to be subsumed under the principles of contradiction and identity; otherwise it would indeed *be* a contradiction for Owen Barfield to speak of polarity in *Speaker's Meaning* as "the principle of seminal identity."

II

If we return now to Eliot's "Tradition and the Individual Talent" with the foregoing proposals in mind, I think it is soon clear that his famous attempt there at a more dynamic conception of tradition, his insistence, for example, that, with "the introduction of the new (the really new) work of art among them," the "ideal order" already formed by the "existing monuments" undergoes real modification — is an assumption that must rest ultimately on polarity.[6] The "modifying" agency itself is essentially one with the "imaginative faculty in modifying the objects observed" propounded by Coleridge 100 years earlier.[4b] The agency in both cases bespeaks polarity because it alone accomplishes the vital condition of mutual transformation: in one instance, between the existing monuments and the new work of art; in the other, between the objects observed and the observer.

Still, Eliot's argument as a whole in "Tradition and the Individual Talent" is not consciously based on polarity. For, even as he sought to reinvigorate our understanding and appreciation of tradition as far more than "the reassuring science of archaeology";[47] and even as he insisted that, rather than praise a new poet's originality, "we shall often find that not only the best, but the most individual parts of his work may be those in which the dead poets, his ancestors, assert their immortality most vigorously";[48] nevertheless, it soon becomes apparent to the reader of the essay that polarity (by which I do not mean the word itself) is by no means Eliot's own governing conception. This emerges for us in particular when he proceeds from the proposals about tradition as such to amplify them by taking up the matter of a poet's individual consciousness ideally developed throughout his career. It is Eliot's well-known argument in favor of "depersonalization." He writes of this development as follows: "What happens is a continual surrender of himself [the poet] as he is at the moment to something which is more valuable. The progress of an artist is a continual self-sacrifice, a continual extinction of personality."[52-53] These words, at first reminiscent of Keats's "negative capability," lead swiftly to a further assessment that sounds acutely foreign to the spirit of Keats: "It is in this depersonalization that art may be said to approach the condition of a science."[53] It is here, when he proceeds to explain more fully the "approach" to a "condition of science" operating in poetic-activity-as-depersonalization, that Eliot reveals a real point of divergence from polarity. "I . . . invite you," he tells us, "to consider, as a suggestive analogy, the action that takes place when a bit of finely filiated platinum is introduced into a chamber containing oxygen and sulphur dioxide."[53] This is an invitation we do well to accept, for it is also the critical juncture in "Tradition and the Individual Talent," at least from the standpoint of polarity:

The analogy was that of the catalyst. When the two gases previously mentioned are mixed in the presence of a filament of platinum, they form sulphurous acid. This combination takes place only if the platinum is present; nevertheless the newly formed acid contains no trace of platinum, and the platinum itself is apparently unaffected; has remained inert, neutral, and unchanged. The mind of the poet is the shred of platinum. It may partly or exclusively operate upon the experience of the man himself; but, the more perfect the artist, the more completely separate in him will be the man who suffers and the mind which creates; the more perfectly will the mind digest and transmute the passions which are its material.[54]

Eliot undoubtedly chose this analogy primarily to reinforce for the reader his conviction that lasting poetry cannot and should not be understood by some vague "emotive" criterion, or some facile idea of "sublimity." He chose it, clearly, to counteract just the sort of false idolatry on behalf of originality which (to recall again Barfield on Coleridge) superficially equates it with novelty or eccentricity. He chose it, one also has to say, to counteract the "Expressive" viewpoint about the nature of poetry, a school with which it is conventional for us to associate Coleridge himself.

The fact is, however, that Eliot's analogy of the poetic process with that of catalysis is inadequate to the particular kind of transformation his own argument concerning both tradition and the individual talent and the relation of the poem to its author required. To separate as he does the mind of the poet from the experiences of the person so drastically as to require us to think of the former as an "inert, neutral, unchanged" catalyst in the presence of the latter is surely to overstate things in favor of objectivity, poetic distance, or whatever term we prefer to describe what is perhaps an admirable and necessary distinction between the poet and the poem. That is just the point: Eliot clearly sought a *distinction*, but instead presented a *division*. Coleridge, it is interesting to remember, so often reminds us that in such matters we must learn to distinguish where we cannot in fact divide. In any event it takes only a little reflection to perceive that, whatever the precise relationship between the "mind that creates" and the "man who suffers," it is one that is bound to be at bottom reciprocal. To speak of reciprocity, however, is not then to assume half-automatically that the relationship is in equilibrium. It is not only possible but far more likely that in a reciprocal relationship one side or its opposite is in predominance. We are back, in other words, to the issue of polar-concentration. As a genuine spokesman for the "classical temper," Eliot most understandably wished to emphasize the extent to which the poem is not just the personal expression of the man who writes it. His appropriate predominance was therefore at the pole of the poem rather than the author, as earlier the same "temper" put him at the pole of tradition rather than the individual talent. But what happened this time was, he set out to convey his natural predominance so strongly that he actually ended up, by means of the catalyst analogy, denying any reciprocity at all!

It is easy, of course, to quarrel with Eliot's scientific analogy, and one could do so, certainly, without the least awareness of or concern with the principle of polarity. One might object, for example, to such an image of the poetic sensibility as much too scientific, much too cold, too detached. I would only want to maintain, in this regard, that to grasp polarity is also to see why such an image might otherwise tend to strike us as too cold or too detached. Polarity, after all, is preeminently a vital and living relationship, wherever the dominion of its occurrence. Indeed it is "not only a form of thought but the form of life."

At the same time, it is not my purpose to try to "show up" T. S. Eliot by pointing to the difficulty with his catalysis analogy. My real point is that the analogy failed his *own* argument in the essay and that that failure has to do with polarity. That he was close to, was in fact working toward, a profound understanding of polarity in his essay is finally the case. This can be shown by addressing for a moment something that is invariably overlooked by the many interpreters of Eliot, whatever their critical viewpoint: there is a curious and apparently inadvertent "lapse" in the catalysis analogy itself, a momentary contradiction to the internal logic of the conceit. It occurs in the last line of the passage quoted. Here is the last part of that passage once more: "The mind of the poet is the shred of platinum. It may partly or exclusively operate upon the experience of the man himself; but, the more perfect the artist, the more completely separate in him will be the man who suffers and the mind which creates; the more perfectly will the mind digest and transmute the passions which are its material."

The lapse I refer to is Eliot's use of the word "digest," or, we could say, the implications really embedded in the phrase "digest and transmute." Surely the poetic-mind-as-platinum cannot be said to *digest* the materials it causes to transmute; surely the platinum does not digest the oxygen and sulphur dioxide. Has not the point of the analogy been just the reverse, that the platinum will trigger a chemical change without itself being affected or changed? But again, I suspect Eliot's sense of the matter is easily understood. He surely meant the word "digest" to convey his conviction that the true poetic mind will be able to assimilate, master, and refine the strong passions attending human experiences, rather than directly permitting them to surge out raw (i.e., regurgitate) into the poem itself. Nothing could be more appropriate to his overall perspective in the essay and to his "classical temper." The contradiction, or lapse, thus involves only the analogy with the catalyst as such. But, as such, it amounts to a "happy lapse," an instinctive reintroduction of reciprocity, an instinctive sense that the relationship is living and two-directional, unlike catalysis proper, in which there is only the reaction or movement in one direction, the catalyst itself remaining "inert, neutral, and unchanged." And even had Eliot not committed his inadvertent "lapse," not only would his dynamic conception of tradition show him moving in the direction of polarity, but the very fact that he chose the analogy he did serves in the end to measure just how much he recognized the need to convey *some* conception and image of *actual transformation* as the foundation of all that he was trying to say. As a poet himself possessing imagination and as the strong critical theorist he was by nature, it was all but inevitable that T. S. Eliot would come to expound consciously, adequately, and unforgettably in his later writing the seminal principle that had just managed to elude him in "Tradition and the Individual Talent."

III

There is probably no more universal complaint about essays purporting to deal with large matters philosophical and aesthetical than that they hardly ever seem to aid us directly in reading and appreciating particular literary works of art. Perhaps the complaint is unwarranted, at least for those who (like the present writer) view such issues a proper and worthy object of exploration in themselves. Nevertheless, inasmuch as I have been making such strong claims on behalf of polarity and have spoken with at least the tone of authority about its connection with the whole question of originality and received tradition, I shall try briefly in this final section to relate these contentions to Eliot's great imaginative poem *Four Quartets.*

Much has been written about Eliot's "dialectical" or, as it is also described, "contrapuntal" method in the *Four Quartets.* This is said to arise from the close ties between the four poems and the musical idiom of the quartet as well as the sonata — in this case especially the final quartets and piano sonatas of Beethoven. There can be no doubt, certainly, that these final works by Beethoven impressed Eliot greatly, particularly the composer's ability somehow to convey the selfsame enormity of scope and epic magnitude characteristic of the great symphonies, while at the same time harnessing it almost miraculously within the musical perimeters of the quartet and sonata forms. Eliot's *Quartets* present us with the same achievement in poetic verse, an accomplishment that makes them among the most remarkable poetry ever written. Here are poems that treat profoundly such matters as the relation between time and eternity, the meaning of history, the redemptive process through suffering, the nature of sainthood, the condition of mysticism and grace, the function and value of art and poetry — to name the most obvious subjects explored; and yet, these subjects of such staggering magnitude are compressed, miraculously, within the poetic equivalent of chamber music, each poem of which divides in turn into five "movements" (or four movements plus a coda) like the sonata.

The issue about these extraordinary poems I should like here to address concerns their unity as a single work. Eliot invited this perspective primarily by his decision to publish them together in one volume as *Four Quartets* (1944), after first having written and published them individually over a period of eight years: "Burnt Norton," the first, appeared in 1936, four years before "East Coker" (1940), after which swiftly followed "The Dry Salvages" (1941) and "Little Gidding" (1942). In view of the separation of "Burnt Norton" from its three successors and the opinion of numerous scholars that Eliot did not yet have his plan for the full sequence at the time of "Burnt Norton," it is of some significance that he chose nevertheless to retain the two epigraphs for "Burnt Norton" in the final volume of *Four Quartets*, in effect making them the epigraphs for the whole sequence, there being none chosen for the other poems.

These two epigraphs are from the *Fragments* of Heraclitus, and they translate as follows: "Although the Logos is common, yet most men live as though they had a private insight of their own"; and, "The way up and the way down are the same way." The importance of Heraclitus to Eliot's thinking at the time of the *Quartets*, and to the meaning as well as the method of the poems themselves, has been much noted by his interpreters. It is generally recognized, for example, that Eliot's treatment of time, change, flux, decay, the difficulties assigning "beginnings" and "ends" in the eternal process of human experience and endeavor, corresponds to the Heraclitean view of reality as ceaseless flux. A similar correspondence is suggested, of course, by Eliot's "contrapuntal" method, his mode of constant alternation and modulation. Then, too, it is generally understood that each of the *Quartets* comes to assume some relation with one of the four elements, again recalling Heraclitus: the presiding element in "East Coker" is earth, in "The Dry Salvages" water, and in "Little Gidding" fire; only in "Burnt Norton" is the analogous relationship with air less conspicuous, perhaps because of its genetic separation from the others as already mentioned.

If, as I have argued earlier, "Tradition and the Individual Talent" can to some extent be illuminated as Eliot's expression of a dynamic relationship that could ultimately be grounded only in polarity, perhaps it is preeminently in his *Four Quartets* that he came to grasp polarity most profoundly — to exhibit and express it consciously as a relationship, in addition to continuing to possess it as a poet with imagination. Such a development in Eliot's consciousness would help to account, I think, for his preoccupation in these poems with the thought of Heraclitus. It should be noted, moreover, that the first of the two Heraclitean epigraphs constitutes a repudiation of the "private insight" so suggestive of the general concerns of Eliot's earlier philosophic mentor F. H. Bradley, whose thought figures prominently in *The Waste Land* as well as "Prufrock."

Several times in the course of *What Coleridge Thought* Owen Barfield points out that Heraclitus is the philosopher Coleridge believed to have first promulgated the universal law of polarity, the first to state the actual principle of life. It was also the belief of Coleridge that after Heraclitus the law of polarity was "2000 years afterwards re-published by Giordano Bruno." Barfield provides the following comment on these two views of Coleridge:

A logical contradiction is mere negation; contemplated as "paradox" it becomes, in a sense, affirmative and positive; but it is still static. But the essence of polarity is a *dynamic* conflict between coinciding opposites. Coleridge, as we have seen, cites Heraclitus as the first promulgator of the law of polarity; and the element of conflict, the quality of psychic oppugnancy [the actual striving for predominance by each pole] between opposites is evident there in a way it hardly ever is in [Giordano] Bruno. Heraclitus lived and thought before Aristotle; that is, long before that first great step forward in the "disanimation" of nature, which culminated philosophically in Cartesianism.[3b]

Eliot's concern in *Four Quartets* not only with Heraclitean flux generally, but also with "the reconciliation of opposites" in particular, has of course been noted more than once. F. O. Matthiessen, for example, points out that the opening phrase of "East Coker," "In my beginning is my end," is close to Heraclitus' "The beginning and the end are common," and therefore indicates "the recurrent attraction [Eliot] feels to the reconciliation of opposites which characterizes that pre-Socratic philosopher."[8a] Likewise Matthiessen observes of the following line (also from "East Coker") — "We must be still and still moving" — that it proves "the reconciliation of opposites is as fundamental to Eliot as it was to Heraclitus. Only thus can he envisage a resolution of man's whole being."[8b]

Individual lines like these indeed appear throughout *Four Quartets*, all of which, we could say, bespeak Eliot's penchant for "the reconciliation of opposites" and for Heraclitus. And yet, the phrase "the reconciliation of opposites" does not always *convey* the very relationship it in fact expresses — polarity. One could almost say of "the reconciliation of opposites" as Matthiessen employs it here, and as it is so very often employed in literary criticism, that it too is a "most admitted truth" that needs to be "rescued from the impotence caused by the very circumstance of its universal admission." To do so requires that we attend to more than the presence — even the recurrent presence — of lines that exhibit paradox and opposition, however memorable. It requires that we seek for that dynamic, nay "oppugnant" relationship which at the same time — indeed, for that very reason — unifies the work. I believe something like this can be done, perhaps best by our looking again in a certain way at the musically "recurrent themes" that are often said to relate one quartet to another. For example, we find in "Burnt Norton" the oft-quoted lines dealing with the "still point":

> At the still point of the turning world. Neither flesh
>   nor fleshness;
> Neither from nor towards; at the still point, there
>   the dance is,
> But neither arrest nor movement. And do not call it
>   fixity,
> Where past and present are gathered. Neither movement
>   from nor towards,
> Neither ascent nor decline. Except for the point,
>   the still point,
> There would be no dance, and there is only the dance.
> I can only say, *there* we have been: but I cannot say where.
> And I cannot say, how long, for that is to place it in time.[7]

These lines, almost invariably read as an expression of Eliot's "mysticism" — occasionally Eastern, but more often Christian and Western — relate in a quite special way to the following set of lines found in "The Dry Salvages":

> Men's curiosity searches past and future
> And clings to that dimension. But to apprehend
> The point of intersection of the timeless
> With time, is an occupation for the saint —
> No occupation either, but something given
> And taken, in a lifetime's death in love,
> Ardour and selflessness and self-surrender. [136]

And these lines in turn relate in a quite special way to the following group found in "Little Gidding":

> And what the dead had no speech for, when living,
> They can tell you, being dead: the communication
> Of the dead is tongued with fire beyond the
>   language of the living.
> Here, the intersection of the timeless moment
> Is England and nowhere. Never and always. [139]

What is essentially occurring with these three passages or segments is the dynamic reciprocity which is to be found again and again throughout *Four Quartets*. It is the process of transformation, in this particular case the transformation of the "still point" *into* the "point of intersection" *into* the "timeless moment." It is an example of what is really Eliot's most fundamental and profound parallel with the view of Heraclitus throughout the *Quartets*, the transformation of the elements *into each other*, the seminal Heraclitean life-principle. Granted, these same passages will yield richly to interpretation that bears on the particular context and within the single poem in which each occurs. One can, especially, examine them within that more local field as component elements in "juxtaposition" with various passages that precede or succeed them in Eliot's ongoing "counterstatement" and "modulation" — as indeed they have been understood. One can, finally, focus on the "tension" or "paradox" within the lines themselves and refer to the poet's "reconciliation of opposites" in the way F. O. Matthiessen has done. But I would suggest that our grasp of such passages as actually transformative, interpenetrative, and "seminally identical" to one another is not only important in its own right but helpful to point up the basis for overall unity in *Four Quartets* as well as to appreciate and deepen the Heraclitean tie. Is it really so important, after all, that we recognize each poem to be associated with one of the primal elements of the universe, if we then fail to respond to the dynamic interrelationship itself among the elements propounded by the pre-Socratic philosopher?

It might be objected, of course, that my proposal here really amounts to our recurrent themes put a little differently. I think no one would maintain that the Heraclitean law of transformation itself really amounts to "recurrent themes." The question, in other words, is whether Eliot actually embodies or, in the Coleridgean sense, recapitulates that law. That he does so can be seen in the following way: the "still point" passage, which, as mentioned before, most readers think of as either Eliot's "mysticism" or at least as representative of some superior intellectual or spiritual condition, may in fact be intended by the poet as a false resolution, a conception which, like several proposed in "Burnt Norton," is meant expressly to be "corrected" later on in the succeeding poems. In this connection I once heard an eminent professor of philosophy refer to it as one of Eliot's intended "blind alleys" early in the sequence.

There is something to be said for such a "negative" reading. To begin with, the Heraclitean epigraph repudiating the "private insight" does seem applicable to the "still point": for both the conception itself and the qualities associated with it have a most private, subjectively idealistic tenor to them. Correlative to this is the entire description of the "still point" as an assemblage of negative attributes; i.e., it is "neither from nor towards," "neither arrest nor movement," "neither ascent nor decline." Moreover — "I can only say, *there* we have been: but I cannot say where/And I cannot say, how long, for that is to place it in time" — these concluding sentiments are by no means inevitably flattering. The "still point," then, can be understood as an all too pristine, self-indulgent, eccentric, and arcane proposition; one that, significantly, lacks any attachment to real time, history, or place. This would of course put it in direct opposition to the "point of intersection" and then the "timeless moment" later in the sequence: the first of these insists on the positive manifestation of the eternal in real time (i.e., the lines occur just as Eliot is about to proclaim the doctrine of the Incarnation in "The Dry Salvages"); the second insists that the eternal is fully incarnate in both real time and place (i.e., at that very moment in Little Gidding in Huntingtonshire).*

Now the point is, why might the majority of readers prefer to interpret the "still point" positively, indeed respond to it and treat it as though it were a conception pretty much along the same lines as what one might actually say about the "point of intersection" or even the "timeless moment"? Have such readers merely been tricked into a "blind alley," something like the readers who are said so often to miss the irony in a Henry James story? Perhaps in a sense they have, inasmuch as I do believe Eliot intended his mystical-sounding concept from "Burnt Norton" to exemplify the "private insight" of

---

* In this connection one should note, however, that Elizabeth Drew in *T. S. Eliot: The Design of His Poetry* (New York: Charles Scribner's Sons, 1949), p. 148, says of Eliot and Heraclitus: "All things exist in tension, but to Heraclitus the 'reconciliation of the opposites' means their creative interdependence in accordance with a universal law but not their transcendence. He has no concept of a 'still point' where all the emotional oppositions are 'gathered' and reconciled and conquered by having *meaning* in terms of resolution. So that Eliot's interpretation of 'the way up and the way down' is not that of Heraclitus." This is the sort of conclusion about the *Quartets* that this essay — especially the final pages of it — is attempting to challenge.

which Heraclitus complains in the epigraph. But this does *not* mean that the "still point" is merely to be rejected; it means, rather, that it must needs be reunderstood later *as* the "point of intersection" and then the "timeless moment" — this last the fullest embodiment of the Heraclitean counter-proposal that the "Logos is common." Such a "misreading" of the "still point" on the positive side is therefore not nearly the mistake we might have thought, and in no sense are we confronted with a "blind alley." Inasmuch as the "still point" is in dynamic, reciprocal relationship to the later conceptions, those later conceptions are also present in it; they are indeed the fulfillment *of* the "still point," and the "still point" a potential version of them — a fact that logically contradicts the direct opposition between the "still point" and the later conceptions. Like the Heraclitean law itself, we have a dramatic case here of polarity, of interpenetration, not merely juxtaposition: the way up *is* the way down.

We also have, however, a striking case of polar-concentration or polar-predominance. In fact, the whole matter of someone's "misreading" the "still point" is really the issue of polar-predominance. The "still point" (and in general the vision rendered by Eliot in "Burnt Norton") is in effect the full predominance of the "private insight," which then gradually proceeds to transform into its own opposite, the "common Logos," by the time of "Little Gidding." The two middle poems, moreover, present us with stages in the process of that very transference (which is why they, too, exhibit a "seminal identity" in their use of "recurrent themes" with the first and the last poems). To put this another way and keep to the example under focus, the "point of intersection" in "The Dry Salvages" is the transference itself of the "still point" into the "timeless moment" — which is then the completed predominance *of* that transference from the pole of private insight into that of "common Logos."

This is also why the vision of "Little Gidding" exhibits the same dynamic apprehension of the meaning of tradition found in "Tradition and the Individual Talent" — "And what the dead had no speech for, when living/They can tell you, being dead: the communication/Of the dead is tongued with fire beyond the language of the living." That is, we have by now in the *Quartets* the full predominance of the pole of tradition or of accumulated human history and experience over that of the individual moment, self, ego. It is the parallel relationship universally to that of art in the earlier essay — the "classical temper." One could therefore say, again in Coleridgean language, that art recapitulates the very relationship of mankind to the individual person. But, unlike the earlier essay, Eliot is now in such full and conscious possession of the polar relationship that, for example, the portrayed speaker who can kneel and pray aloud in the secluded chapel at Little Gidding —

> Sin is Behovely, but
> All shall be well, and
> All manner of thing shall be well [142-3]

— is at that "timeless moment" in full possession of all the dynamic energies of what is *not* his own private religious sensibility (a condition corroborated by his prayer being the language of the fourteenth-century mystic, Dame Juliana of Norwich), but rather the cumulative prayer of all who have lived and died before him in the past; whether it be a well known "king at nightfall" like Charles I, or one who was once known but "died forgotten," or even one so fully unknown as to be marked by an "illegible stone."

At the same time, notice that there is no more powerful instance of an individual "persona" totally alone, praying indeed "in private," than this same speaker in the chapel at the conclusion of "Little Gidding"; and in *that* sense, the "dramatic event" sense, one could say that the very polar-concentration of "Little Gidding," located outside the self and the particular individual, is for the moment transformed into its "private insight" opposite (again corroborated by the speaker's choice to utter aloud not a "common" or familiar prayer as such, but the extraordinary, "novel" words of redemption by Dame Juliana) — until we look back once more at the "meaning" or "thematic" sense of the episode, in which case it will transform for us back *again* into the "tradition" pole. That is polarity, the relationship in which the opposing poles can and will transform into each other back and forth in polar-predominance, because they have been mutually transformed by their relationship *to* each other.

Draw a rectangular box in perspective — not too precise perspective (for the receding lines must be kept parallel, instead of converging) — and look at it. It has a front and a back, a top and a bottom. But slide your hand across it in the required direction and look again: you may find that what you thought was the inside of the top has become its outside, while the outside of the front wall has changed to the inside of the back wall, and vice-versa.[1]

Finally, the extent to which such transformation is continuous, once we find ourselves confronted with polarity rather than merely with dichotomy, may be indicated by our recalling the unforgettable lines at the close of "Little Gidding":

> We shall not cease from exploration
> And the end of all our exploring
> Will be to arrive where we started
> And know the place for the first time.[145]

This turns out to be none other than a dramatic rendering in verse of Coleridge's view that "genius produces the strongest impressions of novelty, while it rescues the most admitted truths from the impotence caused by the very circumstance of their universal admission." Coleridge's conception as the expression of an actual relationship has depended on polarity. Eliot has totally grasped the polar relationship in *Four Quartets*. Thus Eliot ends up here clothing Coleridge's conception in the figure of a journey, in which Coleridge's "novelty" emerges as Eliot's "exploration," Coleridge's "admitted truths" the place "where we started," and Coleridge's "rescue from impotence" the knowing of that same place "for the first time." Both affirm the "reconciliation of opposites"; but, more importantly, they are here the same opposites, novelty or originality and received truth and tradition; and, more importantly still, they are reconciled in the only way they *can* be reconciled — through polarity. The "romantic temper" we associate with Coleridge and the "classical temper" we associate with Eliot are opposing poles in full predominance. They are therefore, despite the inevitable extraordinary degree of conflict and oppugnancy between them, not in dichotomy but in "seminal identity" to each other. And so they can and will exhibit the capacity to transform into each other like these two utterances by S. T. Coleridge and T. S. Eliot.

REFERENCES

1. Barfield, O. *Saving the Appearances: A Study in Idolatry*. New York: Harcourt, Brace & World, n.d., p. 11.
2. ———. *Speaker's Meaning*. Middletown, Conn.: Wesleyan University Press, 1967, pp. 38-39.
3. ———. *What Coleridge Thought*. Middletown, Conn.: Wesleyan University Press, 1971, (a) 6; (b) 187.
4. Coleridge, S. T. *Biographia Literaria*. Edited by J. Shawcross. Vol. I. London: Oxford University Press, 1907; rpt. 1962, (a) 59; (b) 59.
5. ———. *The Friend*. Edited by B. E. Rooke. Vol. II. Princeton: Princeton University Press, 1969, p. 74.
6. Eliot, T. S. "Tradition and the Individual Talent." In *The Sacred Wood*. London: Methuen & Co., 1920, p. 50. Subsequent references will be to this edition and will appear in brackets following the quoted material.
7. ———. *The Complete Poems and Plays: 1909-1950*. New York: Harcourt, Brace & Co., 1952, p. 119. Subsequent references will be to this edition and will appear in brackets following the quoted material.
8. Matthiessen, F. O. *The Achievement of T. S. Eliot*. New York: Oxford University Press, 1935, (a) 184; (b) 195.

THE BURDEN OF CULTURE AND THE DIALECTIC OF LITERATURE

ROBERT O. PREYER

I

This paper attempts to say something of the dialectic of literature as it swings from mediated experience to direct confrontation of the actual and then back again. It begins with the situation of a perplexed prophet, Alfred Tennyson, and moves on to consider the implications of Hardy's poetry, written, we sometimes feel, as a direct challenge to the Tennysonian mode of apprehension. Those implications are extraordinary, but let us begin at the beginning.

It is clear that Tennyson thought of himself as one of the classical artists, that is, an artist who offered a "criticism of life" by reference to some implicit or explicit scheme of values. Following in the footsteps of Milton and Spenser — perhaps we could also say, of Dante — he was a nineteenth-century representative of the longest and best honored tradition of English poetry, that which took its origins in the classics and in Christianity. He belonged with those artists who felt quite capable of judging and placing experience according to a controlling myth or value scheme or vision that seemed, on the whole, to do justice to the human situation.* If we evaluate a controlling myth or vision by considering the extent and depth of the penetration of actuality it makes possible for those who have employed it, we can see why Tennyson embraced the Christian humanist view: all great writers in the past had done so. Yet this great body of explicit and ordered significancies, of experiences judged and valued, given form in myth, and fable, and epic, seemed to exist somehow apart from modern conditions. One feels the strain as Tennyson wrestles with the problem of bringing this available wisdom into some sort of relevance with contemporary concerns. It ought to work — yet something in the content of modern life in an industrial economy resists

---

* In the language of contemporary systems analysis "Christian Humanism" would be designated as the name for a "model" that was no longer useful as it once was in describing the real world. I cannot avail myself of this terminology because it assumes that the ontological problem that bedevilled the Victorians has been solved. That is to say, writers who employ the terminology of models consider them to be fictions and not the same thing as the systems they represent. See on this topic, Welsh, A., "Theories of Science and Romance, 1870-1920," *Victorian Studies* 18 (1973): 135-54.

portrayal according to the system of symbols evolved by the humanistic vision.

What we encounter in Tennyson's writing very frequently is a remarkable failure of tone. The poems over and over again are deeply ambivalent; they lack the authority and assurance of the great masters in his tradition.

As an example of this we may note Tennyson's curious habit of disavowing the authority of his speakers. The dominant male in *The Princess* has fainting fits. The hero of *Maud* is half-mad; we are not to take his opinions very seriously. The early "Thoughts of a Suicide" is watered-down to "Supposed Confessions of a Second-rate Sensitive Mind not in Unity with Itself" in a further revision. When "The Charge of the Heavy Brigade" (1882) reappeared in 1885 it flourished an epilogue in which "The Poet" playfully defends his military ardor from "Irene." Examples of this sort of shilly-shallying are plentiful. Fitzgerald pointed out that sometime after 1835 a prologue (entitled "The Epic") and an epilogue were added to "Morte d'Arthur" (1833) to provide "an excuse for telling an old world tale."[7] "The Epic" describes a Christmas meeting of four old friends, Parson Holmes, the Poet Everard Hall, the speaker, and the host, Francis Allen. Their conversation is carefully limited to topics of the day — "Now harping on the Church-commissioners, / Now hawking at geology and schism" (II.15-16) — until Everard is asked to explain why his early Arthurian poems were never published. The explanation follows:

> "O, sir,
> He thought that nothing new was said, or else
> Something so said 'twas nothing — that a truth
> Looks freshest in the fashion of the day;
> God knows; he has a mint of reasons; ask.
> It pleased me well enough." "Nay, nay," said Hall,
> "Why take the style of those heroic times?
> For nature brings not back the mastodon,
> Nor we those times; and why should any man
> Remodel models?"   (II.29-38)

Nevertheless the poet is prevailed upon to read "Morte d'Arthur," a poem that far transcends in theme and accomplishment the trivial apologetics that frame it. It is, of course, a powerful rendition of a traditional myth having to do with the death of a hero and the sad plight of a survivor who can find no authority to fill the void that the death created. In obvious respects this elegy is a precursor to the "Ode on the Death of the Duke of Wellington," though occasioned, perhaps, by the deaths (within two years of each other) of his father and his best friend. Yet the accompanying matter indicates that Tennyson is uneasy in his use of this particular episode from the "matter of Britain," no longer secure in his efforts to relate a traditional poetic mode and matter to contemporary experience. He wishes to be positive in his social and political stance, to discuss current affairs as an interested citizen. Yet he is ever drawn to stories that suggest that the old order is dying or dead, that no means of replenishing its authority is available to the survivors:

> Ah! My Lord Arthur, whither shall I go?
> Where shall I hide my forehead and my eyes?
> For now I see the true old times are dead,
>
> . . .
>
> And I, the last, go forth companionless,
> And the days darken round me, and the years,
> Among new men, strange faces, other minds.
>   (II.278-80,287-9)

Arthur replies by citing the Great Chain of Being ("For so the whole round earth is every way / Bound by gold chains about the feet of God" [II.305-306]), but this is cold comfort for Sir Bedivere. The truth of the matter is that Tennyson *does* feel abandoned in the modern universe and pretends this is not so. "On God and Godlike men we build our trust," he cries out in the Wellington ode (I.266) — but he is burying the great duke and like Carlyle, his political mentor, he looks around in vain for a new Cromwell.

Here is the root of the trouble: the tradition of Christian humanism offers little help in the process of selecting leaders (and formulating policies) in an unheroic age. If we were committed to a belief that Providential Order and Divine Governance are displayed in the transactions recorded by historians, well and good: the Christian humanist has an explanation (God's mercy or justice) for the rise to power of saints and sinners alike. But this cornerstone of Christian humanism, so frequently celebrated in the literary works that mediated the tradition, crumbles away in the nineteenth century. Men write sermons and even write about *God in History,* but the idea is no longer functional.[2] God is claimed by all interested parties in political and social disputes.

Neither Carlyle nor Tennyson was prepared to eliminate God from his account of history; on the other hand, they could scarcely fit Him in except as a possible occasion for the otherwise inexplicable or anomalous. God, in short, is equated with the unknown, the unknowable, even the irrational.* We stand here at the very limits of a long and impressive tradition, defending we know not what against what reason suggests is so. It is no wonder, therefore, that the Tennysonian tone veers from querulousness to bluster, from

---

* English writers were incapable of the response made by Dostoevsky to this situation. In a letter of February 20, 1854, he wrote, "Even if it were proved to me that Christ were outside the Truth, and it was really so that the Truth were outside of Christ, then I would still prefer to stay with Christ rather than with Truth." Epigraph to Wasiolek, E., *Dostoevsky: The Major Fiction* (Cambridge, Mass.: Harvard University Press, 1964).

that of a "little Hamlet" who knows that he must do what is right (but cannot decide what, in fact, is the right thing to do), to that of an impatient cavalier who gives passion the rip, somewhat in the fashion of Shakespeare's Troilus:

> Nay, if we talk of reason,
> Let's shut our gates and sleep. Manhood and honour
> Should have harehearts, would they but fat their thoughts
> With this cramm'd reason. Reason and respect
> Make livers pale and lustihood deject.   (II,2.46-50)

This instability of feeling and attitude shows up, of course, in *The Princess*, the two Locksley Halls, *Maud*, and many other places: it appears as a failure of tone. Tennyson is unable to achieve a consistent and interesting point of view that "places" contemporary experience and institutions in a significant relation to the cultural tradition. We may well ask, how can such a poet speak as a guardian of his culture and spokesman for the values of an historical society? It is impossible to be "simple, sensuous, and passionate" and at the same time deeply ambivalent and perplexed. In Milton's poetry all the cultural past is linked with contemporary experience and inherited values provide positive direction for action in the present. The same outspoken fearlessness and simplicity is present in the actions and utterance of the great duke: Wellington, apparently, had no doubts and hesitations in his commitments. But Tennyson was without certitude. He could only lament their passing, and hope for "one far-off divine event, / To which the whole creation moves" (*In Memoriam*, Conclusion) — namely, the emergence of the "Christ that is to be" (*In Memoriam*, CVI) when (and if) biological evolution happens to be accompanied by a moral evolution. But this hope is tentative: "Vastness" and other poems indicate that Tennyson can also affirm that man does not change and that original sin is part of his nature.

The objection, then, is to Tennyson's instability of feeling and attitude, his inability to achieve a consistent point of view about modern experience and institutions within the Christian humanist framework. He was to compose great passages out of this experience of vacillation and uncertainty; but they were the products of the suffering isolated artist, not the spokesman for the tribe. Tennyson did not possess the deep and pondered assurance, the poise and mastery, which we associate with Milton and other Christian humanists.

We have looked at the evidence for calling Tennyson a perplexed prophet. There is a loss of conviction or vitality in his expression of cherished values and points of view; and this finds parallels in the work and thought of other men as well. At times there is something hectic and shrill in his expression; at other times it seems wheedling and self-pitying. He is a man, apparently, who cannot be sure that his vision is adequate to his experience, but who nevertheless must cling to it since he knows of no other sources from which to replenish that vision. At times it must have seemed that this vision was dying with his generation, that it was not being transmitted with conviction and emotional fullness into the hearts and minds of the new generation growing up in a secular industrial society. So he denies, from time to time, that there is anything to be restless about. Or again he seems to mask social anxiety as moral indignation: any violations or freeing of sexual customs, any tampering with marriage or even the relations between capital and labor upset him. He is prepared, at times, to support punitive legislation, censorships, and other sorts of prohibitions. That is the worst side of this very great poet — and I insist on the greatness elsewhere if not in this paper.[6]

II

I would like to turn now and consider the body of poetry that is apt to appear as a rejection of this sort of thing. I mean an objective art, or better perhaps, an art that does not carry a heavy and troublesome weight of ideology. I am thinking now of an "imagistic" art in which the "value-frame" is removed from view and ethical and social commentary remain unspecified.

The extreme formulation of this revulsion against an Arnoldian version of art as "a criticism of life" or "the application of ideas to experience" provides us with William Carlos Williams' red wheelbarrow, a tiresome and banal object that is simply registered as being present. But perhaps the most powerful poetry is not written by will to express any ideological position as to the nature of the real. I prefer to think of Thomas Hardy, a writer who belonged to the same culture but who expressed an attitude toward it that was equally ambivalent, although ambivalent in a quite opposite direction, as the true anthithesis to Tennyson. Hardy is a poet who will not, and indeed cannot, find much comfort in conventional or available explanations and valuations of experience. He will not pretend to have found answers to the problem of pain, the injustices and accidents of living, the perplexities of love. His mind is strong enough to leave us in hesitations and doubts, without any "irritable reaching after fact and reason" that so offended Keats on another occasion.[3] We simply need to recall some of Hardy's typical endings:

> These purblind Doomsters had as readily strown
> Blisses about my pilgrimage as pain.

> Everything glowed with a gleam;
> Yet we were looking away.

> That I could hope there trembled through
>   His happy good-night air
> Some blessed Hope, whereof he knew
>   And I was unaware.

No answer is provided the "dim moon eyed fishes" who inquire "what does this vaingloriousness down here?" All we know is that the iceberg and the S. S. *Titanic* were "twin halves of one august event"

> and each one hears,
> And consummation comes, and jars two hemispheres.[4]

What is the status of the Spinner of the Years who ordained this conjunction? We are not to know. Or in perhaps the finest of all such problematic endings, we inquire in vain for the status of the speaker, the ghost in "My Spirit Will Not Haunt the Mound":

> And there you'll find me, if a jot
> You still should care
> For me, and for my curious air;
> If otherwise, then I shall not,
> For you, be there.

The pain is real, the separation and loss irremediable, but the status of the spirit remains either purely subjective or at best hypothetical.

Hardy, obviously, would not look for comfort in conventional or available explanations. He tells the reader he has no answers, and such honesty must have seemed positively aphrodisiacal to men like Graves and Sassoon who have survived the wreck of so much patriotic rant and corrupt piety. These were men who could not help knowing how "official" war poetry concealed actualities. They were aware that their experience of war would have seemed unbelievable to the author of "The Charge of the Light Brigade" and to most of his contemporaries. Art existed for these survivors as something that must be antagonistic to the dreary idealisms about war that served, back home, to "illuminate," to "place," and apparently to "dignify" the sacrifices of those over there. Henley's "The Song of the Sword" (1892, dedicated to Kipling) depicts the proper attitudes the culture wished to associate with warfare, a suitably grand and heroic elevation of the actuality:

> Clear singing, clean slicing;
> Sweet spoken, soft finishing;
> Making death beautiful,
> Life but a coin
> To be staked in the pastime
> Than the transfer of being;
> Arch-anarch, chief builder,
> Prince and evangelist,
> I am the will of God:
> I am the Sword.

The "actuality" is found in Sassoon's "Counter Attack":

> We'd gained our first objective hours before
> While dawn broke like a face with blinking eyes,

Pallid, unshaven, and thirsty, blind with smoke.
Things seemed all right at first. We held their line,
With bombers posted, Lewis guns well placed,
And clink of shovels deepening the hollow trench.
   The place was rotten with dead; green clumsy legs
   High-booted, sprawled and grovelled along the saps
   And trunks, face downward, in the sucking mud,
   Wallowed like trodden sand bags loosely filled;
   And naked sodden buttocks, mats of hair,
   Bulged, clotted heads slept in the plastering slime.
   And then the rain began — the jolly old rain!

These examples illustrate the characteristic dialectic in literature. We see how it is that a more objectivist art becomes a prevalent mode when classical value-frames begin to lose conviction, something that happens in Tennyson and the Georgian writers. As I have presented the matter thus far it may look like a simple "progress" from an art gone decadent and academic to something wonderfully vivid and fresh, "barefoot into reality." "Compared to the Georgians," Bernard Bergonzi remarks, "the Imagists were the first poets of a demythologized world, concerned to make poetry from the naked, isolated object, stripped of all outworn mythical accretions."[1] The naked object as it presented itself to the senses was, in theory, what the late William Carlos Williams wanted poetry to present. If Tennyson feels that the poet should depict the attitude that should surround the fact — whether it be the fact of love, or loss, or war, or death — these others describe the immediate experience, the physical fact and feeling. And yet, as *The Wasteland* and *Ulysses* and a host of other works inform us, no subject can remain for long wholly stark and impoverished of mythical accretions. George Poulet, Eric Auerbach, Bachelard, and a rash of phenomenologists demonstrate to us the metaphysic implicit in a relentless imagism. J. Hillis Miller's recent books point in the same direction. And Samuel Hynes makes the case very neatly for Hardy:

If he refused to let unseen reality into the front door of his poetry — or philosophy or theology — it slipped in the back door as superstition. If it could not clothe itself in symbol and metaphor, it could appear as omen and abstraction. . . . Hence the phantoms, ghosts, and dreads in the poems; hence also the presence among the meticulous particulars of abstract words — Crass Casualty, Time, Change — and personifications — Overworld.[5]

I have gone on long enough. The object has been to depict something of the dialectic of literature, the swing from mediated experience to direct experience and then back again as it could have been experienced in Owen Barfield's lifetime. I shall add simply that it is a movement many experience and that the tension that results from this vibration back and forth is necessary and healthy. It is this tension that keeps us alive and anxious rather than fat, dumb, and complacent. Without this dialectic it is hard to see how (as the Lord tells us in the prologue to Goethe's *Faust*)

> A good man, struggling in his darkness,
> Will always be aware of the true course.

REFERENCES

1. Bergonzi, B. *Heroes' Twilight: A Study of the Literature of the Great War*. New York: Coward-McCann, 1966, p. 198.
2. Bunsen, C. *God in History*. 3 vols. Leipzig, 1857-8; English translation, London, 1870.
3. Forman, B., ed. *The Letters of John Keats*. 2d ed., London: Oxford University Press, 1942, p. 72.
4. Hardy, T. "The Convergence of the Twain."
5. Hynes, S. *The Pattern of Hardy's Poetry*. Chapel Hill & London: University of North Carolina Press, 1961.
6. Preyer, R. "Tennyson As An Oracular Poet." *Modern Philology* 55, 1958: 239-51.
   ———. "Alfred Tennyson: The Poetry and Politics of Conservative Vision." *Victorian Studies* 9, 1966: 325-52.
7. Tennyson, H., *Alfred Lord Tennyson: A Memoir*. Vol. 1, London, 1898, p. 189.

ON MODERN POETRY, POETIC CONSCIOUSNESS, AND THE MADNESS OF POETS

by

R. K. MEINERS

In this essay I am going to speak of some characteristics of what seems to me the prevailing mode of consciousness, at least until very recently and perhaps even now, in modern poetry. It will be soon apparent that I am not concerned here with writing a critical essay in the usual sense, for I shall be spending little time in discussions of particular poets or nuances of poetic styles. Those are very important things, but on this occasion I am more interested in the mode of consciousness revealed by the poetry than in the poetry itself (the distinction is artificial; Coleridge might say they could be *distinguished*, but not *divided*). I will also attempt to suggest what seem to me to be some of the consequences of this mode of consciousness, both in our literature itself and in the way the literature reveals characteristic themes and problems that, it is not too much to say, penetrate all of our society.

These are most complex and debatable issues, and the course that I try to pick through them will fall into four sections. The first section deals with some preliminary issues and alludes to the work of a number of the most important and representative poets of mid-twentieth-century American poetry. The second section is devoted to commentary on a crucial modern metaphor and certain qualities of modern poetry and modern consciousness that I believe are latent in this metaphor. The third section is concerned with an equally crucial modern myth. In the final section, I shall turn to a discussion of some of Owen Barfield's views of human consciousness and the evolution of consciousness to see what light they may shed on the issues raised in the earlier three sections. I have hopes that these four sections, dealing as they do with large, difficult, and arguable questions, may nevertheless coalesce into a commentary on some crucial issues; but even if the essay turns out to be no more than a handful of nuances and suggestions, I will feel rewarded if *they* point in the proper direction.

I

I want to begin by calling into attention the example of a number of American poets who seem to me to belong together, not only chronologically, but spiritually. They belong to that generation that began to publish its work at just about the time that Europe was sinking toward the Second World War. The poets are: Theodore Roethke, John Berryman, Robert Lowell, Randall Jarrell, and Delmore Schwartz. They all belong to what I think of as the tragic generation in American poetry (borrowing a phrase from W. B. Yeats). It is not my purpose to speak at length of these poets — that would require a book — but rather to try to evoke a sort of generational consciousness, a shared pattern of experience that runs through their poetry despite the very striking differences between their various styles. I believe that it is peculiarly important to talk about a question like the mode of a poetic consciousness, its assumptions and characteristic forms, at this time for two reasons. The first is hardly arguable, though the second may be.

The first reason is that consciousness *as such* is the major subject, at least by implication, of nearly all modern literature and philosophy. To this point, I have perhaps been speaking somewhat obliquely, and this is not all due to idiosyncrasy. For the tools of obliqueness — such as humor, irony, and indirection — are the devices we have invented to protect ourselves from the omnivorousness of consciousness once it has detached itself from any necessary relation with either the physical world or any conceivable world of thought. (It is a very rare modern man who feels himself attached in any way to ideas: they are mere moments of consciousness.) I can be straightforward on this point: consciousness is the central subject of modern literature, and it is a fearful and destructive subject, particularly when consciousness is conceived of as the inhabitant of a kind of hollow flask, the flask being the round of my skull. All that is *me* is in here, and everything else is *out there*: in between is the Nothing that waits and waits, the famous silences and voids of modern literature. There are other subjects in modern novels and poems — paralysis, dissociation, sexuality normal and abnormal, economic dilemmas, social and political alienation, and so on — but they are all enclitic to the subject of consciousness. Nearly two centuries ago, S. T. Coleridge wrote in his notebook that "psychologically, consciousness is the problem . . . almost all is yet to be achieved." We have learned a great deal since that time, but not how to live with the problem. In another note Coleridge made a sharp distinction between "mind" and "consciousness," and then he remarked in one of those clairvoyant asides that permeate his writing: "consciousness being the narrow Neck of the bottle." We have not gotten out of that neck yet.

The second reason that it is appropriate to talk about poetic consciousness is, as I mentioned, perhaps arguable. But the tone of my remarks may have hinted that I believe we have come, both in the smaller world of philosophical and artistic discussion and in the larger world of society, to a genuine state of crisis in our view of human consciousness and its relation to the world. I shall be suggesting that I do not believe that what is being called the ecological crisis and the state of mind in — for example — Lowell's *For the Union Dead* or Berryman's *Dream Songs* are entirely unrelated.

I have mentioned the names of Roethke, Berryman, Lowell, Jarrell, and Schwartz. They seem to me the most important poets of their generation. Their poetries do not resemble each other in any overt way, though they often wrote on similar subjects, and a little discriminating reading in the writings of the men in question will soon show that they were constantly on each other's minds: they mention one another either directly or by allusion in many places. Why do I group them together? And why do they seem to me the tragic generation in American poetry? I can only give some rudimentary suggestions here.

There is the mere fact that they were all much of an age, and that age was the years between the Great Wars and preparatory to Our War. There are the other facts: four of the five dead prematurely; one certainly a suicide and probably two. The deaths of Roethke, Jarrell, and Schwartz haunted the later poetry of Berryman and Lowell, and we can only wonder at the impact of the last tragedy on Lowell. It is an unavoidable fact that all five had very serious mental troubles, and that mental illness effectively destroyed Delmore Schwartz's career and his very life. But more than this: it is the extent to which madness and anguish were the *subjects* of the poetry of these men, and the extent to which a sense of acute mental and social crisis permeates the tone of nearly all of their work. I realize that these are quite pervasive qualities of modern literature, but even given the general condition, my remarks hold particularly true of these writers: even in the case of Roethke, who is the most joyous of these poets, and in the case of Berryman, who is among other things a wildly comic poet. What I am saying, with no documentation, is that there is no place in American poetry (and probably in no other poetry, either), where there is such a powerful sense of harassment and turmoil as in these five poets. And even when their poetry triumphs over this harassment — as it frequently does, in Jarrell's special children's world (but by no means always), or in the later work of Roethke and Schwartz — we never lose sight of its spectre and immanent presence. I quite realize that there are other tones, other themes, to be found in these poets; but I trust that I am fairly suggesting a common center toward which they all incline.*

The major quality in these five poets, which makes them to me a tragic generation, is a sense of exhaustion and depletedness. It is, furthermore, an

---

* I should, properly, here quote some representative passages from the works of these five writers, but space considerations prevent me doing so. I trust that their work is sufficiently familiar, and that the charitable reader may recall that work and grant that I have not unduly distorted its characteristic qualities in my admittedly peremptory summary.

overpowering sense of the isolation of the individual consciousness, "the mind at the end of its tether." Given another occasion I would qualify these bald assertions; and in the cases of particularly Schwartz and Roethke I would suggest that they were moving toward some alternative mode of consciousness, especially in their later work.

In 1939 Randall Jarrell wrote an essay that he called "The End of the Line." All the alternatives had been tried, he said, and the young poet found himself with no principle left for preferring one form to another, nothing to lead him to write this way, that way, or another way. I am saying that I believe it was the end of the line in an even larger sense, and that what was happening was that the continual drain upon the resources of the poet's individual consciousness, a consciousness that had been sharply separated from all other being by at least three centuries of European and American intellectual tradition, had finally taken too great a toll. And by implication that a commensurate process had been taking place in European and American society. To reinforce these speculations I must now turn to consider what I have called a crucial modern metaphor.

II

As I said at the beginning, the second section will be devoted to discussing a metaphor and the third to a myth. One cannot be a member of the critics' union unless he has at least one piece of myth criticism to establish his bona fides, so I am seizing this opportunity. Very well. Marcel Raymond has talked of "the modern myth of poetry." *I* have in mind what we might call the orthodox modern myth of the *poet*, and it centers upon the figure of the poet as sufferer. Often the figures of Prometheus or Orpheus are invoked, but there are radical differences between this mythology and the classic; for here both the Promethean and Orphic figures are internalized, made into motifs of consciousness. This is generally true of the use of mythic figures in modern psychology: they are turned into emblems of consciousness. If one were to say that was also true of the classical figures, I would reply that such a position begs some crucial questions into which I cannot go here: basically it involves a projection of a logical consciousness onto prelogical experience.*

I will postpone looking directly at this myth and turn instead to the metaphor I mentioned, which is closely allied with the myth. The metaphor often appears independently, and often the myth is suppressed or displaced, appearing only in the residual rhetoric of the metaphor. In any case, the metaphor usually turns around the major questions of life, death, love, and art;

* Barfield has illuminating passages on the subject in *Poetic Diction, Saving the Appearances,* and elsewhere.

and it usually employs the images of flame and fuel, or fever and disease — though there are plenty of variations like worms, cankers, rust, and so on. Here I will introduce some examples. There are so many possibilities that I hardly know where to begin, so I have scattered the examples across a very wide spectrum. This is from Shakespeare's 73rd sonnet:

> In me thou see'st the glowing of such fire,
> That on the ashes of his youth doth lie
> As the deathbed whereon it must expire,
> Consumed with that which it was nourished by.

And here are a few lines from Dryden's first description of Achitophel:

> Restless, unfixt in Principles and Place;
> In Power unpleas'd, impatient of Disgrace.
> A fiery Soul, which working out its way,
> Fretted the Pigmy Body to decay

From the nineteenth century, here is a passage from Shelley's "Epipsychidion":

> Then, from the caverns of my dreamy youth
> I sprang, as one sandalled with plumes of fire,
> And towards the lodestar of my one desire,
> I flitted, like a dizzy moth, whose flight
> Is as a dead leaf's in the owlet light,
> When it would seek in Hesper's setting sphere
> A radiant death, a fiery sepulchre,
> As if it were a lamp of earthly flame.

And here is the conclusion of Charles Baudelaire's shattering poem, "The Voyage," in Robert Lowell's version:

> It's time. Old Captain, Death, lift anchor, sink!
> The land rots; we shall sail into the night;
> if now the sky and sea are black as ink
> our hearts, as you must know, are filled with light.
>
> Only when we drink poison are we well —
> we want, this fire so burns our brain tissue,
> to drown in the abyss — heaven, or hell,
> who cares? Through the unknown, we'll find the *new*. (72-3)

I am tempted to quote Walter Pater's "hard gemlike flame" passage to illustrate the deliquescence of metaphor to cliché, but I will forbear. Instead, here are two final examples, by men more nearly our contemporaries. The first is from that incredible "Sonnet to Orpheus" by Rilke, which begins: "*Wolle die Wandlung. O sei für die Flamme begeistert*," and in Rilke's most Orphic manner takes us into a state of continual metamorphosis:

Will metamorphosis! O be radiant with that Flame
where things are always elusive, which boasts of changes;
that projecting Spirit, which masters the earthly,
loves the movement of figures, and delights in the moment
of mutation

Here is something less Germanic, closer to home; a passage from Robert Lowell's "Night Sweat":

For ten nights now I've felt the creeping damp
float over my pajamas wilted white . . .
Sweet salt embalms me and my head is wet,
everything streams and tells me this is right;
My life's fever is soaking in night sweat —
one life, one writing! But the downward glide
and bias of existing wrings us dry —
always inside me is the child who dies,
always inside me is his will to die
one universe, one body . . . in this urn
the animal night sweats of the spirit burn.

That should be enough examples. Of the five poets I mentioned earlier, only Lowell has been represented in these quotations. It would be easy to show that one version or another of the metaphor permeates their work, but I dare not take more space for examples. I wish to emphasize that I fully realize I have taken many of these passages from their contexts, that they are open to differing interpretations, that I am riding a hobbyhorse. But subject to those limitations, I would like to make some comments on the basic metaphor animating these passages and to attempt to suggest some implications that I see in it.

The fundamental metaphor likens the consciousness of the poet to a flame which, as it burns, consumes its fuel and thus itself. To put this another way: life is the fuel of art, and art feeds on, and often exists at the expense of, life. There are numerous analogues to this metaphor, and two are very common. One of these involves a slight change in the vehicle, and the second a change in the tenor. In the first, the consciousness of the poet is compared to a fever, which wastes in the disease of his life and produces his art: Lowell's "Night Sweat" is a perfectly good example. The second variation is one well known in the Petrarchan tradition; in it the mind and love of the lover are compared to the consuming flame. It antedates the artist metaphor, and I suspect that both the actual metaphor and the attitude toward love and passion it implies furnished much of the historical basis and residual rhetoric for the later development of the artist metaphor.

I am reasonably certain that this metaphor is distinctively modern, using "modern" in the very broad sense of postrenaissance. I do not believe the metaphor is found in medieval or classical literatures. We frequently find the phoenix image in earlier literature being used to illustrate questions of both love and art, but this is a quite different matter. The image of life as the fuel for a consuming flame begins to appear, I believe, quite clearly in the renaissance, usually applied to the case of the lover devoured by his love. Gradually, it begins to be transferred to the realm of artistic experience, and by the middle of the nineteenth century it is a cliché. It is beyond my scope or competence to suggest the manner in which this image may be related to the earlier traditions of courtly love, the various competing theologies of divine and human love in the Christian church, and so on. But I believe I can risk several generalizations about the progress of the metaphor in the modern mind, and some of its implications.

The first generalization is this: it is a metaphor that emphasizes change rather than permanence; it emphasizes process. The movement, however, is a finite process rather than an infinite one; sooner or later the fire runs out of fuel (thus the "burnt-out" figure of speech with which everyone is familiar). The second generalization is this: the metaphor that compares the mind of the poet to a burning flame has certain parallels in its contemporary philosophical thought, and we may say that the metaphor proceeds at just about the same rate that epistemology proceeds to dominate European intellectual thought, and it begins to turn into a rhetorical and literary truism during the same period that an articulated psychology of consciousness emerges. The third is this: M. H. Abrams' *The Mirror and the Lamp* is deservedly celebrated for its research into the implications of the image of the lamp used as a metaphor of the active mind in romantic art and thought, but perhaps one thing he slighted in his work was the fact that one cannot have light without heat. The fourth generalization is a presupposition of the finite quality of the process: the metaphor is both reflexive and predatory. The poet's art *devours* his life. It turns inward, and eats up the ground of its own being, because it has no other place to go. The fifth and final generalization may stand as a sort of epitome and summary of the preceding four: the metaphor of the devouring flame emerges in European literature as a literary and linguistic counterpart to the development of a view of human consciousness, which sees that consciousness set off, sharply divided (not merely distinguished), from all other existence. The Cartesian separation of the world into *res cogitans* and *res extensa*, into "subject" and "object," if you will, is often pointed to as a crucial example of the beginning of this development in modern philosophy. And Descartes will serve well enough as an example so long as we understand that his work is *only* an example of a much wider development taking place in the mind of European man. But the fact is, it is usually tacitly presumed that Descartes was only making clear that relationship of man's mind to the universe that had *always* existed, had earlier philosophers but had the wit to see the situation. With *this* attitude is born the peculiar arrogance that suggests that older philosophies, *because they are old*, are both quaint and untrue, and that the "modern" mind has an access to truth denied to earlier periods: that it is more trustworthy *because* it is modern. On this point I dare not attempt to bestow any argument. An assertion must suffice: I agree with Owen Barfield in thinking that the modern conception of the human being as a self-conscious individual is itself the result of an evolution of human consciousness, and that far greater effort must be spent in attempting to understand this evolution than has yet been made.* It will not do to think that human nature has always been the same — though that is the common assumption — and that we merely understand it better than our ancestors. Nor, even more importantly, will it do to say that history will and must grind to its inevitable conclusion. We *must* become more aware of our part in the evolutionary process and the changing relationship between human consciousness and the rest of nature, which is the dynamic of that process.

To return to the literary manifestations of these problems, it may be said that in the metaphor of the devouring flame the poets have shown their awareness of the results of a sharp cleavage driven between consciousness and being, but there has been little suggestion to date that poets, or anyone else, can do anything about the situation.

I say "anyone else" advisedly. It is often said that the poet is quite different from other persons, or that his activity has little relation to the greater society; that his activity and indeed his experience is in striking contrast to, for instance, that of the scientist or engineer. This is a very misleading view. Our literature is only *too* exact a counterpart of our society at large. We see on all sides the results of a view of the human mind that has sharply separated the mind from the world and man from the rest of nature, including other men. What we are witnessing in our politics, in our technology, and in our art are the results of a process that has been drawing on its capital for far too long to the place where there is now little left to draw upon. The "capital" in this case is all the rich results — and who can deny their very real value in many instances? — that followed from the separation between mind and world, which made possible the birth of not only modern philosophy, but technology and science as we know them. But by now we have plundered the earth for fuel for engines (for the earth is merely *out there*), and we are very close to destroying it. Our art, with no taste for or basis in the classical "imitation," has turned inward into our lives, our consciousness, for substance; and we have plundered our lives and consciousnesses for fuel for passion and art, and we are very close to destroying them.

* See such essays as "On the Consciousness Soul" and "The Form of Hamlet" in *Romanticism Comes of Age*, and all of *Saving the Appearances*; indeed, all of Barfield's work, though these and portions of *Poetic Diction* perhaps deal most directly with the issue.

III

Now I want to turn, much more briefly than the subject deserves, to the myth that may be said to more or less underlie the metaphor of which I have been speaking. A crucial modern myth, I have called it. Actually, I wish to speak of what mythology has become for us: a kind of symbolic pattern, an archetype of our conscious and unconscious experience. It is very easy to suppose that this is what myth has always "meant." Indeed, that is just what we *do* assume, all the time. But in my view this is quite misleading, and in fact the classical mythologies looked back to a period when man's being and the animating being of the world were experienced as an undivided unity.* In at least some of the classical myths — that of Oedipus, for example — we can see the emerging of man's conscious individuality from an earlier period of undifferentiated unity (remember the Sphinx's question). If my use of the word "myth" in the present context is to have any meaning, two things must be kept in mind. In the first place, the "myth" must be understood to be a kind of shared pattern of conscious and unconscious experience. In the second place, this "myth" in both form and content refers to postlogical rather than prelogical experience: it is a myth not of the emergence of consciousness, but of the individualized consciousness cut off, separated from all other existence.

The myth is, as I have suggested, usually constructed along the lines of the Promethean or the Orphic archetype, but attention is fixated on the concluding phases of the archetype: not on the benefits of consciousness (Prometheus) nor on the mysterious communion of the artist with nature (Orpheus) — if these factors enter at all, it is usually either nostalgically or ironically — but on alienation, the dismemberment, the *penalties* of consciousness that are at the center of attention. Indeed, there are times as I read and think about our experience and our poetry when I feel that extremity has become a kind of technique of rhetoric: madness is a motif of decoration, and suicide only the ultimate trope and guarantor of sincerity.

> Your face broods from my table, Suicide.
> Your force came on like a torrent toward the end
>   of agony and wrath.
>
> (Berryman, *Dream Songs*, 172)

The suffering poet. The wreck of consciousness. The cliffs of the mind. The pattern is so well established in the romantic-symbolist-modern tradition

---

* Anyone who thinks I am making conventional neoprimitive noises is quite mistaken. I am speaking literally. If that seems obscure or unbelievable, I cannot argue the case here, but refer the reader to, among other sources, R. B. Onians' *The Origins of European Thought*. Barfield has a great deal to say on this subject, especially in what he has written concerning "original participation" in *Saving the Appearances*.

that it would seem a mark of tact to avoid more description of it (let alone teaching it). What is there to be said when we can refer to commentators like Rimbaud, or Freud, or Dostoevski? To poets like Lowell, Berryman, Plath? If more is needed, we can read Erich Heller's *The Disinherited Mind*; or Norman Brown's *Life Against Death*; or A. Alvarez; or others; there is no paucity of sources.

And yet, we *must* find ways to talk of the disasters of consciousness, of the isolation of the poet, of the loneliness at the center of life. No matter how dispiriting the topic, we must comprehend the condition if there is to be the slightest chance of breaking through it. I think I have probably done more than my share of talking *about* it, both in this essay and elsewhere.* Instead of more examples and discussion, I will devote the rest of this section to a sort of diagram, something like those hypothetical *gedanken experimenten* with which Albert Einstein and Niels Bohr used to challenge each other.

Imagine a horizontal line *XY*. *X* may be labelled Memory, *Y* Apocalypse (the limits of consciousness extended backward and forward in time, both poles dependent upon consciousness). This horizontal line is intersected at its midpoint by a perpendicular line *AB*. *A* is Clairvoyance, *B* Ecstasy. The intersection of the lines forms the center of two concentric circles, one much smaller than the other. The smaller circle may be called self-consciousness; the larger circle, with lines *AB* and *XY* as its diameters, may be called simply consciousness. Put in another way, the smaller circle may be labelled *consciousness proper*; the larger, *projected consciousness*. The upper segment of the vertical line represents the Promethean movement of consciousness, upward (to use spatial terms) into clairvoyance; the lower segment is the opposing Orphic movement, downward into the unconscious and ecstasy: the rapture of the depths.

This is very crude. But it must substitute here for both exposition and argument. Take it as a sort of spatial image of orthodox modern conceptions of consciousness and of the myth of poetic consciousness. There are a number of crucial further points to be made about modern notions of consciousness. The first is that *it alone is creative*. In terms of the diagram, meaning and energy are generated in the smaller circle of self-consciousness (including the personal unconscious, the lower half of the circle), and move outward. In other words, this is in opposition to earlier theories of inspiration, in which the poet's vision was given by the Muse, or God — something other than his own being. The poet is now *creator* (we teach courses in creative writing). He does not imitate the life of the universe; he draws life out of himself and

---

* Especially in *Everything to be Endured: An Essay on Robert Lowell and Modern Poetry*. Columbia, Missouri: University of Missouri Press, 1970; and *see also* my essay-review on Delmore Schwartz in *The Southern Review* 7 (1971): 314-37, from which the following "diagram" is adapted.

bestows it on the universe (remember the pathetic fallacy). The second quality of modern notions of poetic consciousness is that it is *inescapable*. There is nothing, save dead matter, that is *not* involved with consciousness: and *it* is involved in the act of knowing. Even the *un*conscious (including Jung's collective unconscious), is defined in relation to consciousness. All is drawn within this closed sphere; my world is my creation: my glory and my prison ("I have heard the key / Turn in the door once and turn once only / We think of the key, each in his prison"). It is this last quality that accounts for the ubiquity of such conceptions as those of repression, on the one hand, and projection, on the other.*

In terms of my diagram, whether the mind seeks the way down, into the Dionysiac unconscious, or the way up, into Apollonian wisdom, its limits are still to be found within a closed circle. The major traditions of modern thought have so far failed to solve these problems inherent in the Cartesian and Kantian traditions that the very possibility of a prior world of consciousness in which the individual consciousness participates is as yet all but unthinkable. Owen Barfield says it is taboo, and he is right. For the orthodox modern mind, consciousness is private, a closed container. And the modern myth of the suffering poet — with all the truth than any valid myth always contains — generates its energy out of precisely this fact. The individual consciousness is isolated, sealed off. The genie is shut in his flask. He may ornament the walls of his cage, he may kick at them, he may go mad: but he cannot get out. He has two choices: to amuse himself in lassitude, or to generate enough friction to incinerate himself.

IV

The final section of this essay will be relatively short, but I would like to think that, at least by implication, it will be the most important. First, I want to separate myself from a suggestion that may seem to be clinging to the earlier pages of this essay. Certainly the conditions that I have been addressing, the sense of alienated and isolated consciousness, have often been described before, both in and out of literary contexts. But once the condition has been described, what then? That, indeed, *is* the question, and I suppose it is only because I, like everyone else, have so often avoided that chilling question that I am attempting these suggestions. Better to appear credulous, naive, or worse, than to keep turning one's eyes aside.

* An entire book is concealed in this sentence. Perhaps I will one day try to write it. Meaning — so the conception goes — is exclusively the product of self-consciousness and is projected onto phaenomena. Older notions of meaning *drawn in* from the world are foolish and deluded.

An implicit suggestion is often made — and it may seem to be the direction implied in my own earlier pages — to the effect that we must return to the past to realize that the modern consciousness has gone drastically wrong, and that what is needed is to return to older modes of thought. This impulse is sometimes called "primitivism," sometimes "conservatism," depending upon who is describing it. Both words seem to me inadequate, but that is not the issue. The issue is whether we should attempt to revive older ideals and forms. Different ideals are suggested in different contexts: classicism, agrarianism, traditional Christianity, and so on. Now I do not want to dismiss such motives with a characteristic slighting remark about "neoprimitivism" or something similar. For to do so may seem to suggest that we can learn nothing from history, and the burden of my remarks is precisely that we *must* learn from history. Nevertheless, I see little real possibility of resurrecting earlier modes of thought and setting them to solve problems which, by their very nature, they were never called on to face in their original contexts.

Another suggestion, which seems in its various forms a very popular one, as one can verify by some browsing in a paperback book store, is that the solutions to the problems of modern consciousness are to be found in the mystical tradition. The limits of the human personality are real, the dimensions of the universe ineffable: let us turn (so the argument goes) to the Perennial Wisdom, or to the Orient, the Occident having come upon bad days. I am even more reluctant to give any impression of dismissing such possibilities than in the former case. There is much in the mystical tradition, Occidental and Oriental, to be learned. But I am afraid that for me there seems small possibility of the Occident really finding within Oriental wisdom the solutions to problems it has itself created, no matter how much it can indeed learn from the East. And as for the possibility of resurrecting the Neoplatonists, or Jacob Boehme, or Blake, or some other representative of Western mysticism, I think that, again, this is indeed something to be done — although "resurrecting" implies a certain deadness in that tradition, which I do not think warranted. But our problems are so permeated with conditions prevailing since the scientific revolution that we earnestly need to develop adequate postrevolutionary frames of reference, and Meister Eckhart and Jacob Boehme (even William Blake, though this is less true of him), for better or worse, lived in a prerevolutionary climate of thought.*

What I am suggesting is that, to my mind, it is worse than useless to attempt

---

* Those familiar with Owen Barfield will realize how much I am indebted to his writing in this section (not only where I have mentioned him). I do not wish to saddle my opinions on him; nor would I have it thought I have sanguinely borrowed his. Some of the points made in the last paragraph are similar to those Barfield makes in the preface to his translation of portions of Rudolf Steiner's *Von Seelenrätseln* [*The Case for Anthroposophy*].

to turn aside in any way from the burdens and difficulties of consciousness. We can only "escape" those difficulties by becoming *more* conscious, by *transforming* consciousness and learning to assess correctly its status, and by learning that the modes of viewing consciousness, which are sanctioned by philosophical orthodoxy, are more in the nature of conventions and models than of demonstrated conclusions; as such they are not sacrosanct, not unchallengeable. The "answer," insofar as I can presume to give one, is that we must go even further into consciousness. And going into it, we may find that we shall emerge through the "neck of the bottle" to which Coleridge referred in the passage quoted earlier. Does this sound like another hortatory metaphor? I do not mean it at all that way, but as a description as exact as I can manage in a short space. For some awareness of and reflection on the history of human consciousness should show that the development of modern self-consciousness out of earlier views of consciousness, as well as the development of those earlier views themselves, has been a precipitating, constricting process. It has proceeded by cutting off certain possible modes of experience, and by "cutting off" self-consciousness from general consciousness (thus, among other things, making possible the precision of modern scientific method). What I am suggesting is that modern self-consciousness is indeed the *neck* of the bottle, but that the solution is not to turn aside into the vatic ecstasies of silence and unconsciousness, but to move *through* the neck.

That is all very well, it may be said (by a charitable reader) — but how? If I may gather my audacity for one last time, here are some considerations that seem to me most relevant:

In the first place, we must become far more aware of the development and evolution of consciousness itself, as opposed to more customary histories of *thought*. For example, it is only by reflection on the developing modality of consciousness that one could justify describing the emergence of self-consciousness of a kind of constriction, as I have done.

In the second place, I think that we must recognize not the *untruth* of the "myth of the poet and poetic consciousness," which I have attempted to describe, though the reverse might seem to have been implied in the earlier pages. Rather, it is necessary to recognize *its profound truth*. Because we have a faulty conception of evolution, we assume that the isolation of the self-consciousness — which is quite true, and an indisputable feature of our experience — is the entire story. We assume on the one hand that we have quite left behind earlier stages of consciousness and that they have nothing to say to *our* unique situation. On the other hand we refuse to recognize the possibility that our own constricted self-consciousness may be but one more step, a very necessary step, in the continuing process of transformation. And so we cut ourselves off from both past and future and isolate ourselves in the mute present. The orthodox myth of consciousness is radically true as an emblem of this condition, and our poets have vividly represented this situation's feeling and dramatized its moment. But we congratulate ourselves too much on our misery and uniqueness when we make our version of human experience an exclusive one.

In the third place, and I think this is the most important point I can make (it is implied in the foregoing): there is a need to challenge radically a number of crucial assumptions that have imbedded themselves in our ordinary thinking, our special studies, and in our very language. In particular it is necessary to challenge the proposition that the human intelligence is inherently isolated from the totality of nature. Is it not possible that the human intelligence *does* stand in a relation of polarity to nature? Is the proposition worth considering? There is no way I can possibly deal with the concept of polarity and its implications here. The best I can do is to refer to Barfield's recent book *What Coleridge Thought*, and perhaps particularly to the chapter "Coleridge and the Cosmology of Science" (though *it* cannot be read in isolation from the rest of the book, nor the book in isolation from the rest of Barfield's work).

Although this essay is already long, I will enter two short final paragraphs. There is enough of the evangelist about me to want to conclude on some final exhortation, and enough of the ironist to make me feel ludicrous doing so. But it seems necessary for anyone who feels at all the way I have described to attempt to bring some other sense than that of either inevitable disaster or mere stoical endurance into one's thinking and teaching. "Tragic sense of life" used to seem to me a beautiful phrase, and attitude. In a way, as Unamuno used it especially, it is; but it will not suffice, not for me. In my own case, of which I speak with reluctance, I am trying to begin to take the injunction, that consciousness must be transformed, seriously. My best example of this will conclude this essay.

If one as wise as Owen Barfield has seemed to me to be continually recommends Rudolf Steiner as one immeasurably wiser, well, then, I had better do some investigating. So far my investigations have discovered some strange vocabulary, some really inept translations, a plenitude of *echt-Deutsch hoch-philosophisch* syntax; and some notions that seem, on first reading, truly outlandish and outrageous. But these are the reactions of a timid and orthodox mind; and beyond that first range of hills I also begin to see some of the wisdom to which Barfield refers. This last exposes me pretty completely, and that is not a good position for an ironist. But so be it. When one has looked along a good many other conventional and unconventional paths and has found them all leading, by longer or shorter routes, to the same locked doors painted the same drab colors, perhaps one ought to explore the one path one has discovered that appears to lead to something substantially different, or at least to a door one has never before experienced. Even if that path be described as "occult," "esoteric," or with other gaudy adjectives. The stakes are as high as they *can* be. As Barfield says in the preface to *Poetic Diction*: "The possibility of man's avoiding self-destruction depends on his realizing before it is too late that what he let loose over Hiroshima, after fiddling with its exterior for three centuries like a mechanical toy, was the forces of his own unconscious mind."

MILTON'S ICONOCLASM

by

PAUL PIEHLER

ORIGINAL PARTICIPATION

Among the most fruitful, and at the same time the most elusive, of the concepts Owen Barfield has introduced into literary studies is that of "original participation." It is a phrase obviously impossible to define in a few words, since it refers to the essential quality of a consciousness different from and anteceding our own. It is hardly enough even to refer the reader to the chapter entitled "Original Participation" in his book *Saving the Appearances*, for the whole book is largely a commentary on this concept. Let me instead attempt to evoke a type of experience in which one might sense something of "original participation" even today. One is walking alone on a country road at night. The darkness grows more intense as the road enters a wood, and one begins to feel a certain indefinable uneasiness. To avoid any danger of "imagining things," one locks one's mind into a certain attitude of resistance. The trees — at all costs they must remain trees, for one begins to fear that any slackening of mental resistance would permit something alien and rather menacing to start manifesting itself in the trees, something possessed of a quality akin to consciousness. In resisting this feeling one is resisting a manifestation of "participation" — that is, the awareness, behind phenomena, of a quality "of the same nature of the perceiving self, inasmuch as it is not mechanical or accidental, but psychic and voluntary."[2a]

In this age one is unlikely even to confess the existence of such feelings to other people and still less to make it an important element in one's interpretation of human history. And yet, if Barfield is correct that this type of participation underlay, to a greater or lesser extent, human consciousness until the seventeenth century, our understanding of history must remain superficial without some comprehension of that earlier cosmos in which spiritual and physical perceptions were fused together.

My present concern is with that critical moment in our history when original participation gave way to our modern nonparticipated universe, in which objects are perceived merely as objects. Thus the following is in one sense a footnote to such chapters in *Saving the Appearances* as "Some Changes" and

"Before and After the Scientific Revolution." In the former, Barfield demonstrates, for example, the seventeenth-century change in the concept of blood, in which the older, participated meaning of blood is polarized into two meanings, a metaphorical one and a literal one.[2b] The new ability to see the body as a "literal" or mechanical system may be associated with Harvey's discovery of the circulation of the blood, but also, one may suggest, with the decline in the comprehension of the psychosomatic element in the human system. As for the embodiments of the "psychic and voluntary" agents behind phenomena, they lose the independent existence they enjoyed in a participated cosmos. In Barfield's words: "We must no longer look for the nature spirits — for the Goddess Natura — on the far side of appearances; we must look for them *within ourselves*."[2c] The process of internationalization affects, as we shall see, not only nature spirits but a whole class of spiritual beings, here termed *potentiae*, which in a participated cosmos function simultaneously as subjective and objective entities.

One might expect such evolution of phenomena to be particularly evident in the history of poetry, since poetic expression itself involves the continual interplay of metaphorical and literal, internal and external perception. And the specific seventeenth-century crisis in participation one would expect to find most clearly in the work of the most intellectually daring and profound of its poets, John Milton. We have space enough here to glance at two of his major works, *Comus* (1634) and *Paradise Lost* (1667), to attempt to sketch a development from the poetry of participation to a poetry of iconoclasm. In *Paradise Lost* the separation of metaphorical and literal perception reflects, as I hope to show, contemporary iconoclastic destruction of objects believed to embody a dangerous confusion of the material and spiritual worlds.

ALLEGORY

We may distinguish two main types of participated poetry: myth, where literal and metaphorical are fused inseparably together, and allegory, where there is a simultaneous awareness of both the identity and the separateness of these elements. Thus allegory is an "otherspeaking," a continuous utterance of the spiritual in terms of the material, with the participated nature of the material world making it easy and natural for the poet to walk simultaneously in both worlds. The tradition of participated allegory in the Western world, traceable back to the second-century *Shepherd of Hermas*, reaching its highest point in Dante's *Commedia*, and brilliantly if intermittently present in the *Faerie Queene*, was remarkably consistent in its main characteristics. Let me attempt to list them, briefly:

1. The hero of the poem finds himself in a condition of crisis, spiritually

in profound doubt or anguish, literally in a dark wood, dungeon, or other adverse circumstance. There may be an intense and frightening degree of fusion of spiritual and physical worlds.

2. In his anguish the hero invokes some benevolent psychic power (*potentia*). He thereupon finds himself in the altered and higher mental state characteristic of visionary allegory, in which the *potentia* (normally a goddess or personification) appears transformed from mere metaphorical status into a living reality.

3. The landscapes and other locales of the visionary world represent similar development of metaphorical imagery and are similarly charged with a more intense spiritual quality. Place and state of mind become fused together.

4. The hero's visionary experience shapes itself into a quest for the spiritual powers and places best capable of aiding him in his perplexity or anguish, a quest that involves comparison of different *potentiae* and locales, with rejection of some, acceptance of others. The quest may involve or take the form of extensive dialogue with the *potentiae* to elucidate the visionary experience in rational terms.

5. The journey into this visionary world thus constitutes a type of literary experience that communicates simultaneously in symbolic, allegorical, and rational terms. The disunited powers of the mind are thereby reconciled into a state of harmony and serenity. Thus in visionary allegory the experience of participation in the phenomenal world is intensified both in respect of inutitive perception and rational comprehension.

6. Visionary allegory also constitutes "participated literature" in a slightly different, though closely related, sense insofar as the reader is offered participation in the process of soul-healing embodied in the poem, through imaginative identification with the hero.

7. Allegory bears within itself much of the history of man's interpretation of the phenomenal world, in that the scenes and events of the allegorical experience are derived from ancient myth in a long and largely conscious evolution. Allegory thus reflects and comments on the larger history of man's consciousness.

Not all the above characteristics are found in every work of visionary allegory, but striking variations in these characteristics normally reveal, on examination, useful indications of the allegorist's specific purposes.

COMUS

For some demonstration of these rather bold assertions concerning medieval allegory the reader will have to look elsewhere.[12] The most that can be indicated here is the presence of these characteristics in *Comus* and their curious appearance in a kind of reversed or negative form of *Paradise Lost*.

Let us first look at those aspects of *Comus* that manifest these characteristics without significant variation. For simplicity in cross-referencing, I shall indicate the characteristics referred to in the previous section by their appropriate numbers. The heroes and heroine are (1) lost in a dark wood whose darkness and confusion reflect, in differing degrees, their inner doubts and fears. After (2) a series of invocations, the children succeed in drawing to their aid a *potentia*, the Guardian Spirit, to guide them safely out of the (3) enchanted wood, whose spirit is manifested in the evil *potentia*, Comus. Their subsequent (4) quest for physical and spiritual safety involves also a series of dialogues, which eludidate their temptations in rational terms and assist them in distinguishing the true nature of the tempter, Comus, and in rejecting him. The experience may also be regarded as constituting (5) an intensification of the normal degree of intuitive participation, in which rational and intuitive perceptions are reconciled in a harmonious solution. We are clearly intended to participate imaginatively in the adventure through emotional and intellectual identification with the lost children. This invitation to participate in the act is made explicit in the final lines of the poem, when the Spirit addresses the audience directly in these words:

> Mortals that would follow me
> Love virtue, she alone is free,
> She can teach ye how to climb
> Higher than the Sphery chime;   (1018-21)

Finally (7), there is constant assertion of the evolutionary continuity of the allegorical tradition. For example, the elder brother's references to the "huntress Dian" (1.441) and "wise Minerva" (1.448) among the manifestations of Chastity implies a sense of the development of the abstractions of allegory out of the spiritual powers depicted in ancient myth. The Guardian Spirit proclaims quite explicitly the continuity of the inspiration of visionary poetry:

> I'll tell ye; 'tis not vain or fabulous,
> (Though so esteem'd by shallow ignorance)
> What the sage Poets taught by th' heav'nly Muse
> Storied of old in high immortal verse
> Of dire *Chimeras* and enchanted isles
> And rifted Rocks whose entrance leads to hell,
> For such there be, but unbelief is blind.   (513-18)

My main point here is to establish, however sketchily, something of the adherence of *Comus* to the form of visionary allegory. Insofar as we have now done this we may distinguish certain significant variations from the normal patterns. In looking at these variations we shall particularly note anticipatory signs of Milton's abandonment of allegory.

Let us look at Milton's Lady at that critical moment when under the stress of wandering in the "blind mazes of this tangl'd wood" she begins to experience (1) the characteristic fusion of internal and external worlds, of outer darkness and inner confusion:

> What might this be? A thousand fantasies
> Begin to throng into my memory,
> Of calling shapes and beck'ning shadows dire,
> And airy tongues that syllable men's names
> On Sands and Shores and desert Wildernesses. (205-9)

And yet, in this frightening situation, similar to that which in Boethius' *Consolation of Philosophy* provokes the vision of the Lady Philosophy or in the *Commedia* Dante's rescue from the dark wood by Vergil, the Lady remains strangely calm:

> These thoughts may startle well, but not astound
> The virtuous mind, that ever walks attended
> By a strong siding champion Conscience. (210-12)

The figure of Conscience within her remains, however, inert and metaphorical and takes no independent allegorical role in the drama. The *potentia* remains internalized. This failure of Conscience to metamorphosize into full visionary reality argues no lack of capacity for vision in the Lady, as the next lines make clear:

> O welcome pure-eye'd Faith, white-handed Hope,
> Thou hov'ring Angel girt with golden wings,
> And thou unblemish't form of Chastity,
> I see ye visibly. . . . . (213-16)

As in the case of Conscience, the vision of these spiritual powers is not followed by their manifestation as characters of the drama. If she needs any protection, it will be physical rather than moral, for her initial confusion, it is now evident, was psychological rather than moral. So her faith is strong enough to reassure her, quite correctly:

> That he, the Supreme good, t'whom all things ill
> Are but as slavish officers of vengeance,
> Would send a glist'ring Guardian, if need were,
> To keep my life and honor assail'd. (218-22)

Thus the Lady makes no direct invocation of spiritual guardians at this juncture. Instead she calls upon the aid of Echo, "sweetest Nymph that liv'st unseen," for straightforward assistance in locating her brothers. But remembering how often Milton's poetic juxtapositions imply more than merely logical connection,[9a] we may find Echo here a particularly appropriate *potentia* for one who turns inward for inspiration and succour, this in respect of both her own qualities and as a lover of Narcissus (237). Thus though the echoes of her song do not, despite her plea, carry as far as her brothers, the scene has been set for her debate with Comus, in which she will have to rely on what Wordsworth calls "the mind's internal echo."[14]

The incarnation of the *potentiae* within the Lady makes possible a new type of body-spirit dichotomy. Where Amoret in the House of Busirane (*Faerie Queene* III, xii.) is totally helpless and silent within the power of the enchanter, the Lady is subject only to Comus's physical control — a matter of flesh and nerves. Within the intellectual and spiritual realm she can put up an effective resistance to Comus, who is conceived on allegorically more conservative lines and functions simultaneously as an eternal menace and the voice of internal temptation.

Let us now turn to the brother's invocations. These imply varying but more restricted relationships between man and the visionary world. On first entry, the elder brother bursts into immediate invocation:

> Unmuffle ye faint stars, and thou fair Moon
> That wont'st to love the traveller's benison,
> Stoop thy pale visage through an amber cloud,
> And disinherit Chaos, that reigns here
> In double night of darkness and of shades;   (331-5)

The elder brother lacks his sister's perceptual access to the visionary powers but, on the metaphorical as opposed to the specifically visionary or allegorical level, the invocation is effective enough. The phrase "ye faint stars" seems a groping, metaphorical reference to the powers represented by the Guardian Spirit, the first line of whose first speech has associated him with the "starry threshold of Jove's Court (1.1)." His "regions mild of calm and serene air" (1.4) are contrasted with the "smoke and stir of this dim spot" (1.5), from which, it seems implied, the stars would indeed look faint. The concluding phrase of the Spirit's opening speech, "I must be viewless now" (1.92), thus prepares us for the elder brother's plea, "Unmuffle ye faint stars (1.331)."

The appeal to the moon and stars to "disinherit Chaos" implies a similar linkage between spiritual and physical worlds, dependent, no doubt, on Milton's acceptance of the traditional philosophical association of the concepts "forest" and "chaos" in the term "silva."[12] In the dark forest the negative powers of the unconscious mind are at their strongest, where rationality is deprived of its supporting external correlatives in the physical world. Where the elder brother perceives the domain of Chaos, a double night reigns, the darkness of the physical universe and of the shades that afflict the soul.

Thus the elder brother, even if lacking the Lady's powers of perception into the world of visionary allegory, retains at least the power of metaphor: in Blakean terms, the twofold vision. The "single vision and Newton's sleep" is rather to be seen, and subsequently corrected, in the more earthbound and skeptical mood of the younger brother. His answering speech hardly reaches the level of invocation but implies a toning down of the elder's loftier plea into more homely wishes: "might we but hear / The folded flocks penn'd in their wattled cotes . . . [343-5]."

In his limited vision he fears for his sister's stability of mind: "In this close dungeon of innumerous boughs" she may have fallen into "wild amazement and affright [349-56]." The elder brother, possessing the twofold vision, is able to make distinction between internal and external terror and to recognize the same power of mature distinction in his sister. Thus he has no fear

> . . . that the single want of light and noise
> (Not being in danger, as I trust she is not)
> Could stir the constant mood of her calm thoughts, . . .   (369-71)

She has, he recognises, the inner light — the *potentia* is internalized:

> Virtue could see to do what virtue would
> By her own radiant light, though Sun and Moon
> Were in the flat Sea sunk . . .   (373-5)

whereas:

> . . . he that hides a dark soul and foul thought
> Benighted walks under the midday Sun
> Himself is his own dungeon.   (382-4)

The confident tones of the elder brother's response reflect his profounder understanding of his sister's spiritual maturity. But note the strain his explanation put upon the whole mode of consciousness implied by the poem. If virtue is its own light, what need shall we eventually have for that light of Heaven which is "participated," simultaneously physical and spiritual? The ancient concept of light divides into exclusive categories, a "literal" subject for study by scientists *or* a source of metaphor for poets.

The debate of the two brothers concludes with the elder brother's success in persuading the younger of the power of chastity to protect its adherents against their foes, to open to them the world of "clear dream and solemn vision," or to "converse with heavn'ly habitants [457-9]." The younger brother's acceptance of such conceptions, in the speech "How charming is the divine Philosophy," leads immediately to the manifestation of the Guardian Spirit in the guise of a shepherd. Both brothers have now attained a level of consciousness at which such beings are perceptible. Thus the elder brother's invocation is answered, as all invocations in the poem, in strict accord with the mode of consciousness implied by the appeal. Since the brothers are not able to perceive the spiritual world directly, as their sister is, and have invoked the spiritual world ambiguously through its physical manifestations, the guide comes disguised in the earthly form of a shepherd, adapted to their spiritual capacity.

In conclusion we should note that while the main lineaments of medieval allegory are preserved in *Comus* the demarcations that distinguish man and *potentia* are becoming slightly blurred. The Guardian Spirit fulfills the *potentia*'s role of spiritual instructor so far as the audience is concerned, but in his incognito as Thyrsis he functions as a character on the same conceptual level as the children and imparts no specific spiritual instruction to them. The esoteric understanding of the wider polarity of earth and heaven, embracing that of wood and castle, is reserved to the audience alone.

In fact the Lady, with the *potentia* internalized, is clearly very capable of looking after herself intellectually, and in the debate with Comus becomes a teaching voice, almost a *potentia* herself, rather than a character in whose process of enlightenment we are expected to participate. Similarly, the elder brother functions, in his more limited capacity, as the medium for the spiritual instruction of the younger. The significance of these new relationships between man and *potentia* will become clearer as we look at their further development in *Paradise Lost*.

PARADISE LOST

While *Paradise Lost* by no means gives the impression of an allegorical poem, it has in fact many points of correspondence in theme and image with the earlier poetry of visionary allegory. Let us see what happens when we attempt to relate it to the seven aspects of allegory we have previously distinguished.

The poem opens (1) with depictions of intense mental and physical turmoil, includes spiritual disintegration and reintegration among its major themes, and concludes in some measure of reconciliation and harmony. Invocation (2) of spiritual beings is a persistent feature of the work, and such powers are constantly encountered by Adam and Eve in the roles of instructors or tempters. The landscapes (3) of Heaven, Hell, and Paradise dominate the poem, the first two functioning in obvious and explicit polarity. Satan's quest (4) for vengeance constitutes one of the strongest elements in the plot of the poem, and each new development of the plot is accompanied by explanatory dialogue of some type. The poet makes constant reference, implied and explicit, to the tradition of myth (7) in which the poem is operating, an employment of tradition that constitutes an important element of the poem's meaning.

When we turn, however, to the fifth and sixth of our categories, those that are specifically concerned with the quality of participation, we find a drastic change of tone, a resolute and explicit rejection of participation, that calls in question all the resemblances we have noted. Let us see how the forms and images previously associated with visionary allegory function in a poem of the new, postmedieval, participation-rejecting consciousness.

Milton's invocations (2) are quite different from anything one might find

in the works of an allegorist, a Boethius, Dante, or Chaucer. In such poetry
we associate ourselves with the poet's invocations of a *potentia*, and when
she manifests herself to assist the visionary, she also acts simultaneously on
the reader himself, as participant in the experience. But of course in *Paradise
Lost* it would be impertinent and absurd for us, as readers, to attempt to
participate in this fashion in Milton's invocations. We can hardly identify
ourselves with the aged blind poet, favored by Urania but rejected by men.
As C. S. Lewis pointed out, Milton becomes an image in his own poem —
"the image of the Blind Bard — and we are told about him nothing that does
not help that archetypal pattern."[9b] With the poet installed as archetype, no
wonder that Urania is never manifested in the poem. For Milton, as archetype,
now himself becomes the *potentia*, the "Guardian Spirit" of the poem. It is
he who, inspired by the shadowy Urania, will justify the ways of God to
man, a task that Boethius or Dante would have left to a Lady Philosophy or
Beatrice. As the figure of Conscience was embodied within the Lady of
Comus, so Urania has been merged into the role of the poet himself.

But with the poet and *potentia* identified, through whose eyes, it may be
asked, are we to see the action of the poem — with whom may the poet
associate himself? Adam and Eve arrive too late on the scene and their experiences are related in too detached and critical manner for the reader to
feel a strong sense of identity with them. Some readers have been tempted,
against all discouragement, to accept Satan as hero.[3] In his case, we can feel
that Milton does more than isolate Satan from our sympathies. Rather he
seems almost to be attempting to break us of our habit of participation by
some kind of aversion therapy, as one would break a dog of a bad habit.
On one hand we are tempted to feel massive sympathy for Satan. There is
a normal expectation for the sympathetic characters in a work to be presented first, and this is of course enormously reinforced here by the presentation of Satan at his highest point of courage, resilience, and self-awareness —
in the face of unparalleled adversity — having defied "th'Omnipotent to
arms" without suffering annihilation. In terms of the old participated literature there could hardly be a more attractive hero in terms of situation, but
of course the slightest attempt at real sympathy is checked by the fact that
Satan is in terms of the story, the Devil, our archenemy. Similarly, the
reader has to resist the plausible rhetoric of the debates in Hell, which tends
to lure him into a measure of agreement, if he fails to resist participation
and preserve a cool detachment from the proceedings.[8] Participation here
seems literally Satanic.

Thus around the figure of Satan a great tension of attraction and repug-
nance has accumulated, a tension that has always made *Paradise Lost* a matter of strong debate among its readers. Those who are temperamentally more
impressed with the situation of Satan rather than his reputation will naturally

try to upset the complacent reading of the poem by those who are content to abide by the labelling. Thus Blake tells us in the *Marriage of Heaven and Hell* that Milton is on the devil's side without knowing it.

But let us look further at this matter of labelling. How do we know that Satan is wrong? Not exactly because of his name, or his "bad behaviour," which can always be reargued on the basis of the facts provided, as does William Empson in his book *Milton's God*.[7] Fundamentally, it is because devils in a participated cosmos represented external forms of what we see today normally as internal negative impulses alone. The horror of devils is in fact part of the basic way in which they are perceived; it is an essential part of their representation. Lacking such horror, the devil can be no more than a man in fancy dress, even if he does behave, in human terms, rather badly.

So in fact Milton's confusion of man and *potentia* takes a double form. Not only does he turn himself into the archetype of the poet — as if in the *Commedia* Dante had turned himself into his own Vergil — but he also reduces Satan, and indeed all his other spiritual beings, to a human level, so that they function only in an external, nonparticipated fashion. There seems here a relationship to Milton's angelology — his taking over contemporary Platonistic theory to give his spiritual powers material bodies of a particularly refined type. Since they are no longer simultaneously internal and external beings, they obviously stand in need of some kind of refined materiality not to be dismissed as purely subjective. Therefore these materialised spirits may tempt, deceive, instruct, or enlighten Adam and Eve, but only, essentially, as beings on the same level of reality, as human characters in the poem might have functioned.

Let me attempt to demonstrate this evolution of the *potentia* in one critical instance where Milton's externalizing of a spiritual power leads to a breakdown of the narrative logic. Among the temptations offered by Satan in *Paradise Regained* is a banquet, which Christ refuses in these words:

> Said'st thou not that to all things I had right?
> And who withholds my pow'r that right to use?
> Shall I receive by gift what of my own,
> When and where likes me best, I can command?
> I can at will, doubt not, as soon as thou,
> Command a Table in this Wilderness,
> And call swift flights of Angels ministrant
> Array'd in Glory on my cup to attend;   (II 379-86)

If Christ has power to command anything he wishes on his own behalf, it is useless for Satan, as a kind of rival magician, to tempt him in this fashion. So the succeeding temptations, particularly Satan's offer of the kingdom of this world at the price of acknowledging him as "superior Lord," become meaningless. It is only if Satan himself represents in one aspect a temptation, a potential weakness in the soul, if there is no division between external adversary and internal voice, that the story can show its true significance, as it does in the accounts of Matthew and Luke, where there is no hint of such distinctions.

Similarly, and even more explicitly, the landscapes (3) of *Paradise Lost* suffer this split between literal and metaphorical perception. Satan proclaims defiantly at the opening of the poem his doctrine of nonparticipation, which will render Hell a tolerable dwelling:

> Farewell happy Fields
> Where Joy for ever dwells: Hail horrors, hail
> Infernal world, and thou profoundest Hell
> Receive thy new Possessor: One who brings
> A mind not to be chang'd by Place or Time.
> The mind is its own place, and in itself
> Can make a Heav'n of Hell, a Hell of Heav'n.   (I 249-55)

It is almost as if his Fall has this loss of participation as one of its consequences, for his insensitivity to his hellish environment seems to be purchased at the cost of a similar insensitivity to the Joy of the happy Fields. His subsequent escape from Hell and successful expedition to Eden turn out to have no effect on his inner state:[1]

> within him Hell
> He brings, and round about him, nor from Hell
> One step no more than from himself can fly
> By change of place;   (IV 20-23)

In *Paradise Regained* we learn that Satan has been once more in Heaven, but, as Christ reminds him, "the happy place / Imparts to thee no happiness, no joy . . . [I 416-7].

It is of course not only Satan who undergoes this loss of participation as part of a Fall. Adam, dispossessed of Paradise, is promised by Michael "A paradise within thee, happier far [XII 587]." With Adam and Eve seeking a paradise existing only in metaphor, the literal paradise, to point a moral, is destroyed by Noah's Flood. As Michael explains:

> then shall this Mount
> Of Paradise by might of Waves be mov'd
> Out of his place, push'd by the horned flood
> With all his verdure spoil'd, and Trees adrift
> Down the great River to the op'ning Gulf,
> And there take root an Island salt and bare,
> The haunt of Seals and Orcs, and Sea-mews' Clang.
> To teach thee that God attributes to place
> No sanctity, if none be thither brought
> By Men who there frequent, or therein dwell.   (XI 829-38)

Milton's God teaches by destroying; as a good Puritan iconoclast He is zealous for the destruction of objects deemed holy in themselves, that are in our terms "participated," fusing together internal and external. Prynne's comment on sanctification at the trial of Laud (1644) gives the note: "Our homilies say, that the church is called holy, not of itself, but because God's people resorting thither are holy, and exercise themselves in holy things."[11] Thus the sanctity of a place derives solely from the sanctity of God's people. The idea of inherent sanctity is abhorrent enough in an age rejecting participation to provoke widespread destruction of "idolatrous" ecclesiastical art.[12] The significance and ramifications of this iconoclasm seem only slightly understood today, though the iconoclasts themselves were certainly forceful and confident in defense of their activities, as witness the notorious William Dowsing's contention with the dons of Pembroke Hall, Cambridge, in 1643.[5]

Let us turn, finally, to the question of Milton's consciousness of the tradition in which he was working (7), which had been, of course, until his time a poetry of participation. One finds that he is always willing to employ the metaphorical associations of earlier poets for his own purposes, but while doing so, he is careful to reject the conceptual attitudes implied there. The visionary aspect of earlier poetry, so enthusiastically vindicated by the Guardian Spirit in *Comus*, now seems repugnant to him; vision permits the intensifying of participation and is thus quite contrary to the spirit of Milton's biblical literalism.

Not only is *Paradise Lost* not a dream, but, as we learn in a passage early in the poem all other literature is, by implication, but a dream to this: Mulciber's fall from heaven, we are told, was related erroneously by Homer, being but a dim echo of the truth to be found in Milton's "Christian" account (I 738-52). Similarly, in the proem to Book VII we are told that in comparison with the Christian inspiration he seeks, the pagan muse is but an "empty dreame." What is new is not so much the distinction between Christian and pagan, but the sharpness with which the pagan dream is repudiated. Milton's description of Paradise is similarly negative toward pagan poetry.

>   Thus was this place,
>   A happy rural seat of various view;
>   Groves whose rich Trees wept odorous Gums and Balm
>   Others whose fruit burnisht with Golden Rind
>   Hung amiable, *Hesperian* Fables true,
>   If true, here only, and of delicious taste: . . .   (IV 246-51)

With this one may compare the conciliatory attitude of Dante in describing the earthly paradise:

>   Those who sang in ancient days of the Golden
>   Age and its happy state perchance on
>   Parnassus dreamed of this place.   ("Purgatorio," XXVIII
>   139-41)

Milton has need of the poetical associations of the pagan gardens but jealously guards against any possibility of doctrinal contamination. Dante, on the other hand, is not afraid to suggest that the true paradise is the archetype of pagan dreams. Augustine had insisted on both the literal and the spiritual truth of paradise (*City of God.* XIII 21). But for Milton that would be close to admitting that paradise is a state of mind, as well as an actual place.

Thus so far as pagan poetry is concerned, Milton rejects the literal meaning but is willing to use its metaphorical overtones. With the biblical tradition his method seems quite opposite, insisting on the literal while rejecting any allegorical overtones. Here Milton reflects once more the tenor of Puritan thought, specifically in its distrust of allegorical methods of biblical exegesis.[6] Luther condemned such interpretation as perhaps suitable for poets but unworthy of theologians.[10] For Calvin allegorizing is not only mistaken and useless but inspired by the devil.[4] The existence of such opinions among Puritan divines shows that Milton's poetic violence against allegorical interpretations of Eden and other biblical motifs was fully in accord with certain strong currents of feeling in his age. We have come far since Augustine, equally in harmony with the feelings of his age, confessed:

I joyed also that the old Scriptures of the Law and the Prophets were laid before me, not now to be perused with the eye to which before they seemed absurd . . . and with joy I heard Ambrose, in his sermons to the people, oftentimes most diligently recommend this text for a rule unto them, The letter killeth, but the spirit giveth life, whilst those things which taken according to the letter seemed to teach perverse doctrines, he spiritually laid open to us, having taken off the veil of the mystery . . . .   *Confessions* IV 4

Allegorical exegesis, which for Augustine had been a means to overcome a sense of the *perversitas* of the literal text of the Scriptures, is now itself considered a diabolical perversion of the literal text. What is common, therefore, to Milton's attitude toward the two main traditions, pagan and biblical, in reference to which *Paradise Lost* was composed, is his iconoclastic refusal to accept either in its earlier participated form. The literal and metaphorical had to be separated and one of them discarded.

What were the effects of Milton's repudiation of original participation? C. S. Lewis commented on *Paradise Lost*: "The cosmic story — the ultimate *plot* in which all other stories are episodes — is set before us. We are invited, for the time being, to look at it *from outside*. And that is not, in itself, a religious exercise."[9c] Precisely. We are no longer asked to participate in a religious experience, but rather to observe, in a detached fashion, the effect of such experiences on others. In Martin Buber's terms, we have shifted from an I-Thou to an I-It relationship with God and the universe. We are shown round Hell, Heaven, and Paradise almost as tourists guided round a Cathedral, to admire rather than to participate, safe from both the horror and the ecstacy of an encounter with the spiritual worlds of a participated universe, of a Dantean cosmos.

Paradise Lost thus constitutes a major document in the history of consciousness, a prophetic book of iconoclasm, manifesting the destruction of the ancient participated cosmos. I close with one slight indication of the immense consequences of this literary iconoclasm. In *The Recluse* Wordsworth wrote:

> All strength — all terror, single or in bands,
> That ever was put forth in personal form —
> Jehovah — with his thunder, and the choir
> Of shouting Angels, and the empyreal thrones —
> I pass them unalarmed. Not Chaos, not
> The darkest pit of lowest Erebus,
> Nor aught of blinder vacancy, scooped out
> By help of dreams — can breed such fear and awe
> As falls upon often when we look
> Into our Minds, into the Mind of Man —
> My haunt, and the main region of my song.   (31-41)

Here we see the split between the imagery of participation and the "Mind of Man" made complete. The refined Platonic materialism by which Milton sought to give an account of the nature of spiritual beings acceptable to the new nonparticipating consciousness proved too tenuous a bridge between mind and spirit to last long. For Wordsworth, the possibility of the strength of Jehovah "in personal form" being a representation of Godhead within the mind of man, and as such evoking fear and awe, does not seem to exist here. And since these images can only effectively exist in a fused and simultaneous form on both the physical and spiritual level, there can be no room for them in a world of nonparticipated phenomena, of materialistic idols. For in the post-Miltonic world, men forget that all phenomena exist by virtue of the participation of the human mind.

Yet Wordsworth, in the same poem, looks beyond the idolatry of materialism, it seems, to a new form of consciousness, in which participation may be restored, in a higher form, with the "intellect of Man" itself functioning as the activating force behind phenomena:

> Paradise, and groves
> Elysian, Fortunate Fields — like those of old
> Sought in the Atlantic Main — why should they be
> A history only of departed things,
> Or a mere fiction of what never was?
> For the discerning intellect of Man,
> When wedded to this goodly universe
> In love and holy passion, shall find these
> A simple produce of the common day.   (47-55)

In other and more Barfieldian terms, under the "final" form of participation, the earthly paradise will be regained as a "representation" of the paradise within, as the creation of man.

REFERENCES

1. Allen, D. C. "Paradise Lost I, 254-5," *Modern Language Notes* 71(1956): 324-6.
2. Barfield, O. *Saving the Appearances*. London: Faber & Faber, 1957, (a) 42; (b) 83; (c) 129.
3. Bodkin, M. *Archetypal Patterns in Poetry*. London: Oxford University Press, 1934, pp. 230ff.
4. Calvin, J. *Les Commentaires de Jean Calvin*, Edited by A. Malet. Geneva: Labor et Fides, 1962, Col. I. 47.
5. Dowsing, W. *Journal for 1643*. Edited by A. C. Moule. Cambridge: Cambridge University Press, 1926, p. 5.
6. Ebling, G. *Luther, An Introduction to his Thought*. London: Collins, 1970, p. 107.
7. Empson, William. *Milton's God*. London: Chatto & Windus, 1961.
8. Fish, S. *Surprised by Sin*. New York: Macmillan, 1967, chapter 1.
9. Lewis, C. S. *A Preface to Paradise Lost*. London: Oxford University Press, 1942, (a) 40-50; (b) 58; (c) 128.
10. Luther, M. *Works*. Edited by J. Pelikan. St. Louis, Mo.: Concordia, 1958, Vol. 1, pp. 90-1.
11. Neal, D. *A History of the Puritans*. London, 1822, vol. 3, p. 167.
12. Piehler, P. *The Visionary Landscape*. London: Arnold, 1971, pp. 75-7.
13. Roszak, T. *Where the Wasteland Ends*. London: Faber & Faber, 1972, pp. 110-41.
14. Wordsworth, W. *The Prelude* I 55-6. London: Oxford University Press, 1926.

TWO DESCENTS INTO THE UNDERWORLD

by

COLIN HARDIE

The descent into the Underworld has enough "polarity" to interest the author of *What Coleridge Thought*, even if polarity is explicit only in Dante. But Homer exhibits a "myriad-minded," "fusive power of the imagination," and for him the descent is already an ancient theme of oral poetry, lending itself to much sophisticated elaboration. It may even be connected with the long literary tradition of Summerian and Akkadian mythology.[16] In the *Epic of Gilgamesh* the ghost of Enkidu, the hero's friend, is very like Patroclus' in *Il.* 23. But can there be any good reason to discuss the "Nekyia" in the *Odyssey* yet again?[18]

First, the recent discovery in northwest Greece of the Oracle of the Dead "on a rock at the junction of the rivers Acheron and Cocytus," *Od.* 10, 515, near the site of Ephyra in Thesprotia of which Kheimerion was the port, makes it for me certain that this oracle is the nucleus that Homer developed in successive recitations. If so, the Nekyia is basically not a descent (as the scholion MV on *Od.* 24, 1 observes[29]), but an evocation of ghosts to a blood-filled trench on the surface of the land. Secondly, I offer a hypothesis that the pre-Homeric story of Odysseus can be reconstructed from bits and pieces that resisted Homer's authority because they were known to belong to the earlier and more historical saga of an often villainous Odysseus. Oral composition has left traces of the stages by which the poet transformed the saga, chiefly by the use of folktales and divine interventions.[18, 26, 35] I believe in one poet and no interpolations. Interpolation in a great poem by an inferior successor seems much more difficult to imagine than a single poet amplifying his fluid oral text in successive stages. I believe in oral composition, but not in a long period of oral transmission of poems that were written down shortly after their composition.

For Vergil too there is also a recent archaeological discovery of two sites, in fact, near Lake Avernus: the Cave of the Sibyl at Cumae and the "Great Antrum" at Baiae. Dante, with his meager knowledge of Greek, did not know a line of Homer (except in a Latin version), but he knew enough about him to exalt the Greek poet as "the eagle of poetry who soars above the rest," *Inf.* 4, 96, and somehow to divine behind Vergil's villainous Ulixes an

Odysseus with an Aristotelian passion for knowledge. This Ulisse is a symbol of Dante's own devouring enthusiasm for philosophy during his middle period, that of alienation from Beatrice. The *Aeneid* is, of course, omnipresent in the *Comedy*, and Vergil figures in person throughout sixty-three cantos. To touch on the *Comedy* however briefly as an epilogue might be excused (space permitting) if a different date for its inception and a consequent interpretation as far more poetic autobiography than imperialist thesis could be indicated. In Dante the theme of descent receives its most extensive and yet most concentrated development, as a spiritual odyssey, *itinerarium mentis ad Deum*, of which there is no trace in Homer (pace George Chapman). Homer sets the Nekyia on the shore of Ocean, the stream that surrounds his disclike world. Although this world is described as having a bronze canopy of heaven above it and the bowl of Hades below, and although in his accumulative manner Homer adds two extra rivers, Pyriphlegethon and Styx, this is not a pure fairyland like the land of Cyclops and of Laestrygonians, rather it is based on a real place, known to us from history and now also from archaeology. The remarkable building that Dakaris discovered under the eighteenth-century monastery of St. John Prodromus, on a hill significantly still called Aidonati, above the confluence (*Mesopotamos*) of the Gourlà or Souliótikos (Acheron) and Vourós (Cocytus), some two or three miles from Kheimerion, is not Homeric in date, but Hellenistic, an elaborate rebuilding of the latter half of the third century B.C.[6, 11, 12, 21] It was closed down not long after, presumably by the Roman Aemilius Paulus after his victory at Pydna in 168 B.C. and lay desolate until the eighteenth century. But it is beyond doubt the site of the Oracle of the Dead that figures in Herodotus' story, 5, 92 of Periander the Corinthian consulting the ghost of his dead wife, Melissa. Indeed Mycenean pottery found nearby shows that the origin of the sanctuary goes back to that period. This site was embodied in the poetic tradition about the cradle of the Greek people in northwestern Greece that the Ionians took across the Aegean to the islands and to the coast of Asia Minor. This tradition is seen also in Achilles' archaic invocation of Zeus at Dodona, about twenty-five miles inland from Kheimerion, in *Il.* 16. 233: There the Selloi live, a name that is the origin of Hellenes, going back to a time earlier than the Mycenean tablets when initial sigma before a vowel had not yet become an aspirate. The odd puzzle of the Cimmerians is solved by Kheimerion.

It has commonly been thought that Odysseus' descent or evocation, Teiresias, and even "the deepsea yarns,"[35] were in the pre-Homeric story of Odysseus' Return and attracted the main or "monumental" poet to the theme.[1] The wrath of Achilles and Odysseus' return are imagined as themes of oral epic "for [at least] several centuries"[25] before Homer, and his versions of them as orally transmitted for several generations. But why should the poet not have chosen an untouched theme in which he saw new possibilities (as he did in the wrath of Achilles, a minor incident with no effect on the outcome of the war) and preferred to take the peripheral and obscure family and kingdom of Ithaca and raised them to full epic dignity alongside those of Agamemnon, Achilles and Nestor? Odysseus had certainly been drawn into the literature of the Trojan War before Homer, but the poet may have created him as a character in the *Iliad* and then wished to develop him into the quite different hero of a quite different kind of poem, combining everyday life with the supernatural and with adventures in fairyland, and folktales with the heroic saga. The scraps of tradition, incompatible with our *Odyssey*, and not obviously post-Homeric developments (like Telegonus, Odysseus' son by Circe, or Telemachus' marriage to Nausicaa), yield a simple story that is more like semihistorical saga or "chronicle" (if the word can be used of oral tradition). Some of the scraps, such as those in Pseudo-Apollodorus (second century A.D.?, not Aristarchus' pupil 180 B.C.) go back to the early historians, Pherecydes of Leros and Acusilaus of Thebes, not long after 500 B.C. when local traditions were still alive.[2] Thus, after the fall of Troy (from Dictys 5, 12ff.), in the dispute with Ajax over the Palladium (not over the arms of Achilles, since Homer invented them), Odysseus, suspected of having compassed Ajax's death, hurriedly and secretly leaves Troy and, to put pursuers off his trail, sails not homewards but eastwards into the Propontis (Sea of Marmora), according to Malalas, the sixth-century A.D. Byzantine chronographer, who was using a fuller version of Dictys than we have. This perhaps suggested the eventual inclusion in the *Odyssey* of material from the Argonautica (i.e., eastward story, Circe, Laestrygoniaus, Clashing Rocks, Sirens).[23] When the rest of the Achaeans left Troy, Odysseus reemerged in the Aegean, but was cast up by a storm on Salamis where Ajax's father, Telamon, threw him into prison, stripping him of everything — ships, comrades, booty. But the cunning son of Sisyphus and grandson of Antolycus eventually escaped to Crete, where he told his story to his friend, King Idomeneus. It was then a year after the Fall of Troy, and as Odysseus is presumed lost at sea, suitors begin to assemble on Ithaca. Odysseus is given a ship by Idomeneus. He does not, however, sail straight to Ithaca, since he has heard how Clytemnestra has killed Agamemnon, but sails to his former ally, the king of Thesprotia, on the mainland just north of Ithaca. From there he reconnoitres the situation on Ithaca, either himself in disguise or by sending spies; and with two boatloads of soldiers, supplied by his ally, he surprises the suitors at a festival and kills them all. When their relatives demand satisfaction, Neoptolemus, Achilles' son, king of Epirus, is agreed upon as arbitrator, and he orders Odysseus to go into exile and them to repay his estate. Penelope was found to be unfaithful (cf. Pausanias 8, 12, 5; Seneca, *Epp.* 88, 8; and the extraordinary notion that she was mother of Pan, by all [*pan*tes] the suitors) (cf. Tzetzes, *Scholia on Lycophron* 772;

Servius on Vergil, *A*. 2, 44) was dismissed. Telemachus, aged twelve or so, is too young to be more than mentioned. Archaeology confirms that the Mycenean palace on Ithaca was destroyed at this time.

This story is unpromising, because it is undramatic and unheroic. To improve it Homer must return Odysseus dangerously, alone and in disguise (probably as Theoclymenus in Homer's first new version). This solution was imitated by Stesichorus and Aeschylus to improve the story of Orestes' revenge: for in Dictys 6, 3 Orestes collects soldiers from Crete, Athens, and Phocis, and with them surprises Clytemnestra and Aegisthus. But how can a prudent man like Odysseus take such a gratuitous risk as to return alone, even in disguise? Only on two conditions: first, the Oracle of Zeus at Dodona should so advise, just as Apollo at Delphi so orders Orestes; secondly, Odysseus must be able to count on Penelope. How is he to know that she is not another Clytemnestra? The other famous local sanctuary, the Oracle of the Dead, provides another divine or supernatural solution: the poet invents or adapts the recent death of Anticleia, Odysseus' mother, and makes Odysseus consult her ghost about Penelope's fidelity, asking not for advice or prophecy, but for the natural knowledge that the dead once possessed — the proper function of such an oracle. This suggests why she should appear first (apart from Elpenor) in our revised Nekyia, but be put aside in favour of Teiresias, who now has the important message to give. When she reappears after Teiresias, she has, now nine years after her death, nothing definite to tell her son about Penelope and the suitors. But the oral poet wanted the oracle to graft Teiresias on, and, having created the moving scene with Anticleia, was not going to waste it, but to reuse it here and also as a peg for the catalogue of heroines. The consultation of Zeus at Dodona likewise survives in one of the false stories Odysseus tells when he is in disguise on Ithaca, *Od*. 14, 327 - 19, 296, how he missed Odysseus in Thesprotia because Odysseus had gone up to Dodona.

But why did the poet entirely refashion this version, in which Odysseus, disguised as a respectable seer and relying on Zeus and Anticleia, is entertained in the palace and makes his old nurse recognize him and reveal him to Penelope, with whom he arranges the trial of the bow (as the suitor Amphimedon's ghost says, *Od*. 24, 167-9)? Why should Homer make the fabulous adventures (that Odysseus perhaps first told the king of Thesprotia to conceal his humiliation by Telamon) into the true story, and his own new truth into part of Odysseus' lies about himself? It was economical to reuse his own now rejected version (cf. Shakespeare in *King Lear* using "the Source's version of Cordelia's death by making it the 'official' story, spread by Edmund as cover to the murder")[24]; so too Theoclymenus is retained, though he is no longer Odysseus in disguise. But the fairyland adventures could also be expanded and recast to exhibit the poet's moral, which Zeus pronounces in *Od.* 1, that men bring their troubles on themselves by their folly but blame Zeus; the poet is at pains to make the suitors deserve their fate, so that Odysseus should not deserve exile. Only as beggar, not as Theoclymenus, could Odysseus have been so badly treated by them. In our *Odyssey*, Odysseus is landed on Ithaca, perforce alone, because of his and his companions' follies. He and they incur the wrath of two gods, Poseidon and Helios, the Sun, and by deserving their years of suffering also illustrate the moral. Even in the more real world of Ithaca and the Peloponnese, Homer is perhaps too fond of the supernatural, in Athena's constant presence and in the series of bird omens. Fairyland and deep-sea yarns also make easier the passage of extra years when Homer decided to have Telemachus grown up and able to help in place of Penelope. Homer swiftly duplicated Circe (with whom Odysseus spent one year) with Calypso, who detains Odysseus for seven uneventful years. Telemachus also offers the inclusion of the returns of Nestor and Menelaus from them at first hand; and it is between their destinies that Odysseus chooses.

Homer's second version involves the removal of the real Oracle of the Dead from Thesprotia. But this facilitates the introduction of Teiresias, recently dead like Anticleia, but a prophet in this life and after his death to be consulted in Boeotia or Colophon, not Thesprotia. In the transference of Teiresias (as of Circe from the East to the West), the poet is quite open; he points out that Teiresias is unlike the other dead in not needing blood before he can think and speak; nevertheless he is given it, perhaps to raise him to the level of prophecy (cf. Scholion on *Od.* 11, 51).[29] To graft onto the nucleus of evocation a descent into the underworld was also easier away from the precise location in Thesprotia. There may have been a separate cave-sanctuary for descent on the coast of Thesprotia, as Pausanias suggests, and in any case the Ionian Sea there was traditionally regarded as the Stream of Ocean at the end of the world, as we can see from Aeschylus, *Prometheus Vinctus* 837 and Euripides, *Alcestis* 591.[34] Homer must have known about the recent colonisation of Italy and Sicily (which latter he mentions incidentally), but he chooses to ignore it and make the Western Mediterranean empty except for a few small islands. The ghosts in *Od.* 24, 11f. pass Leucas, just to the north of Thesprotia, the Streams of Ocean and the gates of the Sun, and are soon at Persephone's meadow of asphodel. The localization of Odysseus' fairyland adventures is an absurdity, exploded by the great geographer Eratosthenes, but unfortunately defended by Strabo and continued in modern times by a series of photographers and yachtsmen.

At the edge of the world all modes of contact with the dead are readily fused, including the swarming of ghosts as at the Athenian Anthesteria, and Homer had good reason to fuse evocation and descent, though he was well aware of the difference. In the first place, it was another opportunity to introduce the comparison and contrast of Agamemnon-Clytemnestra-Aegisthus-Orestes with Odysseus-Penelope-the Suitors-Telemachus, a theme that the poet handles no fewer than twelve times. The comparison of Peleus-Achilles-Neoptolemus with Laertes-Odysseus-Telemachus is there too, though it is less explicit. The so-called Second Nekyia in *Od.* 24 (with Agamemnon and Achilles), often rejected as a late addition, is very possibly earlier than the scenes with Agamemnon and Achilles in *Od.* 11, since it refers to the earlier version in which Odysseus and Penelope without Telemachus plotted the slaying of the suitors, 167-8. It may then have suggested the extension of *Od.* 11 by the "intermezzo," 333-84, leading to the appearance of Agamemnon, Achilles, the rest, and finally Heracles. It is Heracles whose appearance in Hades when he is really on Olympus (his "image" is a much criticised but well-prepared expedient) explains Homer's second and chief reason for treating an evocation as a descent. Evocation was open to anyone, but the descent of Heracles was a great heroic adventure, the last and worst of his labours, a conquest of death (as in the *Alcestis*) and a defiance of the gods of the dead, not the supplication of an initiate.

Theseus and Peirithous, without divine aid in their criminal enterprise, failed to return. Heracles, with the same helpers as Odysseus (Hermes at *Od.* 10, 277 and Athena *passim*), succeeds, and, after Homer, in a version known to Vergil, he is made an initiate of Eleusis, Pseudoplatonic *Axiochus* 371E, to give him courage. Odysseus is to be raised to the heroic stature of Heracles by facing the danger and terror. When Circe tells Odysseus that he must *descend* to consult Teiresias, 10, 490-5, he and his companions later, when he tells them, are appalled, 496-9 and 566-70 (cf. the preparation of this at 10, 174-5), and on their return Circe greets them as having experienced and survived death, which they have not. Again, Heracles as the great archer is there for Odysseus to emulate when he shoots down the suitors, as Heracles shot the birds of Stymphalus. Odysseus' bow is connected through Eurytus with Heracles, 8, 224. The catalogue of heroines, also much criticized, has the function of elevating Anticleia to the company of the famous women of the past, just as Penelope is ennobled by comparison with the heroines Tyro, Alcmene (Heracles' mother), and Mycene (2, 120 repeated in 21, 107; cf. 18, 212-3, 245-9). On Phaeacia the suspicious Arete seems to be convinced by Anticleia's associates in Hades that Odysseus is to be accepted.

The so-called sinners, Tityus, Tantalus, and Sisyphus (*Il.* 576-600), just before Heracles have also been pronounced a late interpolation, because Homer does not know of reward or punishment in the Underworld for good or bad behaviour in this world, except for perjury (*Il.* 3, 278-9; 19, 258-65). The moralised Underworld is a symptom of the religious revolution of the sixth century B.C. brought about by Pythagoras (who is said to have descended into the Underworld and seen Homer and Hesiod punished for their lies about the gods), by the "Orphics,"[32] and by the development of the Eleusinian and Dionysiac mysteries, in which the descent is initiation into a new life, and the soul, not the body, is "the man himself." But why should the "sinners" be distinguished from their neighbours, Minos, Orion, and Heracles himself, who continue below what they most characteristically practised above? The sinners reenact their punishment, because it had been the most marked feature of their life on earth.[7]

To sum up, the Nekyia is basically an evocation, blended into a descent. Its original purpose was to ask how Odysseus, that is, whether alone and in disguise, should return to nearby Ithaca, an event which depended on Penelope; finally, it was to ask how, that is, by what route, in what direction, to return from afar to Ithaca. In this Teiresias was used to prophesy Odysseus' happy old age and to assure us that the exile of the pre-Homeric tradition was not to occur. Teiresias prophesies of Odysseus, as Proteus does of Menelaus. But Odysseus refused from Calypso what Menelaus was to owe to Helen, translation to the Isles of the Blest; Odysseus chose what Nestor enjoyed, a happy old age at home. The Nekyia is no expression of the poet's belief in immortality or in the Underworld. He uses traditional themes and ideas of the soul, old or new, incompatible or not, as it suits his artistic purpose. His final version is beautifully composed, in two parts, each with three main conversations and then a suggestive catalogue. The last heroine, Eriphyle, who also betrayed her husband, is a link with Clytemnestra, the subject of the first conversation, in the second part, after the "intermezzo." The whole is skillfully adapted to the narrator and his audience; Odysseus, having lost his companions, conciliates the Phaeacians by his concern for the youngest and least useful of his companions, Elpenor; then he addresses himself to winning over the suspicious Arete, by exalting the women who founded famous lines, and finally accedes to Alcinous' request for heroes, not without a certain irony at the expense of Alcinous' male self-assertion and credulity. The whole Nekyia is a brilliant piece of oral reshaping, by fusion of motifs and adaptation to its new place and function in the poem as a whole.[7, 33] Rationalistic and logical dissection of the written text murders the enchantment of an oral performance, but if such "fingering" has "botanized" on the grave of poetry, it can be used to illustrate the masterly oral technique of the "eagle who soars above the rest."

Vergil's Underworld, a descent, not at all an evocation, is permeated by the post-Homeric developments, especially in poems that moralised Heracles' descent and celebrated Orpheus' also, and by all the philosophical speculation of the Greeks, especially Plato's and his myths.[3] Vergil certainly studied philosophy, especially in the years 49 to 45 B.C. with the Epicurean Siro, and he intended to devote himself to the study again after completing the *Aeneid*.

But what his views at any stage of his life were is disputed, and in *A*.6 there is only one explicit (and very difficult) passage in which Anchises commits himself to an extreme dualism of spirit against matter, the body as "the prison of the Soul"; "*sôma sêma*" is the Pythagorean formula that Plato accepted in the *Phaedo,* though later in the *Timaeus* he is not so otherworldly, but closer to Aristotle. This dualism has been described as the most disastrous bequest of the classical world to mediaeval and modern times. Dante had a struggle to overcome it.

Aeneid 6 is not, then, philosophical except in the one otherwordly passage, which is not really compatible with the idea of Augustus as an incarnate god and of the positive and permanent function of the Roman Empire for the peace of world. But is it based on a pattern of initiation, as Servius suggests when he speaks of a descent as the performance of the rites of Proserpina? Was Vergil influenced in particular by the cults and antiquities of Cumae and Lake Avernus? Was there not a sanctuary there where descent was practised, that was usually identified with the site of the Homeric Nekyia? Now such a sanctuary has come to light, not, however, within the crater of Avernus, but outside it at Baiae, namely at Dr. Paget's "Antrum."[27, 28] But I have argued that Vergil did not know of it, since it had been virtually closed down in 186 B.C. when the Romans suppressed Dionysiac mysteries, Bacchanalia, throughout Italy.[14] *Aeneid* VI is for me basically a Homeric and literary exercise, one among Vergil's many adaptations of Homer, though the most extended, most deeply felt, and most magical.[17] Vergil does not describe such an initiation as might make a decisive change in Aeneas. An initiate passed various barriers and tests to come in the end before the goddess and be granted the promise of a happy immortality. Such a ritual is suggested by the so-called Orphic Tablets. But Vergil has made the goal of Aeneas' descent a variation on the original nucleus of Homer's evocation. For Anticleia, Odysseus' mother, he substitutes Anchises, Aeneas' father, who, like Teiresias, supplies advice and prophecy. Just as Homer often mentions Persephone, her groves and her sending or scattering of ghosts, so Vergil speaks of Proserpina as requiring the Golden Bough and receiving sacrifice. But neither hero comes before her (as Heracles or Orpheus, in Vergil's first descents of Heracles and of Theseus and Pirithous, but Aeneas' descent is the mysteries as Aeschylus was accused of. Charon refers to the violent heroic descents of Heracles and of Theseus and Perithous, but Aeneas' descent is peaceable (though like Odysseus he has a sword) and by consent (VI, 399). Vergil seems to follow a post-Homeric version of Heracles' descent, in which he obtained Dis's permission to remove Cerberus, and the Sibyl tells Aeneas that Theseus is eternally punished for his criminal violence.[8]

Of the two archaeological discoveries in the Phlegraean fields, the first, the Cave of the Sibyl, discovered in 1929-30 at Cumae, need not detain us, since the Sibyl's function there as Apollo's ecstatic prophetess is quite distinct from her function as Proserpina's or Hecate's priestess and sober guide to the Underworld.[9] The cave is impressive and Vergil has imaginatively enhanced it. It has been described, however, only in a popular guidebook, without plans or elevations or account of what if anything was found in it to support its dating to the fifth century.[20] But the Great Antrum at Baiae was discovered by R. F. Paget in 1961 and was as adequately published as possible without excavation.[27, 28] There is now hope that the little work needed may be done to examine the tons of rubble for pottery or coins and to explore what has come to notice since Dr. Paget's publication, namely, two small square openings in the ceiling of the central chamber, and another passage at its far side. These may lead up to a second more secret and sacred chamber, with perhaps a trace of wall painting? Further discussion of the whole complex is also desirable. Yet it is doubtful if there ever was an Oracle of the Dead at Avernus. No consultation is recorded, except that Hannibal visited a sanctuary there as cover of a reconnaissance of Dicaearchia (later Puteoli, Pozzuoli), Livy 24, 12. Was the sanctuary then a deserted site or still a going concern? Hannibal knew Greek and might have been interested in the Phoenicians of the *Odyssey*. The historian Ephorus from Cyme in Asia Minor, visiting Cumae about 360 B.C., found no Oracle of the Dead, only the story that there had been one until a king of Cumae, perhaps in the seventh century B.C., had suppressed it, and the oracle had been removed elsewhere. But Ephorus seems to have found the "Cimmerians," *Od.* 11, 14 (where we should read 'the people of Kheimerion,' the port of Ephyra[10, 13, 15]) living underground and emerging only at night from their caves (for which he very oddly used the Latin word for clay pits, "*argillae*"). Was Ephorus perhaps shown the Antrum at Baiae as the house of the Cimmerians? Strabo, 244, who reports Ephorus, found neither oracle of the dead nor the Antrum, since he dismisses the Nekyia as mere fable, even though he accepted Homer's western "geography" as based on fact. Vergil, roughly contemporary with Strabo, seems not to have known the Antrum either, since he makes Aeneas descend at Avernus, not at Baiae. It had evidently been forgotten since its closure in 186 B.C. Its foundation can perhaps be attributed to the tyrant Aristodemus of Cumae (ca. 510 to 490 B.C.), who might well have fostered a new popular cult as rival to the old cults in the hands of his aristocratic enemies. As the Cave of the Sibyl belongs to the same period, he perhaps introduced also Apollo and his Sibyl, perhaps from Asiatic Cyme, since Sibyls are at home in Asia Minor, in place of an oracle of Hera (attested by an earlier inscription to the effect that she does not answer supplementary questions!). What then was there at Lake Avernus itself in Hannibal's or Vergil's time?

Servius (on *A*.6, 136) connects the Golden Bough with the Latin federal cult of Diana at Aricia, south of Rome in the Alban Hills, just above a very similar round lake in a volcanic crater; this cult was not prehistoric as Sir James Frazer supposed, but of Greek origin and datable also to ca. 500 B.C. Perhaps then there was at Lake Avernus a cult of Artemis as the federal sanctuary of Cumae, Dicaearchia (founded ca. 525 B.C.), and later Naples (ca. 470 B.C.), perhaps with other Greek cities nearby, Herculaneum, Pompeii, Surrentum. The sanctuary was probably taken over by the Samnites of Capua, and it is referred to by Livy (23, 35, 12) as at Hamae, three miles from Cumae. In 215 B.C. the Romans surprised the Samnites there during their nocturnal sacrifice and killed two thousand of them. In the next year Hannibal might well have visited the site to reaffirm the Capuans' claim to lead the Campanian federation. The political motive seems more likely than an interest in an oracle of the dead. If so, Hamae (the pail or fire-bucket) was the Greek name of Avernus (which is certainly Italic, like Falernum, Salernum etc.), and when later, in 211 B.C., the Romans captured Capua, they destroyed the sanctuary. It seems to have been revived under the Empire — C.I.L.X,3792, the Rituale Campanum of 387 A.D. from Capua.

The daughter cult at Aricia survived, though not as a federal cult once Rome had wrested the headship of the Latin League from Aricia and built a temple of Diana on the Aventine. Also, in 496 B.C., the Romans dedicated a temple to Ceres, Liber, and Libera (that is Demeter, Dionysus, and Korê-Persephone), taking the cult no doubt from Cumae. Vergil must have been interested in the early relations of Rome and Cumae, of which our knowledge is unhappily so fragmentary, and he did well to bring Aeneas (as previous poets and historians had not) to Cumae.[22] The Sibyl, Apollo's ecstatic prophetess, at Cumae was no invention but historical fact, though probably not after the coming of the Samnites. At Rome she was known as the compiler of the Greek Sibylline oracles, which were not prophecies but ritual instructions on how to deal with portents, plagues, and dearths. Their acquisition was attributed to Tarquinius Superbus, who, when driven from Rome by Lars Porsena, took refuge with Aristodemus in Cumae.

This discussion of the Antrum has been rather long, and its upshot negative, but it was justified perhaps by the novelty of the evidence and the temptation to connect it with *Aeneid* 6. The absence of connection goes to support the purely literary character of Aeneas' descent. As Homer took the form of an evocation and filled it with a largely different content, so Vergil took the form of an initiation and filled it with a preponderantly Homeric content.[17] The danger and terror of a descent are emphasized as in the *Odyssey* before it takes place, *A*. 6, 261, but in the event are scarcely met with. The escape from the Underworld is described beforehand as difficult, *A*. 6, 125-35, but the departure through the strange gate of false dreams (not from the Nekyia, but from *Od*. 19, 560-567) is rapid and easy. Vergil is no mystic, though very likely an initiate, *mystes,* of some cult.[31]

We shall not then expect Aeneas to be changed as by initiation and to become "a new man," any more than Homer's Odysseus. In the second half of the *Aeneid* he never refers to the experiences of book 6, and in his killing of Turnus he is very much the traditional hero, a second Achilles as is Turnus himself. Sir Maurice Bowra speaks of Aeneas "as a different man after he has seen it" (a complete picture of the Afterworld; and complete it is not, since he does not see, but only hears of Tartarus, though sight of it has been promised by the Sibyl, *A.* 6, 134-5). But a page or two earlier Bowra says, "Once he lands in Italy Aeneas is a new man." The phrase "a new man" is indeed used by Statius, Vergil's devoted follower, of the Eleusinian mysteries at *Thebaid*, 12, 501, pointedly in view of its normal Roman, not Pauline, meaning.

Odysseus in his Nekyia is told how to reach Ithaca and of his peaceful old age there; Aeneas in his is warned of a second "Iliad of woes" and shown the outcome of his efforts, the citizens of the city which he visits without knowing it to be the Eternal City. No peaceful old age for him, but the fulfil-ment of Dido's curse, *A.* 4, 618-20, an early death, outweighed by transla-tion to Heaven, which Vergil does not describe. It was left to Maffeo Vegio da Lodi in the fifteenth century to supply the epilogue of a thirteenth book.

If Aeneas is encouraged, not vitally changed, by his reunion with his father and the sight of future heroes, Vergil may be credited with some enhancing of the psychological meaning of descent. Misenus and Palinurus are variations on the theme of Elpenor, Dido on Ajax, and Deiphobus on the Greek heroes at Troy, but they are closer to Aeneas' and to Vergil's heart, and arranged in a significant order as Aeneas works back from present time to Troy (seven or three years before?) via the journey from Carthage and via Carthage itself. From Deiphobus he learns not to look backward to Troy as he so often had (*A.* 1, 94-101; 205-206; 3, 349-352; 4, 340-344; 5, 633-637, 702-703) but forward, 6, 546.

Vergil also exemplifies Jung's pattern of the psyche (very different from Homer's): the ego and its positive and negative "shadows," resting on the "anima" or female component, by which access is gained to the archetype of the "wise old man." Vergil had used this pattern already, twice in *Eclogue* 6 (two shepherds, the nymph Aegle, Silenus, and Gallus; the Muses, Linus, and Hesiod) and again in *Georgics* 4 (the shepherd Aristaeus, his mother the nymph Cyrene, the Old Man of the Sea) where he has even imitated what the critics have found so absurd in Homer, that Circe should send Odysseus to Teiresias. Although in the event Circe seems to know the way back to Ithaca (but she does not without the clue that it is beyond her father, the Sun's, island; so Cyrene knows what to do only when Aristaeus' offence is revealed by Proteus).[7] In *Aeneid* 6 we have Aeneas, the Sibyl, and Anchises. On this pattern Dante has himself guided by Vergil to Beatrice, who leads him to a series of wise old men, which includes his ancestor and father-substitute Cacciaguida and culminates in St. Bernard, and after him the B.V.M. is the mediatrix of the final vision. Vergil also introduces some geographical order to structure his poem, though it is far from Dante's mappable precision. Vergil's Underworld is not like Dante's a complete poem in itself; it subserves the purposes of the whole poem as the most impressive bridging of a thousand years of history between Aeneas and Augustus. Without such bridges origins and consummation would fall apart, and no single action such as Aristotle demanded would be constituted. Like the will of Zeus for the next month or two in the first books of the *Iliad* and the *Odyssey,* Jupiter's plan for mankind under Roman leadership for the next thousand years is stated in *A.* 1, 257-296.

For Dante we must use Dante's own words at *Purgatorio* 33, 136ff: "If only, Reader, I had ampler space . . . but all the pages ordained are now filled."

REFERENCES

1. Allen, T. W. *Homer: The Origins and the Transmission.* Oxford: Clarendon Press, 1924.
2. Apollodorus *Library* and *Epitome.* Edited by J. G. Frazer. 2 vols. Cambridge, Mass. Harvard University Press, Loeb Classical Library, 1921 and London: Heinemann, 1939. *Epit.* 7, 40.
3. Barbu, N. I. *Valeurs romaines et Idéaux humains dans le livre VI de l' "Énéide."* In *Vergiliana,* edited by H. Bardon and R. Verdière. Leiden: Brill, 1971, pp. 19-34.
4. Bömer, F. *Rom und Troia. Untersuchungen zur Frühgeschichte Roms.* Baden-Baden: Verlag für Kunst und Wissenschaft, 1951.
5. Bowra, C. M. *Virgil to Milton.* London: Macmillan, 1945.
6. Brooke, M. "Return Ticket to Hades." *Illustrated London News.* November 28, 1970, pp. 22-3.
7. Büchner, W. "Probleme der Homerischen Nekyia." *Hermes* 72(1937): 104-22.
8. Clark, R. J. "Two Virgilian Similes and the Herakleous Katabasis." *Phoenix* 24(1970): 244-55.
9. Corssen, P. "Die Sibylle im VI Buch der Aeneis." In *Sokrates* 1(1913): 1-16.
10. Cozzoli, U. *I Cimmeri.* Rome: Istituto italiano per la storia antica 20(1968).
11. Dakaris, S. "The Dark Palace of Hades." *Archaeology* 15(1962): 85-93.
12. ———. "Das Totenorakel bei Ephyra." *Antike Kunst* 1(1963): 35-55.
13. Eustathius. *Commentarii.* Vol. I, p. 392 - 1667, 58. Leipzig: Weigel, 1825. Reprint. Leiden: Brill, 1970.
14. Hardie, C. "The Antrum at Baiae." *Papers of the British School at Rome* 37(1969).
15. Huxley, G. L. "Odysseus and the Thesprotian Oracle of the Dead." *Parola del Passato* 13(1958): 245-8.
16. Kirk, G. S. *"Myth: Its Meaning and Functions in Ancient and Other Cultures."* Sather Lectures 40. Cambridge, Mass., 1970, pp. 107-15.

17. Knauer, G. N. *Die Aeneis und Homer.* Göttingen: Vandenhoek & Ruprecht, 1964.

18. Lesky, A. *Homeros.* Pauly, Realencyclopädie Supplement XI. Stuttgart: Druckenmüller, 1967, cols. 125-126.

19. Lloyd-Jones, H. "Heracles at Eleusis." *Maia* 19(1967): 206-29.

20. Maiuri, A. *I Campi Flegrei.* Rome: Libreria dello Stato, 1958.

21. Melas, E. *Temples and Sanctuaries of Ancient Greece.* London: Thames & Hudson, 1973.

22. Merkelbach, R. "Aeneas in Cumae." *Museum Helveticum* 18(1961): 83-99.

23. Meuli, K. *Odyssee und Argonautika.* Berlin: Weidmann, 1921.

24. Muir, K. *Shakespeare's Sources*, vol. 1. London: Methuen, 1957, p. 144.

25. Page, D. L. *The Homeric Odyssey.* Oxford: Clarendon Press, 1955, pp. 21-51.

26. ————. *Folktales in Homer's Odyssey.* Cambridge, Mass.: Harvard University Press, 1973.

27. Paget, R. F. "The Great Antrum at Baiae." *Papers of the British School at Rome* 35(1967): 102-12.

28. ————. "The Great Antrum at Baiae." *Vergilius* 13(1967): 42-50.

29. Petzel, G. *Antike Diskussionen über die beiden Nekyiai.* Meisenheim/Glan: Hain, 1969.

30. Reed, N. "The Gates of Sleep in *Aeneid* VI." *Classical Quarterly* 32(1973): 311-15.

31. Silverstein, H. T. "Dante and Vergil the Mystic." *Harvard Studies and Notes in Philology and Literature* 14(1932): 51-82.

32. Treu, M. "Die neue 'Orphische' Unterweltsbeschreibung und Vergil." *Hermes* 82(1954): 24-51.

33. Van der Valk, M. *Beiträge zur Nekyia.* Kampen: Kok, 1935.

34. Wikén, E. *Die Kunde der Hellenen von dem Lande und der Voelkern der Apenninhalbinsel bis 300 v. Chr.* Lund: Glerup, 1937.

35. Woodhouse, W. J. *The Composition of Homer's Odyssey.* Oxford: Clarendon Press, 1930 and 1970.

ENJOYMENT, CONTEMPLATION, AND HIERARCHY IN *HAMLET*

by

LIONEL ADEY

I

Literature affords few contrasts more instructive than that between the Envoy of *Troilus and Criseyde* and the final lines of *Dover Beach*. The medieval Narrator exhorts his court audience to ground their hopes neither in erotic love nor in a world that "passeth soone as floures faire," but in Christ. As he broods upon the unmeaning chaos left by the ebbing tide of faith, the Victorian grounds what hope he has in human love. For Chaucer and his audience, changes and chances that made the world a darkling plain for such as Troilus, became manifestations of Providence.[9,22,23] Arnold found life unmeaning in itself and in its ceaseless historical flux Christian faith itself was being borne away.

In a portion of a manuscript of the *Troilus*,[11] some early reader has marginally inscribed *"Auctor"* every time the Narrator begins to comment. The difference between *"Auctor"* and "Narrator" is symptomatic of that between medieval and modern views of literature.[8,14] Chaucer's role as *auctor* confers upon him *auctoritas* in saying what all Christians know. Because he wears no mantle of *auctoritas*, Arnold can but record changes in belief. Instructed by his faith, Chaucer could contemplate human life *subspecie aeternitatis*. Arnold could but survey the world from the private world-within-a-world of the lovers.

Inevitably, as Owen Barfield has shown, an observer's nonparticipation drains his observed world of meaning and vitality,[6] but not all Victorian writers share either Arnold's inability to participate in life or his pessimism. Tennyson comes nearest to a like despair, while Dickens presents our most characteristic modern substitute for salvation in the twofold ideal of love in *Bleak House*, Esther's fulfilment in love and her husband's in social service.

Shakespeare marks a midpoint in this progress — if such it be — from the medieval to the modern image of human life. In reaping the reward of sacrificing all to ambition, Macbeth thinks as Arnold might have thought if deprived of love. Yet "Tomorrow and tomorrow and tomorrow" images that species of damnation most familiar to us moderns, not death nor judgment but insignificance.

Hamlet's central dilemma, stated in his speech, "What a piece of work is man,"[24] consists in his ability to "see, not feel"[12] the beauty that he contemplates. That Hamlet regards man against "the brave, o'erhanging firmament," while Coleridge stands in solitude contemplating the sunset betokens an important difference between renaissance humanism and romantic sensibility. For Coleridge can acknowledge but not rejoice at a natural beauty his mind has largely created, while Hamlet's melancholy results from knowing yet not caring that man has so wonderfully been compounded of the dust to share senses with the beasts and apprehension with the angels. Primarily Hamlet is about *humanitas*, what it is to be a man, and that concerns Shakespeare as it does Hamlet.

C. S. Lewis has well adduced the conventional features of the melancholic humour in Hamlet's disposition,[17a] yet Hamlet belongs not only to an age but to all time. He surveys man, earth, and the firmament as Coleridge did Nature, as Pascal the heaven without its sun, as Arnold the world without love. Yet the preceding confession indicates unmistakably the subjectiveness of his vision:

I have of late — but wherefore I know not — lost all my mirth, foregone all custom of exercises; and indeed, it goes so heavily with my disposition that this goodly frame, the earth, seems to me a sterile promontory . . . (2.2.299-303)

Shakespeare can no more be limited to this view than to the visions of Lear and Timon, yet both Hamlet's preoccupation with man's place in the scheme of things and Lear's with man's ingratitude are in some sense part of Shakespeare. The dramatist refuses, however, to intrude his concerns, for a character's inner state of mind reflects the current state of the action and registers as a degree of participation in or withdrawal from human affairs. Thus Macbeth's frustration at his failure to destroy Banquo's seed drives him to destroy numbers of his subjects and renders his inner world inert and lifeless. Brutus compares his soul to a kingdom in rebellion when about to transform Rome to a like turmoil. In *Measure for Measure*, the Duke withdraws from his dukedom but to observe and reorder it. Prospero is providentially cast adrift but to be providentially reeducated and reinstated. Neither world-and-life-denial nor acceptance of the unacceptable will serve. Having healed his court's sickness as an Outsider, Prospero must rule again as an Insider. His enjoyment will be informed by contemplation, his participation by preceding detachment.

Shakespeare is capable of a duality both of involvement and withdrawal. The balance depends perpetually upon the state of the action, which governs each character's viewpoint and inner state. To the characters, Shakespeare is the One in whom unity subsists amid diversity. His own consciousness has

evolved from absorption in the shapeless power struggles of the early histories, or the rhetorical cut-and-thrust of the early comedies, to the magical
refashioning of the contemplated world. In the romances, he conceives not
indeed eternity — as does Chaucer — but a redeemed natural order in which
Grace has raised human love to conscious primacy and so made honour of
men's impossibilities.

In Samuel Alexander's *Space, Time and Deity*, "the enjoyed" is that which
one experiences from within, "the contemplated" whatever one observes from
without.[1] C. S. Lewis applied the terms to *Hamlet* and other Shakespeare
plays in a so far unpublished tractate intended to dissuade Owen Barfield
from belief in the teaching of Rudolf Steiner. In attempting to discredit belief
in supposed intermediate beings between spirit and the soul, Lewis draws an
elaborate analogy between the divine act of creation and the writing of
Hamlet:

Hamlet at some level is Shakespeare: that is to say the subjectivity in Hamlet,
that which says "I," is Shakespeare's subjectivity, in the sense that at the moment
of creation Shakespeare veritably sees through Hamlet's eyes, and except in so far
as Shakespeare is seeing, Hamlet sees nothing. The moment Shakespeare ceases
to see through Hamlet, even if he only raises his eyes from the MS to look out
of the window, Hamlet's soul is annihilated. It will be seen that Hamlet (i.e.,
Shakespeare in so far as he limits himself to living through Hamlet) will be quite
unconscious of such interruptions. Thus if it is argued that Shakespeare does not
really become Hamlet, we must reply that this only means that Shakespeare
constantly reascends out of Hamlet into his own consciousness: but however often
this happens, there remains a real (and enjoyed) Hamlet consciousness, which
is and is not Shakespeare. It is Shakespeare in the sense that whatever is therein
enjoyed is enjoyed by Shakespeare: it is not Shakespeare in the sense that Shakespeare enjoys much which Hamlet can only contemplate (e.g., Polonius) and
much which Hamlet can neither enjoy nor contemplate (e.g., his love for the
dark lady) and contemplates without enjoying much that Hamlet is in no way
aware of (e.g., Ben Jonson).
. . . Hamlet ceases to exist (as a soul — he is still an object, of course) . . .
thinking and feeling cease to go on in Hamlet, when Shakespeare, no longer
enjoying Hamlet, sits back to think of the play as a whole.
Hamlet is a soul (i.e., feeling, etc. in Hamlet occur) only when Shakespeare
limits his consciousness to feeling through Hamlet: and though in the smallest
fraction of time non-Hamlet elements probably intrude upon Shakespeare's mind
while writing, all these fall outside Hamlet's consciousness and are for him nothing.
As soon as there is knowledge of any more of Shakespeare than constitutes Hamlet,
so soon Hamlet ceases to be. There is therefore no more possibility of my knowing the intermediary than of the Player King knowing Hamlet: for to know
Hamlet the Player King would have to be Shakespeare.[18]

A discerning audience enjoys Macbeth, by feeling with him the futility of
his life, yet must also contemplate him insofar as it realises how immoderate
ambition has conditioned his nihilistic vision. The two alternative modes are

necessarily involved in tragedy, since the audience must at one time identify
with the hero and at another time judge him.[16]

Moreover, the two modes alternate, as mutually necessary polarities, in
history and inner experience. Each alone has its abuse, for enjoyment can
lead to self-preoccupation and emotional indulgence, while contemplation
can breed superficial judgment. The progression from watching *Hamlet* as
a groundling to watching it as one of the judicious involves a series of al-
ternations. First one contemplates the action, then enjoys Hamlet, next contemplates him as part of a totality, after which one enjoys Shakespeare's
awareness of life, and finally, if possible, contemplates Shakespeare's career
as part of the creative activity of a generation, while enjoying the Elizabethan
awareness of the world's form and meaning. Inevitably, the scholar's progression involves self-consciousness, for it is impossible to entertain the idea
"Elizabethan playgoer" without simultaneous awareness of the idea "myself,"
as "modern reader or playgoer."

II

Interpretations of *Hamlet*, as recently computed, come out at the rate of one
every twelve days.[29a] Most have three common features. The interpreter will
attend to the play rather than the prince alone.[19] He will take for granted
Senecan and Aristotelian postulates: stoicism, the audience's sympathy with
a hero moving from ignorance to realisation, and by cathartic illumination.
Finally, the interpreter will be aware of tension and juxtaposition:[13a] ideal and
actual, appearance and reality,[21,24] birth and death, funeral and marriage.[29b]

Once accepted Aristotelian principle must be questioned. *Hamlet* experiences ἀγνωρισις[2] only in a very special sense. From the outset he intuitively
perceives his uncle's guilt and when set "naked" on Denmark's shore acknowledges no such bitter lesson as Lear has learned. His realisation is not of his
own character or conduct — to which he was never blind — but of the human
capacity for action, at the Heaven-ordained moment. "The readiness is all"
(5.2.220). Inwardly, he has progressed from helpless passionate involvement
to potent detachment, has come, like Horatio, to suffer all as though suffering
nothing.

This enlightenment is best understood in light of Aristotle's psychology,
with its medieval and humanist accretions. This in turn presupposes a three-
fold hierarchy, within the universe, society, and the soul,[26] that is a commonplace of medieval and renaissance scholarship. Like any work of a dramatist
halfway between medieval collective awareness and modern individual consciousness, *Hamlet* reveals a joint preoccupation with the general *humanitas*
yet with the individual's *haecceitas*. King Hamlet was "a man, take him for all

in all," yet "I shall not look upon his like again" (1.2.188). Hamlet shows "unmanly grief" in not accepting a bereavement common to the species. King Hamlet had been as Hyperion, sun god and model of manly beauty. In Polonius' eyes apparel proclaims the individual man. Poison that "holds enmity with the blood of man" (1.5.65) initiated the action by despatching King Hamlet in the bloom of manhood, and ends it by despatching young Hamlet and the guilty parties.

This brings us to the Aristotelian and Thomist scale of creation and corresponding inner hierarchy, as manifested in allusions to the various levels, mere being and not-being, mineral, animal, rational or human, and angelic.[17b] Claudius is "a thing of nothing." The queen grieved "like Niobe, all tears," like one turned to stone. Denmark is "an unweeded garden"; while kettle-drum and trumpet "bray" the pledges of Claudius, who is a "satyr," and drunken Danes earn "swinish" epithets. A "serpent" wears King Hamlet's crown for which Hamlet will exact retribution "on wings swifter than meditation" or else rot as "the fat weed." Hamlet beseeches "angels and ministers of grace" defend him, sees "heaven ordinant" in the events at sea, relies on Providence for the accomplishment of his task, and is to be sung to rest by "flights of angels." Shakespeare probably never read a line of Aristotle or Aquinas, but the conventional "medieval model"[17c] of the cosmos is implicit in his language.

In Aristotle's inner hierarchy touch ranks lowest, being common to all living beings.[3a] Accordingly, when Hamlet imagines his mother making love in "rank sweat," feeling his uncle's fingers "paddling" her neck, he ranks her with the lower animals. Sound, the medium of rational communication,[3b] and light, the medium of phantasy[3c] and revelation rank higher. Though impervious to reason and emotion, the queen succumbs to Hamlet's pleading after he has shown her inmost part in his "glass." The Ghost appears to Horatio and Marcellus, the most rational and most imaginative of the minor figures, but speaks only to Hamlet, whose mind comprehends both reason and imagination. When examining the skull, emblem of our mortality, Hamlet employs every sense.

The antithesis between the animal and rational principles scarcely needs comment. No villain more insistently manifests the appetitive faculty than Claudius.[4a] Sexual lust impelled him to commit murder. Gluttony[4b] ironically displays itself in his drinking at moments when he must demonstrate his kingly nature by using the higher power of reason to stop a war or supervise a fencing match. Inevitably, we contrast his nature with his brother's.

If in Claudius bodily appetite and mental agility appear side by side, in Hamlet passion and reason hold sway by turns. They need to be considered in relation to the triad of body, mind, and spirit. Hamlet's turbulent emotion in the battlement scene belongs to the body, specifically the heart. His self-aroused emotion in the soliloquy after the Player's speech originates in the mind, but gives rise to physical images. By turns he goes to extremes of emotionalism and ratiocination, for even his self-reproaches for excessive thinking display immoderate anger[4c] and self-contempt and his complementary ideal is a fellow-scholar who has not become passion's slave.[4d] Yet in the end he neither stifles passion nor abandons reason, for the fighting in his soul gives place to a harmony resulting from the growing ascendancy of spirit,[25,29c] whereof the essence is will and purpose. During the sea voyage, this purpose has finally taken hold of him. Having surrendered to the Providence he now recognises in events, he returns "naked," yet armed with implacable resolve. If he no longer schemes, nor rants, his mind has never been so alert to the half-chance, his anger never so open and unforced as in his slaying of Claudius.

Here Aristotle's distinction between ποιεῖν (poiein) and πασχειν (paschein) proves illuminating.[3d] Passive reason, operating through the senses, is analogous to matter and *becomes* all things. Active reason, which *makes* all things,[3e] is superior as is an artist to his material. Hamlet's ironic statement, "Nothing is but thinking makes it so," implies active reason. In making use of memory:

> About, my brains; hum, I have heard
> That guilty creatures sitting at a play
> Have by the very cunning of the scene
> Been struck so to the soul, that presently
> They have proclaimed their malefactions . . . (2.2.592-96)

he reasons passively with regard to his inspiration's source, but actively in shaping his design to unmask Claudius. Subsequently, he fails to despatch his uncle because in his hatred he abuses active reason by trying to shape the perfect form of vengeance. When self-reproachfully comparing himself with Fortinbras, Hamlet describes both reason and action as divine powers:

> Sure he that made us with such large discourse,
> Looking before and after, gave us not
> That capability and godlike reason
> To fust in us unused. (4.4.36-39)

For Hamlet either to have planned a perfect vengeance or to have seized an inappropriate occasion by killing Claudius in the bedchamber would have been a misuse of active reason. Already Hamlet has truly described himself as "very proud, revengeful, ambitious (3.1.125),[4e] but becomes capable of executing justice from the moment he ceases to plan vengeance.[10] By trusting in Providence and waiting upon events, he harmoniously exercises πασχειν, passive reason and his other faculties, for the power of active reason here belongs to Heaven. By becoming the patient, Hamlet becomes the more perfect agent.

Aristotle's distinction takes us further, for:

Το‘ δ’αὐτό ἐστιν ἡ κατ’ ενέργειαυ ἐπιστήμη τῷ πράγματι‘ ἡ δὲ κατὰ δύναμιν Χρόνῳ προτέρα ἐν τῷ ἐντ, ὅλως δὲ οὐδὲ χρόνῳ, ἀλλ οὐχ ὅτε μεν νοεῖ ὅτε δ’οὐ νοεῖ. (Actual knowledge is identical with its object potential knowledge in the individual is in time prior to actual knowledge but in the universe it has no priority even in time; for all things that come into being arise from what actually is.)[3f]

The Gonzago story, the Ghost's disclosure, the arrival of the Players, and the court audience constitute matter brought into relation by Hamlet's thinking and so shaped into the form of the reenacted crime. As the Ghost made actual Hamlet's potential knowledge, his premonition of Claudius' guilt, so the play makes actual Horatio's potential knowledge.[5] As such knowledge is not subject to time, a secret murder must always be potentially knowable, hence the king's guilt becomes more widely manifest until Horatio is to proclaim it to the world. Again, Hamlet turns the matter of Laertes' accusation, the poisoned sword and the chalice into the form of retribution. But active reason pertains to Heaven, for from the human standpoint the purposes of the protagonists are "mistook, fall'n on th'inventors' heads." Hamlet only accomplishes his purpose, when passion serves, instead of frustrating, reason.

Horatio could serve as archetype of the passively rational man. Never judging Claudius amiss, he yet conceives no design of his own. He shows sound moral, discernment too, but his initial disbelief in the Ghost, his warning "You will lose this wager," even his final assessment of the action, betray his limitations. Not by reasoning alone can man discern the operation of Providence nor circumscribe his duty. Hamlet's *intelligentia*, or immediate apprehension,[17d] his power of active reason, his inner conviction and faith transcend Horatio's passive reason, without contradicting it. Hamlet *will* lose the wager, but to put Denmark to its purgation matters more than to survive.

In Hamlet, potential knowledge precedes actual knowledge, but " 'tis not so above" where from the beginning, "the action lies/In his true nature" (3.3.61-62). The nearer a character to the angelic end of the spectrum, the earlier he learns of the crime. The last protagonist to discover the king's guilt is Laertes, creature of passion.

But what of Fortinbras, who at the end still does not know? His role, can only be explained in terms of the social hierarchy. In remarking that Hamlet "was likely . . . to have proved most royal," Fortinbras infers in the prince a potency of kingship, kingliness δύναμις (*dynamis*), that we know to have been lacking in Claudius. But King Hamlet has displayed and Fortinbras will display, kingliness ἐνέργεια (*energeia*),[5] the actuality of majesty. Failing this distinction, the career of Fortinbras would be a mysterious irrelevance. Hamlet admires him beyond his apparent deserts, perceiving kingliness in a martial resolution possessed also by King Hamlet. As though to underline the comparison, the dramatist has Fortinbras smite the Polacks. When chastened by old Norway, Fortinbras channels his energies into legitimate warfare. Victory marks the emergence of kingliness for all to see. The prince of Norway, chosen by Hamlet's dying voice, ascends to restore order and harmony to a kingdom purged but distracted.

Claudius has shown neither potential nor actual kingliness. Lacking this natural, or rather heavenly gift, he must attain power by murder and keep it by guile. Unlike Fortinbras, Claudius must devote himself not to manifesting but to concealing his nature. The legal status of kingship cannot of itself preserve authority and social order. Thus Claudius becomes a "king of shreds and patches," "a cutpurse" (3.4.96-101), just as Macbeth's power hangs loosely as "a giant's robe upon a dwarfish thief." Perhaps a clue to this inner *auctoritas* Hamlet and Fortinbras perceive in each other lies in Antony's tribute to the dead Brutus, of whom the world could say "here was a man," who had acted, albeit misguidedly, for the common good.[17e] So Fortinbras acts, as he sets about restoring order and public confidence. He too is a man, take him for all in all.

III

Our study of *Hamlet* as an exploration of *humanitas*, according to the Aristotelian and Christian model of human nature and social order,[27] has necessarily centered itself on the hero, since Hamlet is Everyman, containing all talents and propensities[25(30)] and so being full of contradictions. Its twin foci, enjoyment/contemplation and hierarchy, can only be brought into relationship through an examination of the play's action.

So far does the Ghost predominate at first, that the opening scene is almost over before Hamlet is mentioned. The skepticism of Horatio — contemplated in advance as the rational scholar — is countered by the reverence of Marcellus:

> We do it wrong being so majestical
> To offer it the show of violence;
> For it is as the air, invulnerable . . . (1.1.143-45)

These and the beautiful lines on Christmas reflect a numinous quality in the apparition. Verily "something more than fantasy," it "harrows" Horatio "with fear and wonder" and for this reason prompts him to use it as an oracle. That the Ghost assumes "a fair and warlike form" does not detract from its serenity and radiance nor preclude its being a supernatural visitant, for like Henry V, King Hamlet has fought as leader of his people. When Horatio resolves: "Let us impart what we have seen tonight/Unto young Hamlet," the cockcrow prevents the Ghost from addressing Marcellus the poet and Horatio the scholar of Wittenberg. Though Horatio needs ocular proof, Hamlet, intuitively aware of the spiritual world, finds no difficulty in believing their account. His questions focus on the Ghost's armour, since that is his father's "form," denoting a martial spirit as his own black denotes grief. More specifically, the armour denotes that actuality, or *natura naturata*, of the soldier-king, into which King Hamlet's potency, or "gifts," had settled, as Polonius has become the politician and Horatio the scholar. An interesting if unverifiable supposition is that the "foul crimes done in my days of nature" (1.5.12)[29d] refer back to a turbulent youth, as with Prince Hal and Fortinbras. Horatio's comparison of the present turmoil to the eve of Caesar's assassination has more than the obvious ironic point: King Hamlet's successor rules by chicanery rather than kingly charisma and force of character.

Then why the Ghost's melodramatic tirades? Since Shakespeare employs rant to dramatic purpose in the Player's speech and the prayer scene, may he not do so here? Rant or tirade in the mature Shakespeare occurs where irreconcilable emotions or mental states subsist in juxtaposition. When beheld as visitant from another world, the Ghost arouses holy dread, but when telling his son of the murder, he is attracted toward his former self. When contemplating earth, he can be grave and majestical, but having resumed his fatherhood, he enjoys again the human anger of brother, king, and husband. Since this "perturbed spirit" wanders between two worlds, his call partakes at once of divine retribution and personal craving for revenge. The states appear separately in Hamlet's tirades against Claudius and in his almost impersonal resolve before the fencing match. As ruler King Hamlet needed to incline toward the pole of detachment or contemplation; as husband and brother he inclined toward the pole of enjoyment. The divine nature is contemplative, the animal nature appetitive and passionate, hence "enjoying," while unredeemed man hovers uneasily betwixt the two.

In the bedchamber, the Ghost speaks more in sorrow than in anger, recalling Hamlet to his role as Heaven's scourge and minister. As Hamlet berates his mother for the very infidelity the Ghost had earlier condemned, the Ghost pleads for her with a compassionate benignity first perceived by the sentries and Marcellus. The sorrowing countenance turned toward Gertrude had earlier looked upon the distracted kingdom and its heir apparent.

As one of the play's fixed stars, Horatio necessarily contemplates passively, nor do we ever "enjoy" him. Forever watching, listening, pronouncing judgment, he predicts with quiet certainty that "Heaven will direct" (1.4.91) the state of Denmark, and remarks "That is most certain" (5.2.11) in confirmation of Hamlet's perception that a divinity shapes our ends. By an exquisite manifestation of Shakespeare's art, Horatio initially recounts the origin of Fortinbras' war by private army and finally welcomes him to the throne.

As to where the other characters or we, the audience, stand in regard to fixity or oscillation, the well-known dualities of Claudius' opening speech in the court scene must be our pointers. Discretion has so far overcome nature that he can think of King Hamlet, but also of himself. Later, he will yearn for divine pardon, yet determine to retain his kingly office. From the proto-type of hypocrisy, a male Duessa, he turns into an earlier Bulstrode, moral, worried, and ruthless. Initially he dispenses advice, always in the listener's best interest, yet always in his own. Whereas the queen appeals to common sense,[17f] Claudius forges a chain of detailed reasoning touching on salient features of Aristotelian and scholastic psychology:

> . . . 'tis unmanly grief,
> It shows a will most incorrect to heaven,
> A heart unfortified, a mind impatient,
> An understanding simple and unschooled. . . . (1.2.94-97)

He reprehends unmanliness, undisciplined emotion, will opposed to divine power, a spirit or "*intellectus*"[17g] untrained, above all passion indulged in defiance of reason. The flaw, of course, lies not in his reasoning but in his motive, the self-interest of the burial image "throw to earth," the pragmatic term "unprevailing" and the improper plea "think of us / As of a father" (1.2.107-8). The king uses reason to serve not the social whole, but himself. Likewise, his mind and spirit serve his fleshly urges. Ironically, the pretended victory of reason calls for carousing and gunfire. As mediator of the divine will, a king stood above his subjects, inclining therefore to detached contem-plation, but Claudius leans toward enjoyment of the lower appetites or, at best, of self-interest. Adultery and usurpation have denied him the power to rule in his subjects' interest rather than his own.

In the court scene, the audience contemplates all characters at the same distance. Even Hamlet looks and acts like a conventional malcontent. After-wards, the audience enjoys his consciousness of an outer world impregnated with his own melancholy, yet also with rottenness and disorder spreading from Claudius' soul.[21] Plant and animal images yield to even lower images when Hamlet turns to his mother's conduct. King Hamlet's love warmed her as the sun, but hers is portrayed by images of touch, the common denominator of senses, appetites and nutritive faculty. King Hamlet is a man unparalleled, a sun god, a spirit. In sharing his father's perception of his mother, Hamlet demonstrates πάσχειν (*paschein*), a passive reason that becomes what it be-holds. He begs his friends give the Ghost's disclosure "understanding, but no tongue." His own unavoidable silence has its potency, for when "foul deeds" (1.2.25) have risen to men's eyes, a final silence will succeed a potential retribution given actuality and form.

While admonishing his sister, Laertes contemplates the prince he even-tually murders. As he describes a crown prince outgrowing youthful wildness, images and words rise from the nutritive level, "a violet in . . . primy nature," through the sensory, "the perfume . . . of a minute" to the psychophysically parallel:

> For nature crescent does not grow alone
> In thews and bulk, but as this temple waxes,
> The inward service of the mind and soul
> Grows wide withal. (1.3.11-14)

In showing how the maturing prince must resolve the matter of youthful impulses into the form of the sovereign will, and so serve the public good, Laertes unwittingly underlines Claudius' failure. The tragedy lies in Hamlet's failure to accomplish this growth save at the cost of his life. Our consoling illumination consists in his nobility but also in kingliness made actual in Fortinbras, under whom the kingdom will regain the pristine health it knew under King Hamlet.

Polonius' advice amounts to passive reason, the administrator's noncommittal observation. If Laertes ironically fails to profit by the advice, the fault may lie in his father's superficial judgment and ethic of prudent self-regard, so at odds with the princely ethic Laertes has outlined.

Polonius' cynical advice to Ophelia, his animal images and ascription of "vows" to "blood," betray one who sees no more in human passion than animal appetite.

Ophelia's account of Hamlet's silent visitation illustrates the shock to the melancholic soul of such a slander as Polonius has instructed Reynaldo to put upon his son. Like his father's spirit, Hamlet can but stare and gesticulate at one too far removed for communication. Ophelia's is the last of a series of observations of Hamlet, by the audience, Laertes, Polonius, and now one furthest removed by reason of her preceding closeness. Only the audience enjoys his feelings, but enjoyment is always counteracted by contemplation.

In his speech, "What a piece of work is man," 29a(34a) Hamlet accurately places man in the scale of creation, having angelic intelligence, serving as exemplar to the beasts, and godlike in capacity to act. Here he speaks of man's power of ποιεῖν (poieiu) or active reason, that enables him to bring potency into actuality. Being independent of the senses, this speculative and purposive intellect resembles the angelic understanding. Hamlet cannot enjoy, but only at this point contemplate, humanity, because he alone has grasped the import of his father's murder, the fact of mutability, and the ultimate vanity of human strivings. This paralysis of his will to live has deprived him not only of princely pleasures but of a capacity for constructive thought, which reappears only when the Players arrive.

That interval in the Player's tragedy speech when Pyrrhus stood "like a neutral to his will" (2.2.483) precedes cataclysmic vengeance. Polonius' incomprehension of the simulated passion arouses in Hamlet an impatience explicable only on the supposition that, as the ensuing soliloquy shows, Hamlet has been moved to self-reproach at his own torpor. He first imaginatively contemplates the Player, then enjoys him, forcing himself into a rage marked, like the Player's, by physical images. Not until self-induced fury has exploded in rhyming and reiterative abuse, "Remorseless, treacherous, lecherous, kindless villain," (2.2.584) does he switch abruptly to self-contemplation. Passionate hatred supplies the motive for the play scheme and active reasoning the means.

The "kind of joy" (3.1.18) Hamlet evinced on hearing of the Players preceded his scheme for using them. Their advent relieved the melancholy that returns in the death wish of "To be or not to be." (3.1.55-90) That soliloquy dramatizes the elemental conflict of Βίος (*Bios*) and θάνατος (*Thanatos*). Life and death[29e] are in turn "enjoyed" by Hamlet, speaking not only as prince of Denmark but as Everyman, naming afflictions he could not have known, hence using the universal, rather than the royal "we." Yet his awareness of life's length reflects his own melancholia and the military image his father's occupation. By tidal movement, he sways between general and specific human consciousness.

Both suicide and killing Claudius can be described as "enterprises of great pitch and moment" (3.1.86). Equally ambiguously, "currents" can refer either to our common drift toward death or an impulse bearing us toward some decisive step in life. Hamlet's frustration and melancholy constitute a spiritual death from which only inflicting physical death can rescue him. Now in imagination he "enjoys" both enduring tyranny and ending it by suicide, but never imaginatively experiences reigning or any other consequence of killing Claudius. His horizon is bounded by death, his own or Claudius', but by the time he sees Fortinbras' army march away, this inner prison wall has given way.

The first stage in its collapse is Hamlet's much criticised bullying of Ophelia. In the nunnery scene, he exercises power by wit and use of language reflecting his superior position in the social and intellectual hierarchies. He answers the sensory terms of her reproach — "Words of so sweet breath . . ./ Their perfume lost" — in moral terms and response to her proverbial jingle "Rich gifts wax poor" (3.1.98-101) by ironic and painfully searching analysis of her rejection. After covering his pique with ironic self-accusations, he distills his anger into general antifeminism and a veiled threat to Claudius. Ophelia can but fit this "madness" into the Aristotelian inner hierarchy and the Elizabethan social order, for his "sovereign reason" (3.1.160) having given way, he cannot use eye and tongue to play the expected roles of the prince and so cannot be to the "fair state" (3.1.155) what reason had been to his own passions and senses. By implication, loss of his inner harmony may portend disharmony within the state. Ophelia cannot rise to logic, nor be expected to see Hamlet's wrath as a sign of revival.

Everyone knows Hamlet's views on acting to be Shakespeare's. But if Claudius is right to detect "something in his soul / O'er which his melancholy sits on brood" (3.1.167-68) the prince-manager could equally well be counselling himself. By anticipating danger, Claudius repeats a central Aristotelian motif, that matter has a potency.[5] Metaphysically, "foul deeds will rise," but psychologically, Hamlet's melancholy incubates an egg that once hatched will prove dangerous. Like earlier "wild and whirling words," what Hamlet says lacks form because an obsession has not yet settled into a resolution.

No wonder, then, that before staging a *mimesis* of the royal crime, Hamlet glances at his own inner turmoil. In the very torrent and whirlwind of his passion he, too, must beget a temperance, if he is to hold the mirror to the Danish court. He deprecates clowning and ad-libbing as a university wit, yet also as a disturbed prince called to be scourge and minister. Already he has shown a propensity for inexplicable dumb show and ineffectual histrionics in place of action.

The Murder of Gonzago, as Owen Barfield has well shown,[7] reflects the main action. Like King Hamlet, the Player King is seen in mime and characteristic guise before being heard. His Queen loves as did Gertrude, but swears fidelity as expected. The Player King diagnoses the human malaise as Hamlet sees it, for

> What to ourselves in passion we propose
> The passion ending, doth the purpose lose. (3.2.193-94)

Will lies captive to passion and to memory, man's simplest inner wit.[17h] The Player King adds what might be Horatio's summary of the main action.

> Our wills and fates do so contrary run,
> That our devices still are overthrown,
> Our thoughts are ours, their ends none of our own. (3.2.210-12)

In no way can this have paralleled King Hamlet's thoughts as he lay down to sleep. The Player King anticipates the end of *Hamlet* from the maladjusted prince's standpoint at this time, seeing fate where later he will see Providence.

The king's cry, "Give me some light" (3.2.269), touches on an archetypal motif in Shakespeare. But does this cry mean that "frighted with false fire," Claudius has imaginatively lived through his victim's experience? Traditionally, light stood for divine revelation and reason within the soul. If Claudius calls for light to dissolve a fictional world more real than the order he has tried to reestablish, the other meanings are perhaps present as resonances, for in the prayer scene, Claudius discovers that neither human nor divine reason can permit him to be absolved of his crime yet retain its proceeds.

These contradictory desires, like opposed currents making choppy water, give rise to the prayer's melodramatic imagery. Though its sensuousness and courtroom argumentation reflect Claudius' disposition, Hamlet, too, seems coarsened as though inwardly "enjoying" Claudius, while outwardly observing him. "Now might I do it pat," reflects Claudius' opportunism; "He took my father grossly, full of bread . . ." his sensuality; and the whole argument and counterargument, from "That would be scanned" (3.3.74-98), the usurper's political duplicity. Hamlet's tone has the hasty intentness often found in one overcoming inner reluctance, clubbing judgment into submission. Claudius echoes Hamlet's facile concluding rhyme, as though to show that the two are nearer here than anywhere in the play. Each seeks to impose his will upon destiny, for both vengeance and bestowal of vocations pertain to God.

The opening stichomythia of the bedchamber scene suggest cannonfire rather than conversation. Misled by anger at woman's frailty, Hamlet has jumped to conclusions. Having successfully held up the mirror to Claudius, he seeks to induce self-criticism by holding up a glass to show Gertrude her inmost part and reveal what it is "to kill a king and marry with his brother" (3.4.29). He loses control of events, for he could not have anticipated her cry nor the shout from behind the arras. Intent upon moral education, he mistakes the voice. Gertrude's anguish on beholding a murder modifies his judgment, for henceforth he confines his accusations to adultery.

A mirror revealing the inmost part would enlighten corrupted reason, but Hamlet turns to wringing an already distressed heart. In describing the "brazing" effect of "damned custom" (3.4.37), he draws on Augustinian moral theology. Likewise, he uses sense experience to enlighten the sinner's mind and bring her "to her senses." "Hyperion's curls" and "an eye like Mars" (3.4.56-57) recall the majestic warrior-king of the opening scenes. Such a "combination and a form" (3.4.60) betokened a man. By contrast, a plant image, "this mildewed ear" (3.4.64), and an animal one place Claudius and Gertrude in the scale of creation. Hamlet turns now to the familiar medieval representation of corrupted judgment as blindness, but extends it to the other senses. So total a breakdown of the five senses has deprived reason of any basis for judgment, hence "reason panders will" (3.4.88).

Even as the queen cries, "Thou turn'st my very eyes into my soul" (3.4.89), Hamlet continues, unable to see that he has achieved his object. Misled by hatred and disgust, he "enjoys" the consciousness of the adulterous woman. Only thus can the Ghost's return be explained. "Almost blunted" may be an exaggeration, but stabbing an unseen victim, while about a business with which Hamlet had not been charged, scarcely constitutes fulfilment of a mission. Attempting to repeat his success in holding up a mirror, and foiled by circumstances, he has turned from enlightenment to playing on a weak woman's emotions. A mirror must be held up to him.

A central irony is that Hamlet should appear mad just when he is becoming sane, when passion is being subordinated to reason and purpose, just as he is recovering that inner harmony of reason and senses without which he cannot function as agent of Providence. The Ghost's intervention turns him from an irresponsible torturer venting hatred and disgust to a spiritual counsellor warning his mother against further self-delusion. Like an earlier C. S. Lewis warning the skeptic not to blind himself by psychoanalysing the theologian,[20] he counsels:

> Mother, for love of grace,
> Lay not that flattering unction to your soul,
> That not your trespass but my madness speaks . . . (3.4.144-46)

Even now, the counsellor has much to learn, for only a daughter's madness and a son's wrath can show him the consequences of substituting passion for purpose. He must learn self-contemplation.

As Claudius, too, loses control of events, he views Hamlet with progressively diminished understanding. His brutally selfish comments on Polonius' death reveal the renaissance villain's "up-so-doun" perspective, from which Hamlet is the "foul disease" (4.1.21). No longer concealing self-regard, claiming neither fatherhood nor his wife's love, Claudius must yet conceal the truth by "majesty and skill" (4.1.31) — oddly juxtaposed words — of political rhetoric. No wonder his soul is "full of discord" (4.1.45). Never again will the audience "enjoy" Claudius, but only "contemplate" him.

Like an unstable compound, Hamlet contemplates and enjoys a multitude of creatures. Rosencrantz and Gildenstern are "sponges," the king an "ape," himself a pursued fox. Soon he beholds maggots and worms at supper on Polonius, yet by angelic *intelligentia* "sees a cherub that sees" the king's purpose. The mercurial compound is resolved by the appearance of Fortinbras' army. Lest we suspect adolescent hero worship, Hamlet epitomizes the disillusioned Captain's appraisal of the war: "This is th' imposthume of much wealth and peace" (4.4.27).

The Aristotelian humanism of Hamlet's soliloquy (4.4.32-66) perfectly balances that of Claudius' rebuke in the court scene. Without "capability and godlike reason" man becomes a beast that sleeps and feeds. Out of self-regard or cowardice, the speaker has been sunk in "bestial oblivion." The Norwegian soldiers, "examples gross as earth," put him to shame. In Fortinbras, Hamlet sees the emblem of active reason, urging on an army become as his bodily organs. Moreover, if to Hamlet, as distinct from Fortinbras, "honour" means no vainglorious pursuit of reputation[4f] but an overwhelming moral urgency requiring action, then well might he be aroused by seeing soldiers acting without such compulsion.

Throughout the fourth act, what has been potential emerges into the au-

dience's view: Ophelia's sexuality; Laertes' choler, uninformed by reason.
Laertes ends where Fortinbras began, in a planless attack by a rabble that
judge but with their eyes. However sympathetically, we must view his grief
as emotional self-indulgence. When weeping for Ophelia, by saying "I have
a speech o' fire" (4.7.189) he characterises himself as the emblem of un-
reasoning anger.

The stark opening phrase of Hamlet's letter, "High and mightly," supplies
a vantage point from which we contemplate a desperate king moving from
expedient to expedient, an unprincipled demagogue become as wax in his
hands, and a queen whose very sentimentality marks a spiritual advance.
"Naked" connotes not only "unarmed," but "unmasked" and "truly aware,"
seeing as God sees.[28] Henceforth a body unarmed but soul reordered will
face bodies armed but souls discordant.

E. Hankiss finds the graveyard scene to mark Hamlet's reorientation
toward death rather than life.[13b] To me, this seems a half-truth. The Clowns
contemplate humanity from the graveyard. Likewise, Hamlet contemplates
human strivings from the grave that makes nonsense of the politician's ambition, the courtier's flattery, and the lawyer's financial manipulation.

Unlike Marlowe's Faustus, Hamlet says nothing to deride divinity, learning, or the productive occupations. His questions elicit answers setting the
action in a historical perspective, his birth coincident with his father's victory
over Old Fortinbras. No longer toying with death as he did when he spoke
the line, "To be or not to be," he tempers physical disgust at the skull with
compassionate remembrance. Indeed, he relives childhood episodes, but his
first person ruminations on Alexander and Caesar suggest that for the only
time he imaginatively enjoys kingly power as well as contemplating its
termination in death. His chop-logic he uses in defending himself against
Horatio's rebuke corresponds to earlier speculating "too precisely on the'
event" (4.4.41), for that rebuke implies that the grave mocks not the ruler's
work, but his ambition.

Now the court again assembles and Hamlet stands aside to watch. This
time the king, queen, and courtiers wear the trappings and suits of woe, while
Hamlet wears what will serve. Earlier, we contemplated him too, but now
enjoy his vision. As Hamlet leaps into the grave, he proclaims himself
"Hamlet the Dane (5.1.252). In the court scene, it was Claudius who had
assured Laertes, "You cannot speak of reason to the Dane / And lose your
voice" (1.2.44-45). Clearly the prince has assumed the right to rebuke
Laertes for an extravagance far transcending "suits of solemn black" (1.2.88).
So far from reasoning with Hamlet, Claudius now commands the queen to set
a watch over "your son." By his exultant claim "Hamlet the Dane," the
prince has set aside the reign of Claudius and joined his father's to his own.

In the graveyard scene, he looks not toward death, but, albeit with disillusioned eye, toward life.

Hamlet's account of his voyage reveals a sea change from the *angst* of total responsibility to a trust that Providence will make use of "Our indiscretions . . . when our deep plots do pall" (5.2.8-9). This relieves him not of the responsibility to execute justice, but of the need to choose its form and occasion. From a secular standpoint, he must take what opportunity fortune offers, but theologically speaking, he has become the agent of Providence. Psychologically, he no longer exerts active reason, as in the play and prayer scenes, but πασΧειν (*peschein*), thinking informed by events and observation. No longer does passion impede action, for as instrument of a higher will he has become a harmonious system of reason, passions, senses and, bodily organs. The turning point was surely the fighting in his heart that led him to discover his death warrant and make use of such chances as having his father's seal about him.

Before stating his own public duty Hamlet condemns Claudius not in a tirade, but a series of precise charges:

> Does it not, think thee, stand me now upon —
> He that hath killed my king, and whored my mother;
> Popped in between th' election and my hopes,
> Thrown out his angle for my proper life,
> And with such coznage (5.2.63-67)

The Osric episodes exemplifies the requisites for success in Claudius' Denmark.[4g] The specious welcome, and all-too-evident emptiness remind us — if in our day we need reminding — how under a tyranny sincere feeling and intellectual curiosity are suspect. Witness Claudius' proscription of Wittenberg and tolerance of the comfortable triviality of Laertes' Paris. Under Claudius, Osric and Laertes typify qualities making for survival.

Horatio's statement, "You will lose this wager," is a rational assessment of probabilities, but having learned to respect suprarational promptings, he urges Hamlet, "If your mind dislike anything, obey it" (5.2.215). Hamlet's New Testament allusion, "There is special providence in the fall of a sparrow" (5.2.213-14), is significant, for this is his hour in Gethsemane. Inwardly, he already dwells in a spiritual world wherein personal survival matters little. In terse monosyllables, he consents to a redemptive process that may also require his death. No longer need he devise the perfect execution nor foster a desire for revenge.[15]

In his apology to Laertes, Hamlet to himself restored displays the essence of princely *humanitas*, rather than its outward show. In offering his usual pledge and gun salute, the king mocks the tradition he falsely claims to embody and preserve. What follows needs no comment here. Moreover, other categories apply: poetic justice, ironic reversal, appearance and reality, *catharsis* and Christian forgiveness. Though Horatio alternates between Roman and Christian impulses, his saying "flights of angels sing thee to thy rest" (5.2.358) corrects any misleading impression given by "The rest is silence" (5.2.356). Hamlet surely means not that death closes all but that the divine will has been carried out, the sickness healed. Henceforth, no perturbed spirits will stalk the battlements.

As by becoming the patient, Hamlet has become the catalyst through whom Claudius' potential ruin has occurred, so Horatio the scholar must ensure that foul deeds rise to all men's eyes. What Hamlet experienced the world must contemplate. Yet Horatio begins by enjoying the world's vision and judging as the world must. Only within a context of historical events contemplated from man's terrestrial viewpoint can Hamlet's story be enjoyed.

Hamlet has accepted Providence, but Fortinbras declares, "For me, with sorrow I embrace my fortune" (5.2.386). A potential king, strong in arm and temper, Fortinbras perceives that slaughter acceptable in battle shows amiss at court. Though anxious to learn of these "dire events," he must fire ensure the safety and health of the whole state, by having Hamlet borne out not in "hugger-mugger" but in full view. Aware that the prince would have proved most royally, he has yet to learn that Hamlet already has. After beholding Hamlet as central figure in recent history, he may by Horatio's agency come to comprehend him. So we partake of Shakespeare's contemplation and enjoyment of his characters, or Heaven's of erring humanity.

REFERENCES

1. Alexander, S. Space, Time and Deity. London: MacMillan, 1920, vol. 1, pp. 12-18, 26-7.
2. Aristotle *Poetics* 1452a 30, 1452b 5.
3. ———. *De Anima* (a) 413a 4; (b) 420b 33; (c) 429a 2; (d) 430a 20-25; (e) 430a 15-20; (f) 431a 1-3. Translated by McKeon, R. *Introduction to Aristotle*. New York: Random House, 1947, pp. 145-237.
4. ———. *Nichomachean Ethics* (a) 1118b 10-15; (b) 1118b 20-22, 1149b 24; (c) 1216b 5-10; 1149b 15; (d) 1124a 15, 1101a 1, 9; (e) 1124a 19, 1125b 10; (f) 1115b 10-17, 1116b 30.
5. ———. *Metaphysics* 1071a 5.
6. Barfield, A. O. *Saving the Appearances*. London: Faber & Faber, 1957, pp. 128ff., 151-2.
7. ———. "The Form of *Hamlet*." In *Romanticism Comes of Age*. London: 1944, and Middletown, Conn.: Wesleyan University Press, 1966, pp. 104-25, ref. pp. 113-15.
8. Bethurum, D. "Chaucer's Point of View as Narrator." *Publications of Modern Language Association* 74(1959): 511-20, ref. p. 515.
9. Boethius. Consolation of Philosophy "I. T." (Translator) rev. H. F. Stewart, London: Loeb Classical Library, 1918, p. 411.

10. Bowers, F. "Hamlet as Minister and Scourge." *Publications of Modern Language Association* 70(1955): 740-49, ref. n.7 and pp. 748-49.

11. Chaucer, G. *Troilus and Criseyde*, Manuscript Rawlinson Poet. 163, Bodleian Library, Oxford. Hand iv (15th century) 3.913-1372.

12. Coleridge, S. T. Dejection: An Ode, line 38.

13. Hankiss, E. "The Aesthetic Mechanism of the Tragic Experience in *Hamlet*." *British Journal of Aesthetics* 6(1965): 368-81, (a) n.6 and p. 370; (b) p. 375.

14. Jordan, R. M. "The Narrator in Chaucer's *Troilus*." *English Literary History* 25(1958): 237-57.

15. Joseph, M. *"Hamlet* and Christian Tragedy." *Studies in Philology* 59(1962): 119-40, (a) p. 124; (b) p. 139.

16. Langbaum, R. *The Poetry of Experience*. New York: Randon House, 1957, pp. 224-26.

17. Lewis, C. S. *The Discarded Image: An Introduction to Medieval and Renaissance Literature*. London: Cambridge University Press, 1964, 1967 edn. (a) 172; (b) 152-69; (c) 11; (d) 88-9, 115; (e) 170; (f) 164; (g) 157; (h) 162.

18. ———. "Clivi Hamiltonis Summae Metaphysices Contra Anthroposophos Libri II" (I: Being; II: Value). Unpublished Manuscript.

19. ———. *Hamlet: The Prince or the Poem?* Annual Shakespeare Lecture of British Academy, 1942. London: Oxford University Press, 1942.

20. ———. "Bulverism, or Foundations of Twentieth-Century Thought." *Socratic Digest* no. 2, 1944 and Hooper, W., ed. *God in the Dock: Essays in Theology and Ethics*, Grand Rapids, Michigan: Eerdmans, pp. 271-78, ref. pp. 272-73.

21. Mack, M. "The World of *Hamlet*." *Yale Review* 41(1952): 502-23, ref. pp. 509-11.

22. Roberts, R. ap "The Boethian God and the Audience of Chaucer's *Troilus*." *Journal of English and Germanic Philology* 69(1970): 425-36.

23. Robertson, D. W. "Chaucerian Tragedy." *English Literary History*, vol. 19, pp. 1-37. (a) 10-11; (b) 36-37.

24. Shakespeare, W. *Hamlet*. Edited by D. W. Wilson. London: Cambridge University Press, 1934.

25. Smith, M. B. *Dualities in Shakespeare*. Toronto: Toronto University Press, 1966, pp. 7-8.

26. Spencer, T. *"Hamlet* and the Nature of Reality." *English Literary History*, 5(1938): 253-77.

27. ———. *Shakespeare and the Nature of Man*. Lowell Lectures. New York: Macmillan, 1942, pp. 101, 109.

28. Tobarina, J. "Nakedness and the Shakesperian Tragic Hero." *Studia Romanica et Anglice* 12(1961): 3-7.

29. Warhaft, S. The Mystery of "Hamlet." *English Literary History* 30(1963): 193-208, (a) 193; (b) 196; (c) 205; (d) 207; (e) 202.

ETYMOLOGY AND MEANING

by

G. B. TENNYSON

Although some form of the word etymology has been known and used in English since the end of the fourteenth century and especially since the late sixteenth century, the disciplined study of etymology cannot be said to have begun until the nineteenth century, as a concomitant or indeed department of the study of philology, which is of course also a nineteenth-century development. Even as late as the time of Johnson's dictionary (1755), there was no formal approach to word origins. Horne Tooke's *The Diversions of Purley* (1786-1805) reveals the growing interest in a more serious approach, but Tooke, like Johnson and his predecessors, often offered purely fanciful derivations and the philological grounds for systematic study were simply not there. Many words, of course, were patently obvious to the reasonably learned, especially those that came trailing still their classical origins. But etymological treatment of these as well as of native and non-classical words continued through the eighteenth century to be etymological only in the traditional sense, a sense that the nineteenth century profoundly altered.

Until the advent of philology, etymology as a word meant chiefly what we today would call its etymological meaning (for etymology has its own etymology too). The word seems to have meant what it reduces to in Greek: *etymos* + *logos*, "true meaning," or even "true word." In Latin Cicero rendered the word as *veriloquium*. With the thought of true meaning in mind, students of language were encouraged to seek the earliest form of the word that could be traced to determine what the word truly meant, indeed what the word meant now. *The Oxford English Dictionary* (*OED*) gives several examples that illustrate this attitude, even while giving definitions that reflect a change in the meaning of the word. Thus, under the main definition of etymology — "the process of tracing out and describing the elements of a word with their modifications of form and sense" — the *OED* offers also the following definition: "The facts relating to the formation or derivation [of a word]. In 16-17 c. occur confused expressions such as 'the etymology comes from,' 'to derive the etymology from.' " If one substitutes for the word "etymology" in pre-nineteenth-century examples the idea of "true meaning" or "true word," such expressions are not confused, though they are not modern.

Virtually all of the pre-nineteenth-century examples cited for etymology and related words in the *OED* (*etymologue, etymologer, etymologic, etymological, etymologically, etymologicon, etymologist, etymologization*, and, above all, *etymon*, of which more later) seem to imply a use of the concept of etymology as "true meaning," "true word," and less often and less clearly as "true or accurate account," or "true history," which would be the modern meaning. Here are a few examples with the specific word being illustrated italicized:

Which word [Musicke] . . . hath been *etymologed* for the signification of the studie of humanities and chiefly of poetrye. (Ferne, 1586)

It were more *etymological* to write montan, fontan, according to the original. (A. Hume, c. 1620)

I try to use no words of which I cannot *etymologically* defend the application. (W. Taylor, 1798)

They who are so exact for the letter, shall be dealt with by the Lexicon, and the *Etymologicon* too if they please. (Milton, 1645) [Probably used in the grammatical sense. See below.]

Chaucer, Gower, and Occleve . . . are supposed by the severer *etymologists*, to have corrupted the purity of the English language. (Warton, 1774)

What is the menynge of the *ethimologeia* and the setting of this name? (John of Trevisa, 1398) [This is the earliest entry for any form of the word in English.]

Etymologie, true expounding. (R. C., 1613)

Etymology, the true exposition or interpretation of a thing. (Willis, 1681)

Etymology, or right wording, teacheth what belongs to every single word or part of speech. (Milton, 1669)

Even this long list does not begin to exhaust the examples from the rich store offered by the *OED*. Many are not so transparent as the ones offered, of course, but the general emphasis in the pre-nineteenth-century uses of etymology and related words still seems clear enough. It is the emphasis on true meaning. Indeed, one definition offered by the *OED* and illustrated by the second citation from Milton is of a department of the study of grammar "which treats of individual words, the parts of speech separately, their formation and inflexion." This use is not listed as obsolete in the *OED*, but the latest citation for it is 1824. It is not a definition found in present-day dictionaries. But it is a definition that accords with the older emphasis on etymology as the true or correct meaning, since grammar at the time was held to be an exact study with unchanging rules.

All of this leads to the extremely interesting word *etymon*, which the *OED* marks as "not naturalized."[19] It derives from the Greek for "true," and means in the first of four definitions offered for it (and one which is marked obsolete): "The primitive form of a word; the word or combination of words from which it has been corrupted. Sometimes nearly = Etymology 1b, 1c." The second definition is *not* marked obsolete. I shall return to it shortly. The third meaning is marked both obsolete and rare. It is: "Original or primary signification." And the fourth and last meaning is similar, and similarly obsolete and rare: "The true name of a thing." Only the second definition would seem consistent with our ideas of etymology. It is: "The primary word which gives rise to a derivative." Interestingly, only one example of its use before the nineteenth century is given and it is not very conclusive. For the three obsolete definitions there are no nineteenth-century examples but a good number from the seventeenth and eighteenth centuries.

The point of bringing in *etymon* here is precisely the fact that it had become obsolete in its earliest sense and had survived, to the very limited extent that it did survive, in a nineteenth-century sense, a sense consistent with our modern understanding of etymology. It seems to me to cast further light on the earlier uses of etymology, suggesting again the importance of the notion of "true meaning" rather than "original meaning." Or, to put the case a little more consistently with earlier usage, original meaning was taken to *be* true meaning.

What seems to have been at work in determining the meaning of the word etymology in the period before the systematic study of philology was the power of the widely held attitude of earlier ages about the past. Prior to the seventeenth century it seems to have been taken for granted that everything, language included, was in a state of decay from an earlier Golden Age and that contemporary civilization was at best a holding action against inevitable deterioration. The seventeenth century, which introduced so much that is characteristic of modern thought, also introduced the notion that perhaps things were getting better not worse, and by the nineteenth century this more "modern" notion was rapidly becoming dominant; in intellectual circles it was already in fact dominant. The citations from the *OED* of the attitude toward the word etymology simply illustrate the change in philosophic outlook.

During the nineteenth century it no longer was taken for granted that the pursuit of the earlier forms of a word was a pursuit for the true meaning. Among the more "objective" inquirers the enterprise became rather a pursuit of the original meaning of the word and an interested following through of the history of the word in its various formations and transformations. Among some other inquirers such a pursuit was automatically a demonstration of the progressive *enrichment* of words as succeeding ages improved the "primitive" language.* It is no doubt to the investigators of the latter school

* The word primitive itself was gradually transformed during the nineteenth century

that we owe the popular conception of Indo-European or Indo-Aryan as a language of virtually nothing but roots and these themselves of the most truncated sort and invariably expressing a gross material notion. But of that more later.

The transition in the attitude toward the word etymology was not, of course, accomplished overnight. Throughout the nineteenth century there are evidences of a mixed attitude toward just what etymology shows. Thomas Carlyle never tired of quoting what was (unknown to him) a false etymology of the word *king* to prove a point he liked to make: " 'The only Title wherein I, with confidence, trace eternity, is that of King. *König* (King), anciently *Könning*, means Ken-ning (Cunning), or which is the same thing, Can-ning. Ever must the Sovereign of Mankind be fitly entitled King.' "[10a] And Ruskin has often been taken to task for his even more extravagant use of what he supposed to be the etymology of the word *wife*. He derived it from weave and argued that therefore woman's place was in the home, presumably at the loom.[21] Perhaps Skeat had Ruskin in mind when he sternly noted that to equate *wife* with a *weaver* (fem.) was "to give up all regard for facts."[24]

But mistakes in etymology alone do not fully characterize the kind of thing that Ruskin and Carlyle and others did throughout the century. In the first place they both, like so many nineteenth-century literary men, had a great interest in etymology, an interest different not only in degree but in kind from that of earlier times. Even their false etymologies attest to an interest, though not an especially new one, and when they are right they show an imaginative grasp of some of the uses to which the proper study of the history of words could be put. In the passage immediately preceding that on the meaning of the word king, Carlyle offers three other etymologies of words for leaders of men, and they are essentially correct. In so doing he shows an understanding of etymology as a window onto the past (and possibly the future).[10b] Ruskin perhaps never exceeded the brilliance of his gloss on Milton's "blind mouths" in the attack on the clergy in *Lycidas*, showing how etymology can illuminate the understanding of literature.[22]

Among the things that Carlyle and Ruskin, and Coleridge before them, began to recognize was the dynamic and evolutionary nature of language, a proposition formerly concealed, insofar as it can be said to have existed at all, in the notion of the decay of language. Carlyle is himself one of the great word coiners in the age, and he early mounted a defense of his habit of creating words to suit his own message.[10c] Of course, poets had been doing the same thing all along, usually without defending it. The difference in the nineteenth century is precisely the consciousness of linguistic creativity and of the historical development of language. It is again part of what may prop-

---

from a meaning with overtones akin to original and uncorrupted to our modern crude and ignorant. It comes from the Latin for first or earliest.

erly be called the nineteenth-century discovery of history. Beyond this, nine-teenth-century students of language thought that etymology might offer a key to the nature of language itself.

Meantime, the more systematic philologists had not been idle. The evidence of interest in language and etymology among literary men is in fact a reflection of the developments in the formal study of language that were taking place throughout the century. By the end of the century, indeed by the time of Skeat's dictionary and the undertaking of the *OED,* study of etymology had reached a high development. Building on the discoveries of a century of learning in philology and comparative grammar, etymology was able to offer complete and accurate accounts of the derivations of words of virtually all modern European languages. There have been no advances in etymology since the end of the nineteenth century at all comparable to those that occurred during that century, although there have been refinements of the method and of particular findings. (Skeat, for example, was unable to draw on the knowledge of Tokharian that is now regularly included in etymological dictionaries.) Although etymology still had things to teach, its method was established by the latter part of the nineteenth century and the study could then properly be described as "the process of tracing out and describing the elements of a word with their modification of form and sense."

Inevitably, with etymology established on firm foundations, there arose an interest in word meanings themselves, based on etymology but not identical with it, a study that became known as *semantics* or *semasiology.* The *OED* records the first use of *semantics* in the sense of "relating to signification or meaning" in 1895 with a citation from Bloomfield, and as a plural substantive synonymous with semasiology not until 1900. *Semasiology* itself had been the earlier term, entering in 1877, and defined by the *OED* as "that branch of philology which deals with the meanings of words, sense-development, and the like." That the later word has tended to drive out semasiology is probably due to the prestige of the early studies in French by Bréal and Saussure in which the word used is *sémantique.*

The arrival of the words semantics and semasiology signal the movement of that branch of philology concerned with words, their origins and meanings, into areas no longer purely philologic. The *OED* again provides the evidence; in a citation from the *Athenaeum* in 1901 the following is averred about semantics: "As applied to language, psychology is not easily distinguishable from semantics or semasiology." The connection was evident even earlier. Under semasiology we find the following citation from F. Haverfield in the *Academy* in 1884: "Philology is now advancing towards a new branch having intimate relations with psychology, the so-called semasiology of Abel and others."

In short, etymology in the narrow sense appeared to have done its work and was ready to be superseded by a more ambitious study. As early as 1865 (as the *OED* records it) Max Müller had declared: "The etymology of a word can never give us its definition." Such an assertion is at once demonstration of the triumph of the modern conception of etymology as word history over against the earlier notion of it as true meaning and herald of a newer study, perhaps resting on the old but going beyond it, to include other disciplines, other insights, and looking indeed for something beyond mere historical record, looking in fact for historical understanding on the one hand and for a philosophy of language on the other.

The time that had elapsed from the first stirrings of the great nineteenth-century development of philology — from, say, Sir William Jones's discovery of Sanskrit in 1786 or, better, from Friedrich von Schlegel's *Über die Sprache und Weisheit der Indier* in 1808 — to the publication of the first edition of W. W. Skeat's *Etymological Dictionary of the English Language* in 1881 is just under a century.[18b] It is roughly the same amount of time that has elapsed since the introduction into English of the word semasiology in 1877 and semantics in 1895 to our own day. The question inevitably arises, has the study of semantics, the study of meaning, made the same strides in this comparable span of time as were made by etymology in its century of development? The answer just as inevitably comes back, no.

Without going into even so cursory a history of semantics as I provided above for etymology, I think one is safe in saying that semantics has by and large failed to live up to its promise or at least to one of its promises. It has done fairly well by the historical-informative aspect, that is, with the expansion and application of etymology itself. For, in addition to the studies that deal with words and their histories, their changes and the light they cast on earlier ages, the results of the study of etymology and historical semantics have also found their way into many related areas of learning. The teaching of literature, to take the most striking example, would now be unthinkable without calling upon our knowledge of the changes in word meanings through the centuries. The most elementary survey course in English literature requires the instructor to explain the historical meaning of Chaucer's *gentillesse* or Pope's *wit* or Dickens's *gentleman* by calling upon the findings of etymology and the applications of them in the study of semantics. Much of this information is acquired by instructors and students alike without a study of etymology or semantics per se; nevertheless, without such disciplined study in the background, anything resembling instruction of older literary works would swiftly crumble. Indeed, in a very real sense, the formal modern study of literature of earlier periods is very much the product of the development of philology in the nineteenth century as the persistence of the word "philology" in the titles of our learned journals of literary study attests.

But what of the case in regard to a philosophy of language and to an understanding of meaning? A great deal has been going on, both under the rubric of semantics and under the larger rubric of the more fashionable term "linguistics." A great deal has also gone on in philosophy. But very little that is currently taking place in linguistic study even assumes any longer that there is such a thing as meaning or that linguistics or any of its subdivisions has any charge to study it. Margaret Nicholson in her American version of Fowler's book *Modern English Usage* notes that Fowler dismissed the term "semantics" in 1925 as a "meaningless term to the average person" (which probably it was), but that the work of Ogden and Richards very largely popularized it in the thirties and that "it is now an accepted branch of the study of language."[16,17] What she does not note is that the same work that popularized the word led very largely to the present view that there is no such thing as meaning after all.[5a] If Fowler were updating his own handbook today he might well be inclined, if he followed popular academic thinking, to denominate as meaningless not only semantics but meaning itself!

As far as philosophy is concerned, the question of meaning has loomed large. Gilbert Ryle complains that "preoccupation with the theory of meaning could be described as the occupational disease of twentieth-century Anglo-Saxon and Austrian philosophy."[23] But, as Ryle's own essay goes on to illustrate, this preoccupation has had relatively little to do with etymology and semantics and rather a great deal to do with logic and mathematics.

The study of meaning, then, has moved away from etymology and even semantics as it was initially understood. And while some philosophers, notably Cassirer, have included the findings of etymology and philology in their deliberations on language and meaning, it is more common to find even students of language ignoring the subject. A recent book entitled *Towards a Semantic Description of English* has no entry in its "Glossary of Technical Terms of the Semantic Theory" for "etymology" or "philology" or even "meaning" for that matter (though there is an entry for "meaningful" and one for "meaningless"; these are of course defined functionally).[12] Perhaps these terms were taken for granted, but the bibliography lists no title that has to do with etymology or philology, nor does it list any philosophical works, like Cassirer's, that draw on these subjects. It seems likely that they were not thought relevant.

Exactly why etymology should have been more or less abandoned by modern linguistics is not my concern, although the thoughtful reader will recognize that it must, like earlier concepts of etymology, for example, be rooted in the philosophic outlook of the time. I am concerned, however, to point out an exception to the generalization about modern semantics that suggests a future for etymology and meaning that seems to me to be more promising than anything offered by the scientized study of linguistics.

In the last decades of the nineteenth century many hands were at work in applying and interpreting the findings of philology to language and meaning on a broad scale. The most celebrated is probably Max Müller, who will be remembered, at least by readers of Owen Barfield, for having popularized the notion of a "metaphorical period" in the infancy of language. Others there were as well, many of whose etymological interpretations have been absorbed, as I suggested above, into other studies, such as literary studies. Thus, while theory was going off to mathematics and psychology, the consideration of the cultural implications of historical word study was going off largely into literature and history. One of the most successful exponents of this latter approach was Logan Pearsall Smith, whose studies of words and their ways still offer instructive and entertaining reading.[25,26]

But the questions raised by the success of the study of etymology were not being confronted, or were only being confronted obliquely, by students of words themselves. Not at least until they were taken up again by Owen Barfield. It is Barfield's work as successor to the nineteenth century that encourages one to speak hopefully of the future of etymology and meaning.

Barfield's study of language and meaning informs everything he has written in the half-century that he has been publishing, though needless to say not all that he has written is narrowly confined to such topics. In works most directly relevant to Barfield's views on etymology and meaning,[1-9] he touches on many of the issues that interested the philologists of the Victorian era; but of these issues, I want to single out only one for consideration here, for it is especially relevant to the foregoing outline of the development of etymological studies in the nineteenth century. It is the use of etymology to illustrate the evolution of consciousness.

To nineteenth-century users of the findings of etymology, it quickly became evident that earlier meanings of terms could tell us something about earlier attitudes toward all manner of things. An interesting little book by Federico Garlanda, for example — chosen almost at random — offers speculations not only on the everyday life of the speakers of the parent language of modern European tongues, that is, Indo-European, but speculations as well on the thought processes of those people, on their concepts of good and evil, and even on the origin of language itself.[11a] Many of Garlanda's conclusions seem today rather rash; certainly they were conditioned by that post-Darwinian conviction that prehistory was primitive in the sense of crude and that the farther back you go the more base and material and narrow becomes human thought until it is lost forever, presumably in nonthought. But it is the fact of this interest, not the approach, that shows the kinship with Barfield. Barfield's approach to the same kind of endeavor is not only free from Garlanda's assumptions (indeed, it offers a splendid critique of the nineteenth-century approach to these matters, although Garlanda is, of course, not specifically mentioned), but it brings to the study of etymology an awareness of something else besides. This something else is what Barfield himself has called the "evolution of consciousness." It is a concept fraught with significance for the study of history, psychology, and philosophy itself, to take only the obvious areas.

Briefly stated, the notion of an evolution of consciousness is that, just as language has changed and developed even during the period when there are records to demonstrate it, so has human consciousness. Today we not only use different words or earlier words with different meanings, we actually perceive the world differently. Our consciousness of ourselves especially is different; we are indeed more *self*-conscious than earlier ages were. Now the notion that there had been an evolution of language was much beloved of nineteenth-century theorists and is nothing new. But the nineteenth-century writers on these matters were also committed (unconsciously or otherwise) to the idea that everything had evolved from a lower to a higher state, that language in this respect was part of a Darwinian evolution that left early language in something like the condition of a Darwinian hominoid. For this reason nineteenth-century writers drew what many today would still think of as obvious and inevitable conclusions from such things as that most or perhaps all of our abstract words derive from words based on sense impressions. Insofar as they went beyond language itself to consider the human mind, they may be said to have entertained some sort of notion of the evolution of consciousness, but it was a notion primarily having to do with the increase in factual knowledge. Barfield's approach is at once more respectful of the past and more radical. Let us consider its main features.

One thing that we see as we go back through the history of words is not increasing simplicity but if anything increasing complexity. The earliest available forms of language as well as, according to Barfield, the findings of modern ethnologists and anthropologists indicate that "primitive" languages are in fact more complex than later forms of the same language or modern languages in general (cf. Lithuanian with its eight cases, said to be closer to the parent tongue than other modern European languages); that "primitive" languages often use whole phrases and what seem to us run-together phrases (the "holophrase") rather than discrete words; that "primitive" languages frequently show an absence of abstract conceptual thinking (e.g., no word for tree but words for many specific kinds of tree); and that various other indications of complexity have an intimate connection with linguistic "primitivism." Etymology in uncovering the earlier meanings of words also habitually finds — and so found in the nineteenth century — a so-called metaphorical and a literal meaning coexisting in the same word (e.g., Greek *pneuma* for "spirit" and "wind").

Faced with this kind of evidence nineteenth-century etymologists did not hesitate to fashion hypotheses to explain it that were consistent with their own view of reality, even if not with the evidence of language. The most striking of these hypotheses — and one that Barfield has exposed for what it is, but one that continues to furnish the minds of many moderns — is the assumption that, if we could go yet further back to the very beginnings of language, we should find "root" words expressing simple physical perceptions — e.g., a root for "tree," and one for "rock," and one for "light," and so on.[11b] "Proto-proto" Indo-Aryan would then presumably be a rather small number of basic sounds, each one (arbitrarily, it should be added) pointing to some physical object. As time goes on, in this scheme of things, men come to expand their awareness and to create words metaphorically by comparing some idea that was dawning in their minds to one of the available roots, thus giving utterance to some abstract notion by saying it was like this or that sensible thing (this is the hypothetical metaphorical period). Later still they begin to take their metaphors as reality, and this gives rise to belief in mythology and other intellectual ills to which our ancestors were thought to be subject. While this view is no longer presented in quite the crude form I have offered it here, it is certainly not dead, though it may be moribund because the topic is no longer of interest. One can turn almost at random to any general book on language to see how the matter is disposed of these days:

The problem of how language began has naturally tantalized philosophical minds, and many theories have been advanced, to which waggish scholars have given such fancifully descriptive names as the pooh-pooh theory, the bow-wow theory, the ding-dong theory, and the yo-he-ho theory. The nicknames indicate how seriously the theories need be taken. They are based respectively on the notions that language was in the beginning ejaculatory, echoic (onomatopoeic), characterized by a mystic appropriateness of sound to sense in contrast to being merely imitative, or made up of grunts and groans emitted in the course of group actions and coming in time to be associated with those actions.[20]

Except for the ding-dong theory (mystic origin of language) all these theories have in common the view of language as having arisen in the uttermost vacuity by something approaching accident and of language as initially simple to the point of imbecility. To be sure, all these hypotheses are generally presented as theory and nowadays are not taken very seriously (especially poor ding-dong), but what they are mainly theories of is our notion of early man as determined by the extrapolation of the Darwinian hypothesis of the second part of the nineteenth century. It is surely for this reason that in popular film treatments of prehistoric man, a great deal of the "dialogue" consists of grunts, these being, to our minds, the natural accompaniment of the behavior of brutes.

Barfield's special contribution to etymology consists in having stepped outside the tyranny of the Darwinian hypothesis as applied to language. And he has done so through the study of etymology itself. What Barfield has done is to look at the findings of etymology as far as they go and ask the simple question: why do we posit these earlier metaphorical periods and still earlier grunting periods when there is no evidence for them whatsoever? What if we consider instead the implications of the fact that, for St. John, *pneuma* meant both wind or breath *and* spirit at the same time or perhaps even yet something else that is more than the two together? There is no warrant to assume that earlier, beyond record, it meant simply wind or breath, that at some point someone used the notion of wind or breath to convey the idea of spirit and that by St. John's time it had come to be falsely assumed that a "spirit" was in the wind or breath. We certainly do not *know* that this is so; we only hypothesize it so. What if we hypothesize it otherwise?

Barfield has hypothesized it otherwise (aided, to be sure, by a vast learning that transcends etymology alone). All indications, especially in language (which has preserved so many earlier ideas, however fossilized they have become), point to the fact that St. John and others actually perceived "breath" and "spirit" to be the same thing. This point must be emphasized; it is not that they chose to adopt the *fiction* that they were the same, nor that they simply inherited the mistaken notion from a now lost metaphorical period that they were the same, but rather that they genuinely *perceived* them to be the same. Nor is this all. Barfield goes on to raise the possibility that they in fact *were* the same. Traditional and radical indeed.

Yet the implications do not stop here. If earlier man acually perceived a unity between the inner character and outer appearances of things, then the meaning of his words was not arbitrary, not a mere social convention; it was part of an objectively real meaning that in fact permeated nature. Here indeed is where metaphor comes into play in Barfield's treatment of etymology. What he has to say on metaphor is always illuminating and frequently profound, but it is another issue from the question of the use of etymology itself, albeit related. Suffice it to say that Barfield recognizes the centrality of metaphor in understanding the nature of language today, but he maintains that it is a later development and that to speak of something like *pneuma* as metaphorical as though it had been coined by Shelley in a fine frenzy is to reimpose contemporary thinking onto a kind of thinking that was quite different, though already starting on its way to becoming modern consciousness.* But rather than the question of metaphor itself, I want to emphasize the notion of the inner and outer coexisting in the word to call attention to Barfield's solution to the problem of meaning in language that for nineteenth-century etymologists was to result in semantics and the eventual abandonment (a twentieth-century achievement, after all) of the concept of meaning as — well,

---

* Barfield has stigmatized this practice as that of projecting postlogical thinking onto a prelogical mentality.

meaningful. A study of etymology reveals to Barfield that meaning was not adventitious but initially given. As we follow his explication of the fortunes of words and of the evolution of consciousness, we can hardly doubt that this is so. Of course this ultimately involves recognizing that his view has metaphysical implication. But, as C. S. Lewis remarks of his own brilliant treatment of metaphor, "so has every view."[13]

Admittedly the one example of *pneuma* must seem thin indeed, and I can only plead space and the availability of Barfield's own more authoritative writings as excuse for not borrowing more from him to illustrate his use of etymology. But I want to go on to point to what the Barfieldian hypothesis leads to as regards the evolution of consciousness. We have noted that Barfield, in company with earlier etymologists but rather more deeply, offers many glimpses into how men formerly perceived the world. This is largely what Barfield's book *History in English Words*[2] or C. S. Lewis' book *Studies in Words* enables us to do.[14] But we are invited by Barfield's investigations to do more, for merely seeing how earlier ages thought, though intensely interesting in its own right, is but a refinement of the study of history and was inherent in the applications to which etymology was being put in the nineteenth century. Beyond that, we are invited to think about the nature of consciousness itself. If St. John, to use the earlier example, actually perceived wind and spirit as the same thing, and if this was indeed the general perception as well as being objectively true, then the very consciousness of men of St. John's age must have been different from ours.

All this may seem like an inflated way of saying what has already been said and what has long been known: men of earlier times thought differently from us. But it is more. Consciousness is far more comprehensive than "thinking about things." Consciousness is the whole awareness of reality, much of it assumed and not thought about as such. By going beyond mere historical differences revealed by the study of words, by examining systematically what these differences point to, Barfield has been able to document, through etymology, the actual developments in human consciousness from the first written records to our own time, as well as to make some educated suppositions about the state of affairs before records became available.

Human consciousness, Barfield shows, has evolved like words from outer to inner, as it were. There has been a progressive detachment of man from his environment, a progressive awareness of each man's own separateness. The ego is not so much an invention of Freud's as a development of Western consciousness.[7] It is more than having different views from medieval men or the ancients on the nature of the lion: we do not *perceive* lions as they did; that is, where we see a tawny-colored quadruped of the cat family with a mane and long tail, they would have *seen* the king of beasts. Modern consciousness is at once more aware of the physical contours of nature and less aware of its spiritual contours; indeed we increasingly doubt that she — or, should I say, it — has any.

As the best single illustration of this point, the reader is referred to Barfield's magisterial treatment of *pneuma* in *Speaker's Meaning* which he shows to have meant *both* wind and spirit.[8a,5b] What Barfield has found in such cases as that of *pneuma* simply sets the history of thought and ideas on its ear and also offers an insight into our own habitual views of the world that can only be called a critique. It is not possible here to explore the ramifications of Barfield's findings. I wanted only to point out how they have built on the study of etymology that seemed to have come to a dead end or to have been lost in dilettantism by the end of the nineteenth century.

And that returns us to our beginnings. At the outset I maintained that the nineteenth-century developments in the study of etymology changed our ideas about the very word "etymology" itself, and I believe the long communing with the *OED* at the beginning of this essay supports this view. But let us for the moment put this in Barfieldian terms: nineteenth-century etymology was the development in the sphere of philology of modern self-consciousness. It was perhaps one of the last areas to experience the release from what Barfield has called "original participation." And characteristically so, for language is intensely conservative and even today carries traces of that original participation that other areas of activity have lost.[8b]

Etymology, then, up to the nineteenth century was only indulging in a remembrance of original participation when it sought the "true meaning" of an English word in its Greek original. Men continued, in other words, to do in language what they had ceased to do in physics and astronomy and medicine and countless other areas: they assumed an identity between words and things, between language and reality. It was, then, not just the tyranny of the past that set men to consult a Greek or Latin original to see what a word truly meant; it was rather the notion that there was some meaningful correspondence between those languages and ultimate reality. It was the notion that was expressed as late as the nineteenth century in the determination of the Reverend J. W. Edward Conybeare that his sister must learn Greek in order that she be able to converse in Heaven, that being the language of the place.[15]

Etymology, as it shifted from "true meaning" to "accurate account" broke away from that thread of original participation and rendered it, dare one say, meaningless or even ludicrous. One cannot but note with a regretful nostalgia the passing of such sentiments as Conybeare's, but at the same time one cannot but acknowledge that the increase in precision and clarity and intellectual understanding gained by the study of etymology in the nineteenth century represents a remarkable achievement. But because that increase occurred during the period when the "idols" (to use another Barfield term) of detached self-consciousness were in almost total command of intellectual life —

when atoms were billiard balls and all phenomena were conveniently "out there" — etymology very soon reached a dead end and deliquesced into antiquarianism. Carlyle's and Ruskin's attempts to join the new knowledge of etymology to the old search for true meaning came to seem mere phantasms. Language too was "out there" and was simply so many counters to be classified and pigeonholed. No wonder that semantics more or less left the matter of etymology behind.

Barfield's redemption, as one must call it, of etymology offers the possibility of gaining true insight, not just more facts, about the nature of human history and the nature of human beings, that is, about ourselves. While Barfield's method is iconoclastic in that it breaks the idols of Victorian etymology, it is also promising in that it provides the opportunity for using etymology as "accurate account" in order to arrive at etymology as "true meaning."

REFERENCES

1. Barfield, O. Greek Thought in English Words. *Essays and Studies* n.s., 3(1950): 69-81.
2. ———. *History in English Words.* Reprint. Grand Rapids, Mich.: William B. Eerdmans Publishing Co., 1966.
3. ———. Imagination and Inspiration. In *Interpretation: The Poetry of Meaning*, edited by Stanley Romaine Hopper and David L. Miller. New York: Harcourt, Brace & World, 1967.
4. ———. The Meaning of the Word 'Literal.' In *Metaphor and Symbol*, edited by L. C. Knights and Basil Cottle. London: Butterworth's Scientific Publications, 1960.
5. ———. *Poetic Diction.* (Rev. ed., 1952). New York: McGraw-Hill, 1964, (a) 14-39; (b) 74, 79-81.
6. ———. Poetic Diction and Legal Fiction. In *The Importance of Language*, edited by Max Black. Englewood Cliffs, N.J.: Prentice-Hall, 1962.
7. ———. *Saving the Appearances: A Study in Idolatry.* Reprint. New York: Harcourt, Brace & World, 1965. This is my own figure and does not imply an endorsement by Barfield of Freudian psychology; *see* pp. 133-4.
8. ———. *Speaker's Meaning.* Middletown, Conn.: Wesleyan University Press, 1967, (a) 56-57; (b) cf. Barfield's example of the still simultaneously literal and metaphorical use of the word "heart," pp. 57-9.
9. ———. *What Coleridge Thought.* Middletown, Conn.: Wesleyan University Press, 1971, pp. 20-1.
10. Carlyle, T. *Sartor Resartus.* Reprint. Edited by C. F. Harrold. New York: Odyssey Press, 1937, (a) 249; (b) 248; (c) 316-18.
11. Garlanda, F. *The Fortunes of Words: Letters to a Lady.* New York: A. Lovell & Co., 1887. (a) In addition to many arresting speculations, Garlanda also distinguishes himself by proposing the substitution of the unfortunate word "glottologist" for "linguist" to denote a student of language; (b) p. 51; Garlanda puts the case succinctly: "all the words in our language — even those that convey the most abstract ideas, come from roots whose meaning is simple and entirely concrete."

12. Leech, G. N. *Towards a Semantic Description of English*. London: Longmans, Green Co., 1969, pp. 248-54.

13. Lewis, C. S. Bluspels and Falansferes. In *The Importance of Language*, edited by Max Black. Englewood Cliffs, N.J.: Prentice-Hall, 1962, p. 50.

14. ———. *Studies in Words*. 2d ed. Cambridge: Cambridge University Press, 1967.

15. Macaulay, R. *Letters to a Friend*. Edited by Constance Babington-Smith. New York: Athenaeum, 1962, p. 163.

16. Nicholson, M. *A Dictionary of American-English Usage*. New York: Oxford University Press, 1957, p. 509.

17. Ogden, C. K., and Richards, I. A. *The Meaning of Meaning*. New York: Harcourt, Brace & Co., n.d.

18. Pedersen, H. *The Discovery of Language*. Translated by John Webster Spargo. Bloomington: Indiana University Press, 1962, (a) 277-310; (b) passim.

19. Potter, S. *Our Language*. Harmondsworth: Penguin Books, 1950, p. 106. Modern dictionaries list *etymon* as a regular word, but Potter gives it in italics as a Greek word. Potter's chapter 9, in which the word occurs, bears the same title as the present essay, though with different import.

20. Pyles, T. *The Origins and Development of the English Language*. New York: Harcourt, Brace & World, 1964, pp. 1-2.

21. Ruskin, J. *The Ethics of the Dust*. In *The Works of John Ruskin*, edited by E. T. Cook and Alexander Wedderburn. London: George Allen, 1905, vol. 18, pp. 336-7.

22. ———. *Sesame and Lilies*. In *Works*, vol. 18, p. 72.

23. Ryle, G. The Theory of Meaning. In *The Importance of Language*, edited by Max Black. Englewood Cliffs, N.J.: Prentice-Hall, 1962, p. 147.

24. Skeat, W. W. *An Etymological Dictionary of the English Language*. 3d ed. Oxford: Clarendon Press, 1898, p. 710. It should be noted that even in error Carlyle and Ruskin were not so fanciful as earlier writers, for their derivations are at least plausible in terms of consonants, though not as regards vowels. The mysteries of vowel change were among the last to be unravelled by nineteenth-century philology. See reference 18(a) above.

25. Smith, L. P. *The English Language*. New York: Henry Holt, 1912.

26. ———. *Words and Idioms*. Boston: Houghton Mifflin Co., 1926.

A NOTE ON BARFIELD, ROMANTICISM, AND TIME

by

R. J. REILLY

All students of romanticism must be grateful to Owen Barfield for his part in bringing to nineteenth-century romantic thought a measure of respectability it had lost in the early years of this century. When the literary history of our time is written and influential critics are discussed, Barfield surely will be mentioned as a matter of course. But as readers of Barfield know, he is more than an elucidator of romantic thought; his own work is itself romantic, an addition to romantic thought; in Eliot's terms it is a continuation but a modification of romantic tradition. One cannot read Barfield's work without being aware of echoes of the past, of Coleridge, and Emerson, and other romantics. It is a past that Barfield is clearly pleased to echo: much of the thought in *Poetic Diction*, for example, he traces to Emerson's *Nature*. It is not too much to say that he is a spokesman for romanticism, that he gives a kind of contemporaneity to older romantics, so that they often seem to be speaking through him.

In this context it is interesting to ask what Barfield meant by a comment he made in *Saving the Appearances*: that the romantic impulse never came to maturity in the nineteenth century, and that the only alternative to maturity is puerility.[1] The statement is clearly derogatory, and one may ask whether Barfield is continuing a tradition that he himself has judged to be sterile. The question is obvious and "leading," and is meant to be. The answer is that he himself has contributed something to romantic thought that had not been there earlier or at least had not been *generally* there. He has insisted that romanticism must be associated with, and culminate in, Christianity; and as a correlative of this he has insisted that romanticism must respect the reality of time and history. I say that, generally, romantic thought was neither Christian nor especially respectful of time; the obvious exception to this generalization is Coleridge. In the following pages I shall suggest that Barfield's thought is what may be called "corrected romanticism" (C. S. Lewis's term for Charles Williams' work) in the sense that Barfield has accommodated both Christianity and time in a way that most romantic thought did not do. But I emphasize that when I contrast Barfield's thought to romantic thought in general I exclude Coleridge's work; I shall, in fact, cite close parallels between their thought. If Barfield has corrected romanticism in general, he has not corrected Coleridge. I believe Barfield would agree that if nineteenth-century romantic thought had been more Coleridgean it would require less correcting.

Now it is generally accepted that romantic thought is almost invariably idealistic and also that it has an affinity with Eastern religious thought. Plato is thus the perfect archetypal romantic, because he combines the strong line of Greek idealism with ancient Eastern religious beliefs, which stress the goodness of spirit at the expense of matter. It is easy to oversimplify in such matters, but certainly a reader who came freshly to Wordsworth, Shelley, Emerson, Thoreau, and Whitman would find certain resemblances in their work, and these resemblances are fairly well described as a mixture of Western philosophical idealism and Eastern religious idealism. Transcendentalism, Emerson remarked, was simply idealism in the nineteenth century, and much nineteenth-century romanticism, we may say, is a fusion of Western and Eastern idealism. Barfield has reminded us of this fusion: "The passage from East to West has always been a curiously fertilising process. 'Time and again,' said the late Sir Walter Raleigh, 'when East meets West, the spirit of Romance has been born.' "[2] It is apparently an easy movement from Plato to Buddha, and not only easy but seemingly "natural," judging by the frequency with which it occurs. Whitman's "Crossing Brooklyn Ferry," as Thoreau observed, is "wonderfully like the Orientals." And the reader of Emerson notes the ease with which the early idealism fuses in the later work with the Hindu rejection of time and space. Thus the poem that precedes his essay "Illusions" (1860) speaks of "The waves of mutation; No anchorage is. / Sleep is not, death is not; / Who seem to die live."

Now two obvious things may be said about this influence of Eastern on Western idealism: (1) the Eastern fondness for insisting on the reality of the world of spirit lends itself peculiarly well to depicting certain experiences of elevation and exaltation; and (2) Eastern thought does this primarily by minimizing, or denying, the reality of the phenomenal world and of time. Illustrations of these points in Western romanticism come easily to mind. We think of Wordsworth's "Tintern Abbey," in which the experience is described as "that serene and blessed mood" that is characterized by the diminution of sensual reality; even the movement of the blood is "almost suspended"; we are "laid asleep / In body, and become a living soul." Or we think of Whitman's "Oriental" poem, in which the ferry serves as the vehicle that takes the speaker out of time and out of his bodily identity, so that "It avails not, time nor place — distance avails not. . . ." Or we think of the passage in Emerson's *Nature* in which he describes the loss of all "mean egotism" and where "I become a transparent eyeball; I am nothing; I see all; the currents of the Universal Being circulate through me; I am part and parcel

of God." In all these cases the speaker is abstracted from the world of matter
and of time; in all these cases his experience may fairly be described, in Eastern terms, as the Flight from the Alone to the Alone, as a temporary escape
from *maya* or an illusory phenomenal world, an escape from time.

Now if we examine Barfield's attitude toward Eastern thought, we find it
generally sympathetic. But in *Unancestral Voice*, the hero, Burgeon, force-
fully rejects the Eastern views of time and matter urged on him by the Bud-
dhist Grimwade. Burgeon does not present the usual Christian arguments
against reincarnation, however. His whole argument is that time is not illusory,
that it is a "given" — a reality in which man is "by nature" immersed. Bud-
dhism, as Burgeon and Grimwade agree, insists on the doctrine of "Mind-
Only" — insists that mind is reality and matter, illusion.[3] This notion Burgeon
refuses to accept. And in *Worlds Apart*, Sanderson also accepts reincarnation
as one of Steiner's teachings but insists that a reincarnation is a repeated earth
life enacted in a real time. Briefly, then, it seems likely that Barfield would
say of the experiences cited from Wordsworth, Whitman, and Emerson that
they are valid experiences but experiences misread or misinterpreted. They do
not prove that man's true reality consists of experience outside of time and
space or that time and space are illusory; rather they prove the reverse. The
transience and rarity of the experiences prove their violations of the norms
of common life, the way things generally go on.

Now to return to the question posed above: why did Barfield call romanticism immature and unfulfilled? Largely, I think, because of this bias toward
time as illusion. Illusory time has no place in Barfield's religious notion of
evolution, nor does it in Coleridge's. If romanticism was to fulfill its promise
it had to see time as real yet not wholly different from timelessness, for it had
to "save the appearances" of Christianity, and Christianity means Christ and
the problem of history, the junction of time and timelessness. To take the
Eastern view of time, as so many romantic writers did, was to take Christ as
"mythic" or "only symbolic." It was to take him as somehow representative,
one of many avatars of God or Buddha. That Christ is symbolic is, of course,
obvious; the problem for a Christian is to keep him from being *merely* symbolic. For both Coleridge and Barfield an iconic God is no God at all. For
Christ to be real, time has to be real, and therefore history has to be real. But
if Christ is both symbolic and real, his context (time, history) must also be
both symbolic and real. Therefore God has to be real man in Christ, and timelessness has to be real time in history. In a word, neither Coleridge nor Barfield is "Easternly romantic" enough to sit easily with Shelley or Emerson.
Time is not *maya*; it is salvational history.

"Time as salvational history" is a phrase requiring considerable explanation. For both Coleridge and Barfield it means timelessness operating in
time, or a relationship between God and man that exists both in and out of

time. In time this relationship is marked by change (the evolution of human consciousness); in timelessness it is presumably static. Yet both Coleridge and Barfield refer to the two aspects of the relationship as parts of evolution. Thus Barfield speaks of "Coleridge's whole idea of evolution, together with its final stage history," and adds, "Both the Bible itself, as an historical phenomenon, and the content of the Bible as history, are to be seen . . . as 'parts' of the whole polarity between God and man, of which evolution is the process in time."[4] This description of Coleridge's view of time and history recalls Barfield's own careful charting of the origin and destiny of man in *Romanticism Comes of Age* and *Saving the Appearances*. Man's first existence is timeless and bodiless; whatever "archetypal" memories he has of an Edenic life suggest a life of spirit, not matter. The whole course of "true evolution" (as distinguished from Darwinian evolution) is from spirit into matter, not a course of increasingly complex material substances. "True evolution" suggests a pattern in time that, not reflects, but *is* in its own way the timeless relationship between God and man. Charles Williams said that all human existence is patterned on the relationship operating in the Trinity; all existence has its being by virtue of what he called "co-inherence," "substitution," and "exchange." I am not sure whether Williams saw this pattern as anything more than imitation or reflection. But Barfield sees the timeless and the temporal as two aspects of the same relation, and is thus less "Platonic" or "Eastern" than Williams. It is of course difficult to conceive of process or change as in any way a part of a relationship whose other part is timeless. But if Coleridge and Barfield are right, then there must be in timelessness something that can be called movement; or there must be something in time that can be called stasis. There must be a kind of likeness in difference, or polarity. Several analogies are available at this point: the notion, for example, of a continuum on which (as in a rainbow) human and divine nature come together at no precise point. Perhaps a better analogy is Henry James's comment on vicarious and "real" experience. In James's metaphor all experience is a web, and it is impossible to distinguish clearly between real and imagined experience. In fact, as soon as one tries to distinguish between "inner" and "outer" experiences, the experiences begin to seem somehow different, yet not really distinct. Milton, we recall, abandoned analogy in *Paradise Lost* and boldly dramatized a kind of movement in timelessness: Christ is in some sense elevated from his original status to that of Son-ship. For both Coleridge and Barfield, Christ, or the Incarnation, is the basis of the time-timelessness polarity: it is Christ who "moves" in timelessness and is somehow static in time.

Now evolution implies the necessity of stages; thus man's temporality, or his polar relation to God in time, is necessary. But this is to say that time is necessary, and therefore patterned, and therefore history. Ancient history and "pre-history" imply a Fall; or as Coleridge said, "In the assertion of original sin the Greek Mythology rose and set."[5] Pre-Incarnation history depicts what Barfield calls man's "apostasy,"[5] man's fall from grace; the history of the Jews is the major example of this. Post-Incarnation history adumbrates redemption in the form of Barfield's evolution of consciousness, a gradually deepening relationship between man and Christ. History, like James's experience, has both an inner and an outer dimension; it is real time, but it is also the medium in which the God-man polarity is evident. In Coleridge's terms, it is symbolic: it participates in the reality of that which it represents.

It is this double vision of time as both real and symbolic that makes Barfield's evolution of consciousness a record in time of man's polar relationship to God. From a "Mind-Only" viewpoint man has no relationship to God in time, the relationship exists only in moments of elevation (abstraction from time) or in death. But for Barfield, man — solid, historical man — is continuously related to God by means of evolution. For what that evolution consists of is man's sense of his relationship to God changing from an unconscious identification with Him before birth to an increasingly conscious sense of God as a different being from himself, yet not a "Wholly Other." The Meggid in *Unancestral Voice* calls Christ "the transforming agent,"[6] the substantive link between God and man, and the ground of all true evolution. Christ, who exists both in and out of time, both as man and as God, is the principle of evolution. By "principle" I mean the underlying identity that man keeps during the evolutionary process, the sameness in difference that keeps him from being transformed into a being other than human. Man changes yet remains man, as Christ changed into man yet remained God, and as God came into time yet remains timeless. For Coleridge and Barfield these relationships are not paradoxes but polarities.

Charles Williams said that the important thing about the gospel stories was not only that they happened but that they are happening. He meant of course that Christ is operative in time now as he was in New Testament time. Williams believed Christ operative in the sacramental system of the visible church. Barfield, I think, would agree with this belief but would find it too restricting and inclined to rely too heavily on the assumption that the sacraments work automatically, like a conjurer's magic tricks, irrespective of the condition of the recipient. For Barfield Christ is not simply a founder of a church that has prolonged his divine power in an institutional way. He is an element of human nature, not merely a witness to possible human perfection but a continuous means to it. He is infinite potentiality for human goodness. He resides in his person-hood within the unconscious being of all men. If post-Incarnation history implies redemption, it implies it in man's continuous (and historical) discovery of the unconscious depths of human nature, and in his increasing ability to bring to consciousness new wisdom out of the unconscious mind. If Christ is "the transforming agent," He is so because He resides in the human unconsciousness, in time.

Now Emerson said something that sounds a good deal like this in the last chapter of *Nature*, and it is worth distinguishing Emerson's view from Barfield's. For Emerson, man sees that "if still he have elemental power . . . it is not conscious power, it is not inferior but superior to his will. It is instinct." He continues:

At present, man applies to nature but half his force. He works on the world with his understanding alone. . . . His relation to nature, his power over it, is through the understanding. . . . Meantime, in the thick darkness, there are not wanting gleams of a better light, — occasional examples of the action of man upon nature with his entire force, — with reason as well as understanding. Such examples are the traditions of miracles in the earliest antiquity of all nations; the history of Jesus Christ; the achievements of a principle, as in religious and political revolutions, and in the abolition of the slave-trade; the miracles of enthusiasm, as those reported of Swedenborg . . . and the Shakers . . . prayer; eloquence; self-healing; and the wisdom of children. These are examples of Reason's momentary grasp of the sceptre; the exertions of a power which exists not in time or space, but an instantaneous instreaming causing power.

Emerson's view of man's potentiality is hardly distinguishable from any number of "occult" assertions of the divinity of man. But the point to be clear about in Emerson's view is its casual reference to time and Christianity. Its examples are random because it is an essentially timeless statement. With a change of examples, Origen might have said it, or Plotinus, or Robert Flood, or a modern Rosicrucian. It assumes a wholly timeless relationship between God and man, which man may exploit by various occult means. In fact it implies at best a blurred distinction between God and man. God, Emerson seems to say, exists in the unconscious mind — or somewhere — and His power may be tapped. Barfield's insistence on history and historical Christianity saves him from such extravagances. Man is not God and never will be. Man's increasing power over nature is not to be confused with his increasing awareness of his intimate relationship with God. Refinements in technology are certainly products drawn ultimately from the unconscious mind (the well of new meaning), but these refinements are not necessarily refinements of spirit; they may indeed be corruptions of it. As Barfield says in *Poetic Diction*: "The possibility of man's avoiding self-destruction depends on his realizing before it is too late that what he let loose over Hiroshima, after fiddling with its exterior for three centuries like a mechanical toy, was the forces of his own unconscious mind."[7] For Barfield, man in his evolutionary process is not approaching closer to God but becoming increasingly aware of his true relation to God. It is from this increasing "moral consciousness" that great things may come. But if they come, they will come by acts of the will, not by what Emerson calls "instinct" or "elemental power." Emerson's examples of human power are precisely examples of unconscious power, and therefore power not understood. What cannot be stressed too often is that Barfield's evolution of consciousness is toward an ever fuller consciousness, a consciousness increasingly capable of moral and intellectual discrimination. Power over nature is perhaps a concomitant element in this process, but it is not the primary end. The primary end is a growing perception of the God-man polarity, a deeper and deeper penetration into the mystery of the Incarnation. Barfield hints at the form that this deeper penetration may take, in a discussion of the poetic imagination and the concept of inspiration. What the imagination now grasps as myth and symbol it may in future grasp as personification and allegory; that is, the human mind may be moving toward a stage in which its intellectual and imaginative perceptions are sharpened, made more precise.[8]

Barfield's description of anthroposophy stresses his belief in the importance, really the necessity, of time. The "kernel" of anthroposophy, he has said, "is *the concept of man's self-consciousness as a process in time*, with all that this implies [italics mine]."[9] If one wonders that Barfield should be an "occult" Christian (as he has been called) rather than an orthodox or traditional Christian, perhaps the answer is that, in Barfield's view, anthroposophy takes history more seriously than a good deal of traditional theology does. Anthroposophy attempts to study the facts of history so far as history is salvational time. Strictly speaking, the God-man relationship cannot be seriously studied except in time, because it is visible only in time. Neither revelation nor theology is the study of man as a phenomenon in time. In this sense Christian history "redeems" time, takes the polar relationship, of which the Incarnation is both the fact and the emblem, out of the realm of belief and into the world we know. Said differently, man's origin in spirit and his destiny in spirit (if that is his destiny) are the "given" facts of faith or revelation. But only man as he exists in time can verify this origin and this destiny. Like Coleridge, Barfield is not only a theologian dealing with dogma but a scientist dealing with facts, the facts of history.

This is the point at which Coleridge and Barfield part company with most of the other romantics. Coleridge and Barfield accept as a "given" the reality of time, as they accept as a given the basic Christian story. Or rather they accept time because it is an obvious part of the Christian story that must be either believed or philosophized away. It may be argued that a study of time and history in themselves yields nothing conclusive in the way of a pattern, not even what Henry James called "the strange irregular rhythm of life." It may be argued, and truly, that both Coleridge and Barfield begin their study of time with certain assumptions based in Christianity. But everyone begins such a study with certain assumptions; the assumptions are what make the study of time necessary. It was Eastern assumptions that in great part shaped most nineteenth-century romanticism. It is Christian assumptions that "correct" that romanticism in the work of Coleridge and Barfield. More precisely, it is Christianity and time that preserve the real polar relationship between God and man, and prevent the two beings from blurring into one. It is not easy to understand, much less paraphrase, Coleridge's and Barfield's view of an evolutionary process that includes both timelessness and time as stages or parts. But one thing seems clear: without a belief that historical time is real, and a factor in man's destiny, the true polar relationship between God and man is endangered. To ignore or minimize time is to change the shape of the hour glass and let all the sand run together.

REFERENCES

1. Barfield, O. *Saving the Appearances*. New York: Harcourt, Brace & World, 1965, p. 131.
2. ———. *Romanticism Comes of Age*. Middletown, Conn.: Wesleyan University Press, 1966, p. 31.
3. ———. *Unancestral Voice*. Middletown, Conn.: Wesleyan University Press 1965, p. 81.
4. ———. *What Coleridge Thought*. Middletown, Conn.: Wesleyan University Press, 1971, p. 154.
5. ———. *What Coleridge Thought*. Middletown, Conn.: Wesleyan University Press, 1971, p. 155.
6. ———. *Unancestral Voice*. Middletown, Conn.: Wesleyan University Press, 1965, p. 16.
7. ———. *Poetic Diction*. London: Faber & Faber, 1952, p. 36.
8. ———. "Imagination and Inspiration." In *Interpretation: The Poetry of Meaning,* edited by S. R. Hopper and D. L. Miller. New York: Harcourt, Brace & World, 1967, pp. 74-75.
9. ———. *Romanticism Comes of Age*. Middletown, Conn.: Wesleyan University Press, 1966, p. 189.

AN "ESSAY" ON COLERIDGE ON IMAGINATION

by

SHIRLEY SUGERMAN

The term "essay" was expressly chosen and I am now using it in its wider and now less usual sense of an *attempt*. For I have found myself, in the process of considering Coleridge's thinking about imagination, not only in dread of where I tread, when I offer this to the author of *What Coleridge Thought*, but also in the thick of the central problems of philosophy: the problem of the possibility of knowledge, that is, what we are fond of calling the subject-object problem, or the relationship of knowing to being, and the problem of the self, here more specifically with the emphasis on the nature of consciousness. Since these both imply the question of the nature of reality, we can see that an examination of Coleridge's central idea involves us in the whole of his thinking and points up his insistence on the "all in every part" quality of life itself. It also explains the reason for calling this an "essay."

And so, to Coleridge — to look at the philosophical structure undergirding his doctrine of imagination: "Repeated meditations," Coleridge writes, "led me first to suspect . . . that fancy and imagination were two distinct and widely different faculties, instead of being, according to the general belief, either two names with one meaning or . . . the lower and higher degree of one and the same power."[5a] We shall look first at the thinking preparatory to Coleridge's distinction: this thinking was a disavowal of the underlying (mechanical, Cartesian) philosophy that made fancy and imagination appear synonymous and made it impossible to distinguish them in *kind*. To establish that distinction, Coleridge writes that he would establish the existence of two different faculties and would also show that this division is grounded in life itself. To that end, he states that his object is to investigate the "seminal principle"[5b] of living things for it "is not in human nature to meditate on any mode of action, without enquiring after the law that governs it."[5c] Secondly, then, we shall examine that "seminal principle" on which he based his theory of imagination.

The prevailing opinion of Coleridge's time was "that the law of association . . . formed the basis of all true psychology."[5d] This point of view, represented by Hartley, who was preceded in it by Hobbes, Descartes, and others, is the philosophical creed that Coleridge disavows, for this view held that ideas were mechanically associated and resembled "successive particles propagating motion like billiard balls."[5e] In this view not only is thinking drawn from material motion, but cause and effect are confused, since the will is seen as an *effect* of association rather than its cause. To Hartley's mechanical theory Coleridge objects on the basis that if it were true, "our life would be divided between the despotism of outward impressions, and that of senseless and passive memory." His conclusion is that this theory is nothing but an indication of "complete lightheadedness." It is the Aristotelian theory of association, which Coleridge refers to as the "universal law of the passive fancy and the mechanical memory,"[5f] that he uses to refute Hartley. So that I must note here that Coleridge does not deny the associative principle completely, for further on in the *Biographia Literaria* he shows how the "associative power becomes either memory or Fancy" as distinct from the imagination.

That the mechanical theory "involves all the difficulties, all the incomprehensibility . . . of intercommunion between substances that have no one property in common," leads Coleridge into the heart of the problem: "For what is harmony," he asks, "but a mode of relation, the very *esse* of which is *percipi*? An *ens rationale*, which presupposes the power that by perceiving creates it?"[5g] Yet the separation of *res cogitans* and *res extensa*, which was introduced by Descartes, made an explanation of the action of each on the other most difficult.

By virtue of a conceptual screen we have separated ourselves from the "outside" and conceive of ourselves as being "inside." How then explain the interaction of thought on matter, to continue Coleridge's argument, for the motion of matter can only produce motion — "matter has no Inward." If "matter has no Inward," it can understand nothing about "depth," it has only to do with "surface." To understand something, we must enter into it — *Einfuhlung* or "sympathetic penetration" is a word I think fits well here — and as Descartes separated mind and matter, any understanding of matter by mind, to say nothing of their interdependence, which of course he denies, is impossible.

I would like to digress here briefly, leave Coleridge, and bring in Pascal and Descartes. For an understanding of what Pascal calls the "geometric spirit," born from the philosophy of Descartes, as contrasted with what Pascal calls the "spirit of finesse," might be helpful here and is relevant to Coleridge's view of intuition and the organic nature of life — and because it is a "way of knowing," a mode of relation to being. The geometric spirit pervades the modern world, as we all know, and is its answer not only to the need for certainty but is also a means of denial of man as spirit, by making him into an object of control. The spirit of geometry moves step by logical step from the particular to the whole — no leaps — no intuition — and directs its attention outward toward the control of objects of the world. In this it has been eminently successful in improving the world we live in. But, there are no hidden depths here: inwardness is sacrificed in favor of the external world, the surface. In the measurable quantities of the outer world, man can feel secure in the grasp of objects and on this objective basis, we can forget that we exist, participate and are underneath it all, involved in life. For in geometric objectivity there is no underneath. The rules of measurement dissolve everything that is below the surface and make the world appear to be calculable, foreseeable, controllable. So that, as Pascal says, "we make an idol of truth itself."[9a] To this he contrasts the "spirit of finesse," which makes it possible to glance into the whole, for it is a way of knowing of the "heart" — by which term Pascal seems to refer to the whole person — that grows out of silence and contemplation and grasps intuitively. It is subtly sensitive to the flowing, shifting, rich textured reality of life as contrasted with the clear "definitions and axioms" required by the spirit of geometry. It is the way we apprehend the multiplicity of reality as a whole.[9b] In this understanding, man as separate and finite, strives toward the whole, the Infinite, and it is in the dialectical tension of those opposites that man's consciousness of himself as part of the whole lies, according to Pascal.

[We] need no less capacity for attaining the Nothing than the All. Infinite capacity is required for both, and it seems to me that whoever shall have understood the ultimate principles of being might also attain to the knowledge of the Infinite. The one depends on the other, and one leads to the other. These extremes meet and reunite by force of distance . . . and find each other in God, and in God alone.[9c]

The inwardness that makes possible the consciousness of the relationship of the finite to the Infinite lies in the subtle way of knowing that is the spirit of finesse. Pascal's reaction against materialism, as fathered by Descartes, his interest in depth as against surface, his understanding of the tension of opposite poles and his comprehension of the organic relationship of the part to the whole made me feel that this brief excursion into his thought, to illuminate Coleridge's thought, might be worthwhile.

"How being can transform itself into a knowing," how "the *esse* then, assumed as originally distinct from the *scire*, can ever unite itself with it,"[5h] is the problem that Coleridge proposes to consider. His assumption is that communion between being and knowing is "conceivable on one only condition; namely, if it can be shown that the . . . Sentient is itself a species of being,"[5i] that "Truth is the correlative of Being . . . that both are . . . identical and coinherent; that intelligence and being are reciprocally each other's substrate."[5j] In developing the philosophical structure of his doctrine of imagination, the problem that Coleridge sets for himself is to explain this concurrence.

To do this Coleridge points to the need for a primary assumption, such as there is in geometry, which is postulated, not demonstrated. For geometry starts *not* with a demonstrable proposition, but with a primary intuition, which corresponds to an outward sense, such as a line or a point. Philosophy, however, is concerned with and requires "inner sense," which in turn requires discipline and contemplation, a "realizing intuition," to arrive at its fundamental postulate. With Coleridge, the "act of contemplation makes the thing contemplated — simply contemplating, the representative forms of things rise up into existence."[5k] But if this sounds simple, let us see what it is that Coleridge suggests as the nature of this act of contemplation! "There is a philosophic . . . consciousness which lies beneath or (as it were) behind the spontaneous consciousness natural to all reflecting beings. . . ."[5l] The consciousness that lies *behind* few achieve, for its "sources must be far higher and far inward" than most of us have ventured. It is from these depths and these heights that "the highest and intuitive knowledge as distinguished from the discursive" is born, and

it is not lawful to inquire from whence it sprang . . . it either appears to us or it does not appear. So that we ought not to pursue it with a view of detecting its secret source, but to watch in quiet till it suddenly shines upon us. . . . They . . . only can acquire the philosophic imagination, the sacred power of self-intuition . . . who . . . know and feel that the *potential* works *in* them, even as the *actual* works on them![5m]

The primary intuition, on which the certainty of our knowledge depends, "is no other than the heaven descended Know Thyself!"[5n] he concludes. For it is in self-consciousness that we find the coincidence of subject and object on which the possibility of knowledge rests. It is this that bridges the gap between knowing and being, since "truth is universally placed in the coincidence of the thought with the thing, of the representation with the object represented,"[5o] in the identity of the dancer and the danced. When Coleridge speaks of subject or subjective, he refers to mind, conscious being, self, intelligence, the representative. When he speaks of object, he refers to the phenomena by which the existence of nature is made known to us, to the represented, to that which is without consciousness. Now, Coleridge points out, we have two innate prejudices, one is that "there exist things without us" that lay claim to immediate certainty; yet since the reference is to what is not-self it is hard to understand how it could become a part of our consciousness. The other position, that "I am," requires the admission of certainty for although it is groundless, it is itself the ground of all other certainty. The apparent contradiction, that the existence of not-self, of which we can *not* be immediately certain, should seem as certain as that of our own being, he resolves by assuming that the "former is unconsciously involved in the latter; that it is not only coherent but identical, and one and

the same thing with our own immediate self-consciousness."[5p] To demonstrate this identity between inner and outer dimension, between subject and
object, self and not-self, and, thence, between knowing and being is the purpose of his philosophy, for he writes this is the "truest and most binding
realism," not that philosophy that "distinguishes truth from illusion only by
the majority of those who dream the same dream."[5q]

Now let us look behind these conclusions concerning the concurrence of
knowing and being, the philosophical preparation for his doctrine of imagination, to understand how Coleridge arrived at them, that is, by understanding
the "seminal principle" that underlies and unifies all of his thinking. With
this principle, familiar to all who know Coleridge's work, he writes: "I will
render the construction of the universe intelligible . . . grant me a nature
having two contrary forces, the one of which tends to expand infinitely,
while the other strives to apprehend or find itself in this infinity, and I will
cause the world of intelligences with the whole system of their representations to rise up before you."[5r] The two forces of which he speaks "counteract
each other by their essential nature . . . [and are] the primary forces from
which the conditions of all possible directions are derivative and deducible;
secondly . . . these forces should be assumed to be both alike infinite, both
alike indestructible."[5s] To speak of the polarity of these forces is to imply
interaction, and since opposites or extremes meet, they imply derivation
from one source or rather one power with two counteracting forces. They
must not be thought of as spatial, temporal, or material but as dynamic,
counteracting forces prior to all direction. We can try to imagine these forces
graphically, for instance, by visualizing a spiral movement illustrating centrifugal and centripetal forces, the former tending infinitely outwards, the
latter counteracting it by a movement inward toward the center, or by a
triangular shape the base of which represents the movement toward diversity,
multiplicity, extensiveness, and the apex of which points toward the unified,
the intensified.

Coleridge instructs us that, after we have examined these two forces

by the process of discursive reasoning, it will then remain for us to elevate the
thesis from Notional to actual, by contemplating intuitively [and we touched
earlier on the nature of the contemplation he suggests] this one power with its
two inherent indestructible yet counteracting forces and the results or generations
to which their inter-penetration gives existence, in the living principle and in the
process of our own self-consciousness.[5t]

By so doing we will know how self and world come into being.

The primary intuition, which as a result of contemplation Coleridge began
with, was the intuition "I am," I know myself. It is that in which we have
faith, "which is fidelity to 'one's own being,' where the roots of conscience
and of consciousness itself are intertwined."[3a] Faith that "I am" implies an

other, for there cannot be an I "without a previous thou . . . and . . . a thou is only possible by an equation in which I is taken as equal to thou, and yet not the same. And this again is only possible by putting them in opposition as correspondent opposites, or correlatives." The "equation of thou with I, by means of a free act (i.e., by an application of the will) negativing the sameness in order to establish the equality, is . . . as . . . these conjointly form the materials and subjects of consciousness . . . the precondition of all experience."[6] "Human consciousness," as Owen Barfield has said, "begins with a free act; it begins with that polarization of unity into sameness and difference, on which 'likeness' is based. . . ."[3b]

If we apply Coleridge's "seminal principle" of the two contrary forces here, one force tending to expand infinitely and the other trying to find itself in this infinity, one toward world and the other toward self, we may see how the interaction of the forces brings self and other into being. Consciousness of self as different from, separate from, "negates sameness" and at the same time establishes, projects, the equal existence of another. The origin of consciousness has its root in man's freedom and lies in the act of the will recognizes the independent existence of another by rejecting sameness and affirming equality. Without the recognition of a Thou, there can be no I. Martin Buber's observation that "*I become* through my relation to the Thou; as I become I, I say Thou" bears on this point. The "primal setting at a distance," making the other an "independent opposite" is requisite to "entering into relation."[4]

The story in Genesis, of the Fall, I believe, is another way of understanding in what way our awareness of ourselves is involved with — is one and the same as — our awareness of otherness. When man turned from God, and from a consciousness originally at one with the Infinite — the state of "dreaming innocence" as Søren Kierkegaard calls it — when he turned to himself rather than the Absolute as his center and point of reference, he became estranged, alienated from God and "*knew*" himself as separate. The fruit of the tree of knowledge is the source of self-consciousness as we know it. The Fall was a fall into a constricted consciousness, a loss of man's original at-one-with-God consciousness, or what Owen Barfield calls "original participation," so that, as Pascal puts it, "there scarcely remains a dim vision of his Author."[9d] Man became aware of himself as *apart from* the whole and at the same time was awakened to the existence of otherness — the world as distinct from and independent of man was brought into being. Salvation, repentance, then, would consist in these terms, in a "turned" consciousness, or what Owen Barfield calls "final participation," which would not be a return to the Garden of Eden but would reconnect man, in his self-consciousness, to the Infinite, so that he would be aware of himself as *a part of* the whole.

A summary of Coleridge's theses in chapter 12 of the *Biographia* might be useful here, seen against the background of the "Essay on Faith." He says that "we are to seek . . . for some absolute truth which therefore must be immediate and original" and not dependent on any other truth; it must therefore be one that is its own predicate. Such a principle can be neither an object nor a subject then, but "the identity of both." "This principle . . . manifests itself in the *Sum* or I AM," which he equates with spirit and self-consciousness and in this "object and subject, being and knowing are identical" by virtue of the free act of the will of the self or subject "constructing itself objectively to itself." Then "if we elevate our conception to the absolute self, the great eternal I AM, the principle of being, and of knowledge . . . are absolutely identical. . . ." This principle of the coincidence of being and knowing, "subsisting in a will, or primary act of self-duplication is the . . . immediate and direct principle" Coleridge is seeking, and is "found only in the act and evolution of self-consciousness." "We begin with the I know myself, in order to end with the absolute I AM. We proceed from the self, in order to lose and find all self in God." He concludes: "Self-consciousness is not a kind of being but a kind of knowing. . . ." Coleridge has led us, through the counteraction of the two forces, from his original intuition of I am, to Thou art, from the self to the independent world of objects, to the infinite "I AM."

The two contrary forces of the one power underlie all of life, which Coleridge sees as an organic whole. We have so far examined them in the "process of our own self-consciousness" and now we must see them at work in the "living principle," before we can go on to a further consideration of imagination. For, as Abrams points out, the principle of polarity "is not limited to the process of individual consciousness. The same concept serves Coleridge as the root-principle of his cosmogony, his epistemology, and his theory of poetic creation alike."[1a] In the *Theory of Life* Coleridge states that he is looking for an "ultimate principle" of life.[7] The "most comprehensive formula to which life is reducible . . . is the power which discloses itself from within as a principle of unity in the many"; or life can be defined "as the principle of unity in multeity." Finally, he defines it as "the principle of individuation, *or* the power which unites a given all into a whole that is presupposed by all its parts." The "degrees or intensities of life" he considers to "consist in the progressive realization of this tendency."

Moreover, he points out that the tendency toward individuation "cannot be conceived without the opposite tendency to connect . . . to detach, but so as either to retain or to reproduce attachment. . . ." This tendency is the law of "polarity" and life then is the "unity of thesis and antithesis" which unite in a "synthesis." Thus "in the identity of the two counterpowers, life subsists; in their strife, it consists and in their reconciliation it dies, is reborn."

Coleridge then illustrates the operation of the two forces — illustrates the process of life from its simplest to its most complex forms. In the biological sphere, the polarity of unity and individuation operates on the most elemental level as reproductive, as for instance in the division of a cell; on the second level polarity functions as the principle of irritability, as for example in the sensitivity of insects; this then polarizes into the third level, with a predominance of sensibility in mammals and finally, "under the predominance of the third synthetic power, both in the intensity of life and in the intenseness and extension of individuality . . . we may leap forward at once to the highest realization and reconciliation of both . . . [nature's] tendencies, that of the most perfect detachment with the greatest possible union, to that last work," man, in whom the polarization of sensibility results in self-consciousness, at once the highest form of detachment and separation and the highest form of attachment in that his self-consciousness is dependent on the positing of otherness, as we have seen. In man, the "whole force of organic power has attained an inward and centripetal direction. He has the whole world in counterpoint to him, but he contains an entire world within himself. . . . Man . . . is a . . . compendium of nature — the microcosm. Naked and helpless cometh man into the world" . . . but, he says, "we complain of our chief privilege. . . . Nor does the form of polarity, which has accompanied the law of individuation . . . desert it here. . . . The intensities must be at once opposite and equal. As the independence . . . in the same proportion must be . . . the sympathy and the intercommunion with nature. In the conciliating mid-point . . . does the man live, and only by its equal presence in both its poles can that life be manifested."

The important thing for us to understand from Coleridge's theory of life is that he sees all life as one and as the process of interaction of the two contrary forces, one tending to expand infinitely and the other tending toward individuation. This process, which underlies all of life, is also descriptive of the process of mind, on the level of imagination, through which we have access to it — through which we can therefore enter into it. Hence, the conceptual screen that makes a dichotomy of inside and outside is an illusion. The "prejudice" that inner and outer are *dis*connected is no *less* illusion because the disconnection is "visible" than the *connection* of inner and outer is illusion because it is *not* visible!

Coleridge's theory of life is also an explanation of the romantic theory of art. It was, as Abrams says,

revolutionary . . . [although it had ancestors], it was in fact, part of a change in the habitual way of thinking . . . which is as sharp and dramatic as any the history of ideas can show . . . . The basic nature of the shift . . . [is] the result of an analogical substitution — the replacement . . . of a mechanical process by a living plant as the implicit paradigm governing the description of the process and the product of literary invention.[1b]

But it goes deeper than this organic metaphor by attributing a " 'creative' power to man as artist or poet," which although not wholly new had been long forgotten, and it emphasized that, in addition, man must look for the principles of art not outward, in the spirits of nature, but *within ourselves*."[2a] If, as it has been described, it is the time between the Gods — "the No-more of the Gods that have fled and the Not-yet of the god that is coming,"[8a] then man is thrown back on himself and it is the task of art — of the poet — to be the "messenger of the Gods."

Coleridge points out, when speaking of the "indestructible power" whose two forces he refers to as "centrifugal and centripetal," that he "assumes such a power as my principle, in order to deduce from it a faculty," or "instrument" that makes possible the interpenetration of the two contrary forces.[5u] He has accomplished his intention (to return to our beginning) to establish the existence of two distinct faculties and has shown that this division is grounded in life itself. From this follows his well-known definitions of imagination and fancy.

The Imagination then, I consider either as primary, or secondary. The primary Imagination I hold to be the living Power and prime Agent of all human perception, and as a repetition in the finite mind of the eternal act of creation in the infinite I AM. The secondary Imagination I consider as an echo of the former, co-existing with the conscious will, yet still as identical with the primary in the kind of its agency, and differing only in degree and the mode of its operation. It dissolves, diffuses, dissipates, in order to recreate; or where this process is rendered impossible, yet still at all events it struggles to idealize and to unify. It is essentially vital, even as all objects (as objects) are essentially fixed and dead.

Fancy, on the contrary, has no other counters to play with, but fixities and definites. The Fancy is indeed no other than a mode of Memory emancipated from the order of time and space; while it is blended with, and modified by that empirical phenomenon of the will, which we express by the word Choice. But equally with the ordinary memory, the Fancy must receive all its materials ready made from the law of association."[5v]

Let us see if, against the background of what we have already examined, with what understanding we have of Coleridge's philosophical principles, we can elucidate these statements a little. Fancy first: that it plays only with fixities, I take to mean that it uses that to which imagination once gave birth — that is, that which is already fixed and definite. These counters or connected images it recalls as "a mode of memory" — "emancipated from the order of time and space," that is, they are not the product of present, immediate experience — they are chosen from other times and places — and are subject to the law of association according to Aristotle, which we mentioned earlier. For his understanding and use of fancy, Coleridge borrowed from that philosophy the concept of the association of ideas, differing from it fundamentally in the manner of association — that is, in his emphasis on the factor of choice and secondly, but most importantly, on the fundamental original source of the material, the imagination.

Now, as to the imagination: the primary imagination is the faculty and agency by which we unconsciously structure the ever changing ("eternal act of creation") phenomenal world by way of the interaction of the noumenal forces of separative projection and productive unity. I would like to point out, parenthetically, that although I have read much of Coleridge's dependence on Kant's philosophy, I find a significant and fundamental difference, if I understand both Kant and Coleridge correctly. Whereas they both agree that the mind structures the phenomenal world, Kant sees this unification and structuring process as taking place by means of the a priori categories of the mind, which results in a rational, conceptual view of reality and which nullifies the "radical heterogeneity"[12] of the elements of the world. In no way does this process depend on the correspondence of the "inner" and "outer" worlds for Kant. In fact, it is precisely this possibility of knowledge he denies. And it is precisely on this correspondence that Coleridge's theory of the imagination rests. In other words, for Kant the possibility of knowledge depends on the given conditions of the subject — the only constant reality is the a priori categories of the mind; for Coleridge the possibility of knowledge depends on noumenal forces that operate in us as well as in all life. In this respect, as well as in the theory of polarity, Coleridge bears some resemblance to Hegel, but with the marked difference that Hegel's epistemology is based on a correspondence between mind and reality that is a purely logical, rational one.

The secondary imagination "echoes" the former in that it, too, is concerned with construction of the phenomenal world, is identical in kind in that it functions by means of the same principle of polarity, but it is directed by the conscious will and therefore in a higher degree, in that it "operates as a function of that freedom which is the essential attribute of spirit."[11] In the multiplicity that it sees, imagination seeks for new order and unity — it is "esemplastic" — it "dissolves, diffuses and dissipates" old unities and ways of seeing and forms new ones and this it does organically, "*ab intra.*" "It is essentially vital" — that is, its essence is the creative process of life itself.

The secondary imagination "re-creates," renews the world by way of a different "mode" of operation, that is, in the mode of art — art meant in its broadest sense of language, poetry, painting, and the like, which are bridges thrown out toward an invisible shore and which bring new worlds into being. This creative function of the imagination implies art as revelation, and as in Hölderlin's understanding, suggests the poet as the messenger of the gods.[8b] Herein lies the significance and implications of Coleridge's doctrine of imagination and the romantic theory of art. It will mean, according to Owen Barfield, that a new act and disciplined effort of imagination will be necessary to propel the impulse of the romantic movement to the point at which "what was first spoken by God may eventually be respoken by man,"[2b] from "within himself," from his enthusiasm (*entheos*, "God within"). Or we might say, to bring us to the point of knowing that God is One and His names are many.

REFERENCES

1. Abrams, W. H. *The Mirror and the Lamp*. New York: W. W. Norton & Co., 1958, (a) 119; (b) 158.
2. Barfield, O. *Saving the Appearances: A Study in Idolatry*. London: Faber & Faber, 1957, (a) 127-9; (b) 127.
3. ———. *What Coleridge Thought*. Middletown, Conn.: Wesleyan University Press, 1971, (a) 155; (b) 164.
4. Buber, M. "Distance and Relation," *Psychiatry*, Journal for the Study of Interpersonal Processes 20, 2 (May 1957): 97-104.
5. Coleridge, S. T. *Biographia Literaria*. Edited by J. Shawcross. Vol. I. London: Oxford University Press, 1962, (a) 60; (b) 64; (c) 60; (d) ibid.; (e) 71; (f) 73; (g) 81; (h) 89; (i) 90; (j) 94; (k) 173; (l) 164; (m) 167; (n) 173; (o) 174; (p) 178; (q) 179; (r) 196; (s) 197; (t) 198; (u) 188; ibid.; (v) 202.
6. ———. "Essay on Faith." In *Collected Works*, edited by W. G. T. Shedd. New York: Harper & Bros., 1853; vol. V, pp. 557-560.
7. ———. *Hints Towards the Formation of a More Comprehensive Theory of Life*. Edited by S. B. Watson. Philadelphia: Lea & Blanchard, 1848, p. 19ff.
8. Heidegger, M. "Hölderlin and the Essence of Poetry." In *Existence and Being*. Chicago: Henry Regnery Co., 1949, (a) 289; (b) 288-91.
9. Pascal, B. *Pensées*. New York: Dutton & Co., 1958, (a) fr. 581; (b) fr. 1; (c) fr. 72; (d) fr. 430.
10. Richards, I. A. *Coleridge on Imagination*. Bloomington: Indiana University Press, 1960.
11. Warren, R. P. "A Poem of Pure Imagination." In *Selected Essays*. New York: Random House, 1950, p. 207.
12. Wheelwright, P. *The Burning Fountain*. Bloomington: Indiana University Press, 1959, p. 96.

THE UGLY AND THE EVIL

by

CLYDE S. KILBY

> Faustus: What art thou, Mephistopheles?
> Mephistopheles: I am. . . .
> The shadow on the world, thrown by the world
> Standing in its own light, which light God is.
> — Dorothy Sayers
>
> . . . sin, which is disorder.
> — C. I. Scofield

A good deal of art criticism in this century has assumed that a thing is good if it is constructed well and bad, or ugly, if it is not. What I wish here is to attempt a limited comparison of ugliness and metaphysical and moral evil with the object of showing that structure alone is inadequate.

We need hardly suggest that the word *ugly* is a commonplace one. Our language is replete with that and its cognates. On the one hand are words whose prefix suggests a negative derived from a positive value — *deformed, disfigured, unsightly, imperfect, unlovely, misshapen, inelegant, ungainly*. On the other hand are words suggesting some objective, positive quality of ugliness — *blemish, crooked, clumsy, awkward, lumpish, monstrous, grotesque*. But it will not do to push this distinction too far, since *blemish,* for instance, is derived from a German word that means wanting in color.

At first it would appear going out of one's way to suggest that the ugly and the evil are to be discussed together. Let it be said, however, that in the history of aesthetics the inquiry into the nature either of the ugly or the beautiful has unavoidably run into something more than structure. To list such inquiries is for the most part to list the great names in aesthetics, including many contemporary ones.

The simplest explanation is that art is an activity of and for man. The creative impulse and act is well summarized in a few lines written by J. R. R. Tolkien:

> Although now long estranged,
> Man is not wholly lost nor wholly changed.
> Dis-graced he may be, yet is not de-throned,
> and keeps the rags of lordship once he owned:

> Man, Sub-creator, the refracted Light
> through whom is splintered from a single White
> to many hues, and endlessly combined
> in living shapes that move from mind to mind. . . .

and concluding with the remarkably comprehensive line,

> we make still by the law in which we're made.[15]

If the whole man, the man *imago Dei*, is involved then a larger perspective is inevitable.

Two or three illustrations will, I hope, enable us to proceed more exactly. The example of a forest destroyed by fire suggests an instance of ugliness to which most people will agree. Yet we can hardly say that a forest fire wholly obliterates either objective form or color. Whereas the predominant color before the fire was green, the predominant color now is black. The remaining trunks of trees and unconsumed underbrush show that form has not disappeared, and there may be a certain amount of uncovering of theretofore unseen form such as hidden stones or the contour of the ground. It might even be claimed that only our prejudice from observing green forests causes us to fail to see the beauty of the burned forest and that no ugliness exists after all. We can, it might be argued, make the very same observations of beauty in the burned forest as in the natural one.

But the ugliness of the burned forest, if we agree that indeed it is ugly, must take account of something else than sensuous proportions and arrangements. This ugliness is less in its appearance than in its very nature as forest. We have to ask what the true nature and being of a forest is, to see its ugliness in ontological terms. We have to consider the forest both "in itself" and in its exhaustive content. We may even need to see it as symbol. In itself, a forest is characterized by the principle of growth, of which greenness is both a scientific fact and at least something of a symbol. A forest is maligned, upset, and deformed when burned. This is one sense in which a burned forest may properly be called ugly.

In a deeper sense still a green and thriving forest is beautiful not alone simply as forest but also as an example of purposiveness throughout nature, of created life, of growth and becoming and "aspiration" rather than death, stasis, and essential "nothingness." In a word, the healthy forest signifies meaning, the burned forest also meaning but meaning of a negative and recusant sort. Form is there actually de-formed.

Consider two other illustrations, one "below" and the other "above" that of the forest, say an automobile and a human being. However streamlined, shapely, and glossy a new auto, we should hardly consider it beautiful if we found it had no engine, transmission, or electrical system. Since an automobile is primarily "for" transportation, its appearance must of necessity be secondary. Its "being" is inner as well as outer. Perhaps we could add that there is an "oughtness" involved — an automobile ought to be handsome but above everything else it ought to be capable of transporting passengers. Even the outward appearance has function also. It is streamlined to avoid wind resistance and its glossy finish serves to protect the body from rust, so that in a strict sense beauty could hardly be claimed for it at all.

In a human being outward appearance becomes less significant than inner quality and meaning. We have all had the experience of knowing someone of physical charm whose inner being as manifest in conduct was sufficient largely to negate outward comeliness. Plain lack of intelligence — being "beautiful but dumb" — may do the same.

Whether it be an automobile, a forest, or a human being, it seems apparent that beauty involves both outward form and inner essence. In the first we call the beauty little more than mechanically functional. In the second function is a less appropriate word, since nature is unique and possesses "being." When we come to a human being, function in the sense applied to the automobile or even to the forest is quite inadequate. To the mechanical and physical must be added another dimension. The saying that beauty is only skin deep is an oversimplification, and of course the same applies to ugliness. Homely people often turn out to be, on real acquaintance, gloriously beautiful.

The problem of beauty and ugliness would apparently be solved if we could hold up two clear examples, one of absolute beauty and the other of absolute ugliness and make them the measure of judgment. The extent, then, to which anything manifested ideal form or total ugliness could be determined. All efforts to discover such a measure gravitate in the direction of metaphysics and the genuinely true nature of man himself.

Jacques Maritain believed that beautiful things belong to the order of transcendentals and are beautiful not alone by manifest form but by a beauty in and from God. "He is the most beautiful of beings, because, as Denys the Areopagite and St. Thomas explain, His beauty is without alteration or vicissitude, without increase or diminution. . . . He is beautiful by Himself and in Himself, absolutely beautiful."[5] Significant as this assertion may be as a center for the organization of our thoughts about aesthetics, it leaves us without the utilitarian measurement we wish for to judge the beauty and ugliness daily about us.

Maritain is thinking of absolute beauty. What of absolute ugliness? It would be good if we were able simply to reverse the principle of beauty and say that ugliness resides in a Satanic nonform and nonunity. Ugliness, however, may be as well organized as beauty. A bank robbery may manifest a finesse that is admirably integrated. The process of a disease germ that destroys its possessor is as well organized as that of the millions of desirable germs that protect our bodies.

To assume that Satan is ugly is in the first place to deny a good deal of Scripture, for there we learn that he appeared among the sons of God, that he is a prince, able to put on the form of an angel of light, and able to think shrewdly and consistently, and such as Milton describes, "Pleasing was his shape/and lovely."[7] In fact, Satan appears to be as "organized," as integrated, and in form as beautiful as God.[3] (The structural similarity of beauty and ugliness, of God and Satan, reminds us of the Scriptural emphasis on the deceptiveness of sin. There is a saying that the best things when corrupted become the worst — *corruptio optima pessima* — and what pride is more abominable than religious pride?)

Only two antitheses to beauty have been suggested. One is an ugliness that is organized, positive, and meaningful, as in the case of Satan provided we believe that his appearance only is beautiful but that his moral and metaphysical essence, while completely organized, consistent, and systematically and harmoniously intricate nevertheless possesses all these characteristics to an evil and ugly purpose. He possesses them to the sole end of making chaotic the beauty and purposiveness of God. Thus we should have, aesthetically, a sort of beautiful ugliness. The other proposed antithesis to absolute beauty is the ugliness of total formlessness, total unmeaning, total nothingness, total illusion.

Randall Stewart reminds us that this view is one of the theological errors of Ralph Waldo Emerson, that in him there is "no conflict, in the strict sense, between good and evil because evil is mere negation, a minus quantity, no struggle between God and the Devil because the Devil is a 'nonentity,' that is, he does not exist."[14] As evil entails not the absence of anything (though of course it may entail neglect), ugliness involves not absence of nothingness but positive and "beautiful" outward form with an inner metaphysical being in antipathy to beauty.

In other words, we must apparently assume both beauty and ugliness to possess form in some manner analogous to the positive reality of goodness and evil. The thorns and thistles identified with man's Fall have as much reality — and, in their way, even beauty — as wheat and grapes. One's profoundest beliefs and insights must play a part in aesthetics because Scripture itself teaches that God and Satan are both aesthetic "objects." In the Renaissance, when men believed in Satan much more than today, Satan was often depicted in plastic and literary art. John Milton has been accused of making Satan the real hero of *Paradise Lost*, and one will not deny that Satan there acts aesthetically, that is, acts a completely organized part. He hates on a magnificent scale and performs in the same way. In Milton, as in the Scriptures, he is anything but a nonentity. But because his entire being and essence are wholly selfish and thus antithetical to God, he is not beautiful but rather "absolutely" ugly. He appears as an angel of light, but it is a total disguise.

The question arises whether we do not commend and take aesthetic delight in anything for being what it purports to be, for being its unique self alone and possessing no aspect of "otherness" or affectation. This is undoubtedly one of the reasons for the pleasing quality of genuine art. It celebrates the individuality of even humble and commonplace objects, making them not less but more themselves in their true being. Is there not a close analogy between the metaphysical and the moral, each appealing in its way to a sense of oughtness within us? The business of so prosaic a thing as a square is to be square, so that an unsquare square is not alone an anomaly but upsetting to some deep urge within us that says it is not what it ought to be.

It is of course absurd to suppose this of a square in a vacuum, so to speak, but man is so constituted that he cannot be completely sure where his symbolism leaves off. "A white lily is not morally pure, since it is not morally characterizable at all but it would be hard to find just what the meaning of moral purity is, if we cannot picture it or think of it in any aesthetic terms whatever."[10]

But cannot Satan be said to possess beauty in the sense of being what he purports to be? Once again his personal essence is against him and he becomes ugly by virtue of being the arch deceiver of the universe. His deception is neither to identify beauty nor goodness but rather to misidentify them. Milton has shown how magnificently Satan imitates God's own glories, and Ezekiel suggests that it was the very beauty of Satan that caused his heart to be proudly lifted up against God. The inmost intent and secret of Satan's imitation is that God's beauty may become ashes and God's righteousness chaos.

I have been attempting mainly to point out the possible antitheses of absolute beauty and absolute ugliness. While this is of necessity theoretical in comparison to the principles of practiced aesthetics, it has, I believe, an important bearing upon certain trends in art and particularly modern art. If what I have said is true, it appears that the art process — I shall not say genuine art — may be used to pervert after the devil's own fashion, that is, all the technical skill and engagingness of art may deliberately be applied to the perversion of good and to the creation of chaos and evil. We see this particularly in under-the-counter pornography as well as in a good deal that is above the counter.

And here we need to distinguish also from the immoral or athetistic artist who produces true art. Every man is *imago Dei* and the nature and "calling" of art may surmount personal defects. Here I mean a devilish-minded artist who lends himself consciously to a work like Satan's. Félicien Rops seems to be an artist in whom the erotic interest takes on at times a Satanic aspect, yet Rops is equally capable of the piercing religious symbol as in his *Satan Semant l'Ivraie*. He can also paint the simple exquisiteness of nature, as in his *Sous-Bois en Automne*.

The attempt to draw analogies between the creativity of God and that of man is precarious, but carefully practiced can yield some valuable insights. I want particularly to mention one such analogy that appears to be the explanation of a difficult aspect of aesthetics. How is it that we delight in the artistic representation of images that actually seen would create loathing and nausea? I mean such pictures as the head of John the Baptist brought in on a salver. A human head is one of the most beautiful things in creation, but a head severed from the body is hideous and becomes more so when the pallor of death has settled on it. The same is true for the innumerable paintings of the body of Christ on the Cross, and we can add such literary themes as Medea's slaying of her own children, the murder of Macbeth, and the like. If art is intended to identify genuine reality, how is it that we are not sickened rather than delighted by such paintings and dramatic situations? How can a Christian in particular literally wish for the fall of a tragic hero? How can we call such art pleasurable and even inspirational? In other words, how can ugliness gain entrance to the structure of beauty?

The most satisfying explanation of this paradox is derived from the analogy of God's sovereignty despite evil. Sin is revolting to the nature of God in a way similar to the manner in which ugliness is revolting to the nature of beauty. Yet art's province, like God's, is universal, and it is concerned with a unified rather than a dualistic world. It therefore cannot limit itself simply to the beautiful any more than God takes account of goodness and ignores evil. Art faces the great paradox as decidedly as theology. To assume that it does not is to allow it little more than prettiness and sentimentality.

As God, by His sovereignty, is able to reconcile so evil an event as Christ's death on the Cross, as well as the multitudinous willful acts of sinful man, so art sovereignly reconciles ugliness, not alone "accounting" for it but, even as God makes the wrath of man to praise Him, transfigures ugliness into the region of beauty. As the devil himself is not outside God's sovereignty, so the ugliness of Medea's infanticide is not outside art's sovereignty. Great art does not dismiss ugliness as unreal any more than God dismisses evil as unreal or as mere negation. On the contrary, by fully accounting for — "redeeming" — their reality in one world whose center of gravity is positive, theological and beautiful, it represents or identifies ugliness as what by its inner essence it really is. By transfiguring ugliness, beauty makes ugliness not beautiful but truly ugly. The artist makes the lamb lie down with the lion without erasing the essential reality of either.

Genuine art is not about soft, pretty things and playful experiences carefully extracted from the actual world, any more than God is a senile grandfather who wants His children to look upon sin as something to be ignored. There is no dualism and indeed no extraneous parts, nothing unaccounted for, in God's cosmos, and the same is true in aesthetics. St. Augustine believed that sin, when punished, becomes a part of the beauty of God. Ugliness does not barely squeeze into the realm of art by some drastic flight of the imagination or some straining of the artistic process but enters as fully as beauty itself. If ugliness is as prevalent in the world as evil, then art would hardly be worth talking about were it to take account only of the beautiful.

We can understand, however, how the ugly might be described as a negation or partial failure of the beautiful, particularly at the level of practiced creativity. Leonard Bernstein describes the various trials made by Beethoven in getting a composition exactly right, a process that would have been outlandish and unnecessary except that some trials were less "beautiful" than others, and of course if less beautiful then uglier. Mark Twain remarked that the difference between "the almost-right word and the right word is . . . the difference between the lightning-bug and the lightning."[1] The art of literature is the art of the right word. Hence the wrong word is the ugly one. Dorothy Sayers says that the act of choosing the right word for a given situation makes every other word in the dictionary the wrong word, its wrongness being contingent upon the rightness of the one chosen.

She goes on to say that the poet in choosing precisely the right word thereby of necessity creates a "wrongness" in the words not chosen. "In making a good which did not exist before he has simultaneously made an evil which did not exist before."[12] Thus by analogy she accounts for evil without charging it to God. She believed that when Shakespeare created *Hamlet* he unavoidably "created" a Not-Being, that is, Not-Hamlet. Thus God could "create" non-being, that is, evil, by bringing good into existence, because "the Good, by merely occurring, automatically and inevitably creates its corresponding Evil."[12] Milton C. Nahm, after a thorough discussion of the historical and philosophical aspects of the ugly, concludes that ugliness is not defect, negation, or privation but that "ugliness is necessary for the conflict of contraries which produces the aesthetic object."[8] If the right word, the right musical tone, the right line and color is the genuine that by its genuineness makes all others for that particular situation or idea untrue, false and ugly, it will be clear that beauty and truth are drawing graciously together.

Ben Shahn declares that he never met a critic who, no matter how he deprecated a work of art, would wish to destroy it. "But," he adds, "the critic within the artist is a ruthless destroyer."[13] The search for the right word or other artistic element puts upon the artist an almost unbearable burden. That condition is inadequately described as technical. It is a burden heavy, among other things, with oughtness. Ugliness, says Stephen C. Pepper, "is moral disapproval of the absence of esthetic value in a situation. It is an ethical rather than an esthetic evaluation. But this moral judgment is very close to the esthetic."[9] George Santayana says, "The absence of aesthetic goods is a moral evil."[11] The square ought really to be a square, not an approximation.

In closing I wish to make several brief observations. One is that when ugliness is considered analogous to evil, all claims for the strict autonomy of art fly out the window. The likelihood of art as a dissociated phenomenon simply disappears and art remains inevitably life-related. This does not mean, of course, that we shall not wish to keep art what it purports to be, that is, art, for when it becomes philosophy, ethics, or plain sentiment, it ceases to be art. Its wish to remain "pure" is a perfectly legitimate desire so long as art avoids asceticism for its own sake. A few modern artists declare they do not want the public to understand or appreciate them. It is this sort of pride that can hardly be afforded.

Secondly, there is an interesting analogy between the freedom of the artist and the freedom of God. One of the outstanding facts of Scripture is the freedom allowed by God to man, even the freedom to deny His reality. It is accompanied by the paradox of sovereignty and everlasting love. The artist likewise gives his creations a "body as it pleaseth him," yet a body in which the full selfhood of the creation resides. Although his materials may resist him, he persuades or loves them into capitulation and, in any case, never allows the ugliness to destroy the unity of his "sovereignty." He produces meaning according to and despite his materials. The freedom consists of the object and its shadow, a unity accounted for by both God and the artist. Even in conversion the obstreperous and mixed or ugly nature of the "object" cannot be avoided. It is a common experience of Christians to recollect, years afterwards, with amazement and shame the incompleteness, on their part, of their understanding of all that was involved.

Thirdly, though ugliness apparently existed before Creation (in the void and formless chaos), it is evident not only that God intended to remove it by His great creative act but also that His plans eventuate in a church "without spot or wrinkle or any such thing . . . holy and without blemish,"[2] and also a time when Satanic ugliness will be universally acknowledged.

Fourthly, the bringing of the world into existence out of chaos was itself the greatest aesthetic act of all history and justifies us in declaring God's antagonism to ugliness as well as evil. We cannot fail specifically to notice the assertions of the first portion of the book of Genesis that God saw His creation to be good and pleasant in His sight.

Fifthly, the beauty of Jesus Christ is the great illustration of the fact that outward form is lesser than inner being. We are told that He had no "form or comeliness . . . no beauty that we should look at him."[4] The woman at Jacob's well, for instance, apparently saw nothing special about Him until after He began talking to her. Yet the Scriptures present Him as the fulness of every virtue and the essence of all holiness. In this truer sense of the beautiful, He is the "rose of Sharon" and the "lily of the valleys." Says François Mauriac in *The Son of Man*:

Undoubtedly He was like many people whose beauty, at once very secret and very striking, dazzled some and escaped others; this is especially true when beauty is of the spiritual order. . . . When we are in love, we are often surprised by the indifference others show to the face which, for us, sums up all the splendor of the world.[6]

REFERENCES

1. Bainton, G. *Art of Authorship*. New York: Appleton Century Crofts, 1890, pp. 87-88.
2. Ephesians 5:27.
3. Ezekiel 28:17.
4. Isaiah 53:2.
5. Maritain, J. *Art and Scholasticism*. New York: Charles Scribner's Sons, 1947, pp. 24-25.
6. Mauriac, F. *The Son of Man*. Cleveland: The World Publishing Company, 1958, p. 65.
7. Milton, J. *Paradise Lost*, IX, 503-4.
8. Nahm, M. C. *The Artist as Creator*. Baltimore, Maryland: Johns Hopkins University Press, 1956, p. 124.
9. Pepper, S. C. *The Basis of Criticism in the Arts*. Cambridge, Mass.: Harvard University Press, 1949, p. 58.
10. Prall, D. W. *Aesthetic Judgment*. New York: Thomas Y. Crowell Co., 1929, p. 305.
11. Santayana, G. *The Sense of Beauty*. New York: Charles Scribner's Sons, 1936, p. 39.
12. Sayers, D. *The Mind of the Maker*. New York: Meridian Books, 1941, pp. 102-4.
13. Shahn, B. *The Shape of Content*. Cambridge, Mass.: Harvard University Press, 1957, p. 34.
14. Stewart, R. *American Literature and Christian Doctrine*. Baton Rouge: Louisiana State University Press, 1958, p. 47.
15. Tolkien, J. R. R. *Tree and Leaf*. London: George Allen & Unwin Ltd., 1964, p. 49.

THE VESSEL AND THE FIRE

by

MARY CAROLINE RICHARDS

for Owen Barfield

This essay began in a time of acute personal encounter with fear, guilt, and woe. It was a time of inner war between anxious dependency and a resolve to change and grow, between a part of me that was in its death agonies and a part of me willing to be born. It seemed to me that the path to peace was through experiencing the conflict and coming to know the adversaries more compassionately. Perhaps a new relationship would form between them. The sense of an "I" within the *me* was quickening. This proved to be important new ground. A picture of human being as vessel, separable from her life-contents, arose. This was a fulcrum, a midpoint: a person who mingles with her life in spiritual dialogue, as co-worker. Because this marks a stage in the evolution of my own consciousness, it seems appropriate to offer it here. Owen Barfield, in his book *Poetic Diction*, first taught me how "the word" divides its meanings after a primal union, how prose and poetry separate, and how poetic imagination now reintegrates the opposites as they have evolved. What follows is an abbreviated rendering of a similar necessity that may occur in living life. Its themes — of war, peace, and violence — reverberate in society.

Metaphors of separating and connecting are felt vividly in the world scene and the individual scene. While crossing this threshold in my own life, I could see that it was an objectively real and common threshold — like that of puberty. Except that this one, crossed later, confronts us with precisely that image of ourselves that is most unacceptable to our daily conscious ego: *the shadow*. The shadow stands there, guardian of the threshold. It is more than one can bear. If one steps through, and faithfully tries to develop a living commitment with one's inner enemy, it will be followed by other steps and births, and transformations, on the inner life line.

This journey may consist in large part of getting to know one's inner family: for example the fearful child, the scornful brother, the sorceress, the fanatical seeker, the possessive parent, who stand in the shadow and create difficulties. Through the years I have struggled to know and to embrace the different members who have spoken to me through dreams or introspection. Gradually there have emerged a motley crew. An inner friend has joined them. Perhaps because I have sought a mothering feminine being as well, such a person has recently appeared in my inner world: a womanly friend and teacher, standing in a group of children with her arm around the shoulders of myself, a four year old, who is looking up at her with beseeching anxious eyes. Both speak in me: the hungry child and the steadying affection of a good mother. At last I have hopes for that worried little girl: here is someone now who respects her and loves her as she is, shadow and all, and who spends time with her; she may begin to feel the love in her own heart, to relax, to play, and to grow.

Inner development may be measured by an ability to be peaceably at war, neither victorious nor defeated.

It is apparent, both individually and socially, that even as we say we favor peace, we, in fact, wage war. Are we hypocrites? Are we insane? No I do not think so. Let us trust the facts of life and be guided by them. This paradox may express a wisdom, if we listen to it dispassionately. If we do not, we may continue to murder our way through life in order that good may prevail.

For in this paradox lie two opposites: the need to fight and the need to love, both. The need for antipathy, the need to say NO; and the need for sympathy, to say YES. To separate; to connect. The reservations we may feel in our body as we brace ourselves against the fearful NO frequently have as their counterpart the reservations we may feel in our body during an intimate YES. There appears to be a physical connection between our ability to bear the tension of conflict and the release of surrender.

Nature tells us we are self-directing, self-correcting organisms, who function therefore by a dynamic of polarities: in-breathing and out-breathing, sleeping and waking, expanding and contracting; seeking balance. Our inner development as persons comes about as we are able to bear the wholeness of these opposites, to experience them as mutually completing, as interdependent and interpenetrating, in some sense simultaneous. To see them, in other words, as ALIVE, AND MOVING, AND INTERWEAVING. Like the distinct and yet interflowing rivers that course through the oceans.

War and peace are both necessities *in what they represent*. Can we have them at the same time? Can we experience conflict and the easing of conflict so that they do not eliminate one another? As soon as we become aware of others, we come into the possibility of external conflict. As soon as we become self-aware, we face inner conflict. We are continuously "at war" with others and with ourselves. But we wish to live "in peace." What's to be done?

Can we imagine a kind of peace that includes the freedom to conflict, a kind of warmth that includes the freedom to withdraw, a kind of union that asks for free and unique individualities, a kind of good that grants the mystery of evil, a kind of life that bears death within it like a seed force?

Perhaps the following picture will help toward this imagination. I had a dream in which a tremendous fire was burning clear across the full length of the horizon. It was moving toward the house where I lived. A woman neighbor and I packed our suitcases and ran away. One person remained behind, he did not run away. He was a friend, the director of a craft school where I sometimes teach in real life. This friend remained, and the fire swept through the landscape, through the house, through the pottery vessels, through the person. I could see it flaming and coursing through everything; but nothing was consumed! After the fire had swept through, I returned, and the director said, "Everything is still here. Only the color is deepened." And it was so. He was intact, and the pots were there, transformed.

The color is deepened!

When color deepens, it adds both darkness and light to itself; it contains more color. Goethe said that color is "the sufferings of light." *The sufferings of light!* That is, what light undergoes, what *we* undergo; as vessels, we are deepened by our capacities for darkness and for light. It is an inner light that wakes in the lustrous stone. It is our darkness, our guilt and guile and greed and hopelessness, that, undergone like a fire, may flame through our consciousness, through our sense of ourselves, deepening our capacities, changing into colored light. Though we may feel annihilated in the process, we are intact.

For war and peace are dispositions of the will. We cannot move our limbs without an inner will to do so. Whatever we do, we in some sense want to do. Whatever happens is prepared for by the voice of nature in the unconscious. It is only ignorance of this voice that enables us to say, "I didn't want to hurt you." We do not know the forces driving us. If we want to create our lives rather than to be their victims, we must inform ourselves about what may be happening on the inside. It is for this reason that self-knowledge is so important. We have to come into life *from the inside*.

Since our will is almost completely unconscious (I am not speaking of wilfulness here, but rather of the deep motivations of our behavior), self-knowledge is difficult to attain. We know little about the world that lives in us: what beings and powers weather us. With what mixed feelings we may discover that the part we play in Art and Beauty and Love is Lucifer's mask. How hard to relinquish the earnest masks of Professional Success, Technical Refinement, and Contempt for Weakness, should they turn out to be not our own faces, but the Adversary's.

The world is a living organism, visible and invisible, of enormous complexity, deep feeling, overwhelming fertility, will-forces so formidable that they maintain the stars in their orbits and the cells in their relationships and the babyhood of mercy surviving in the human jungle. The nuclear bomb everyone is so impressed with *begins* in every cell in our bodies. We sense intuitively the power we have to oppress whoever gets in the way of our dominant self-image. Whoever gets in the way of our conceit and our ambition, our despair. Whoever is our "enemy." The one whom we have not embraced: the enemy is the one with whom we have not surrendered. It follows us everywhere, sleeping and waking, like a shadow.

How shall we come to the condition where we embrace our wretchedness and guilt and woe? Not approve of it, EMBRACE it. How fill with warmth our weakness and deformity and need? How love our foulness, lie down with our leper? When will we be human enough to let the childish demanding self come to the table, to befriend her, patiently to come to understand her soul experiences, to let her be herself, and not to have to carry the burden of our reproaches? When will the loving soul in each of us reach out to comfort the shaky trembling twisted ego? Twisting and turning and telling jokes and shooting 'em up. . . .

Conflict and the easing of conflict is a process through which our human nature may develop. Conflict is a tension between contrary impulses: for instance, the desire to be free and the desire to belong; the desire to be mobile and the desire to be rooted. Guilt is the sensation of an unwillingness to be in conflict; it is the sensation of being accused of being who one is, of being separate and apart and different. And probably unacceptable? Man is born innocent of conflict, innocent of individuation yet to come. Therefore man is born guilty! Childish innocence is unaware of the opposing forces in life. The love it wants leaves no place for the privacies of others. It can be made to feel guilty when an authority requires not only obedience but inner compliance, asking that conflict be repressed rather than celebrated.

Adults tend to feel guilty when they are unwilling to express their strength, which would bring them into conflict with others. They may be unwilling to be at war openly, especially with those they care for. By avoiding conflict, they may think they will be at peace. We may find out different when we abdicate from ourselves to avoid war. We may gain not peace, but duplicity and outbreaks of violence.

Why are we afraid of engaging our strength in the battles of life, the battles for life? Afraid of our energy? Afraid of the power that is in us? Perhaps for good reason. For this is not merely a personal fear, it is as it were a divine fear. We cannot handle our power. We tend to be overwhelmed by it, misuse it, abuse it, waste it. The gifts of fear, shame, impotence disarm us. By fighting the inner battles that our fear and guilt bring us, we become able to bear the power that is ours — when the natural violence of our self-will surrenders in love with its weeping shadow, the power sweetens and reforms, taking on the quality of Person, of Vessel, of Being a part of Being, active and attuned. The dark side of life bears the seeds of light. Perhaps this is why we are advised to consent to the evil in ourselves and in others, and at the same time to struggle with it.

"Resist not evil." And yet, "If thine eye offend thee, pluck it out." What is evil but one-sidedness. . . .

The sensation that may feel like guilt, like self-accusation, is the sensation of becoming a separate person, no longer identified with the lover, the parent, the brother and sister, the group of friends, the place, the time, the society. A separate and unique and unknown being into whom our consciousness has barely penetrated, just far enough to feel the cold winds blow. Chill, self-doubt, shame — these are signs that separateness has soon to be acknowledged, and that the conflict, the drama, is about to begin. We may be anxious and bewildered because some part of us may have no wish to be separate, and yet there is someone in us who is moving and growing as if by inner laws. We may have no wish to grow up, to grow old, to become the senior citizens, the elders of the tribe, and yet there is this law that bears us forward continuously in time. We may have no wish to die, and yet there is this necessity. The "parent" in us afflicts us with guilt as we prepare to take our freedom upon ourselves, as we prepare to "leave home." Perhaps this inner parent too needs to become less possessive of her children?

Conflict and pain are part of the fire of life. They must not be killed. Conflict is an energetic form — it is the way things work. How may we understand this and use it creatively in our lives? We begin by understanding that conflict and pain are not personal, any more than sexuality and old age are personal. What becomes personal is the way we relate to them, how we use them to create our vessel. How we learn from them to deepen our humanity.

When we disentangle our personal emotions from our powers of perception, we see that there is a kind of *play* between inner forces as they struggle in the depths and slowly work their way toward consciousness. There is a *dialogue* between the impulses growing toward independence and those growing toward relationship. There is a questioning and answering, an offering and a resisting. These living processes keep the play alive. We must respect them.

It is not a matter of changing human nature so that it can experience the transformation of its power and the wisdom in its pain. It is a matter of discovering our inner capacities. Voyages of discovery tend to be uncomfortable and perilous and lengthy. We commit ourselves to an unfolding mystery. We may be less ready then to grab at immediate goals. (Mystery may take time, and civilization praises quick results.) And we carefully remember how important we individually can be to each other in such an undertaking.

On a voyage of discovery, we look for possibilities. We cultivate a kind of openness of attitude, a wonder and caution combined. Our patterns of behavior become more flexible, our systems are organic routes. Above all, we cultivate an art of surrender, for we know the new reality must lead us into itself; we do not define it in advance. We look for surprises, knowing we may find our destination very different from what we have supposed.

Surrender is strenuous: *active* surrender. It is an inner activity by which we may enter intimately into the innerness of that which is different from ourselves, from our conscious everyday mind. This is why making love is called surrendering. To come into deep mingling contact with the one who is not us. Not to lose ourselves, but to surrender ourselves. And when we thus make love to life, it flows into our souls as from our beloved. Deepening our color. The flush of the fire.

To enter into the conflict, to feel its spiritual contours from the inside, to be unseparated from it, not to resist. To enter into the resistance, from the inside; not to fake it, not to withhold. To surrender to the whole truth, to become its countenance, not to conceal. For truth will crawl out of all the crevasses, like tiny lichen or blades of grass out of the coldness of stone, and it will with its tiny ray split our foundations apart. The very stuff of existence will bear witness however diligently we work to stifle its cry. (All the truths we do not tell cry loudly through the halls of our being, and echo into the world through our tone of voice, the expression in our eyes, our choice of dress.)

The act of surrender does not get a good press in our culture. Perhaps the reason is that we are in the throes of an individuation process that makes surrender seem threatening. Or it may be a regression: since to surrender to something, we have to be willing to feel its separateness from us. Witness the symptoms of sexual impotence and frigidity, which are unwillingness to surrender. Witness the pursuit of the "high," which tends to make surrender a reflex. The pretensions of the loner: touch me not; I believe in half measures!

The most popular curse is taken from the sexual act, which, ideally, is a sacrament of mutual surrender. Like so many other things in our age, it indicates how unconsciously we live by the power principle. F— you means "I reject you, I reject your power." If we say that a person has been "f—" or "screwed," we mean that he has been humiliated. It is evident that the art of surrendering one's inner being in a transmuting experience of one another that deepens our color, is not part of the popular image of lovemaking. But the truth is that the delirium of the orgasm itself is crude when we know something of inner rapture.

Surrender is actually a concentration of inner power through the process of yielding: yielding in the sense that a plant *yields* seed. The gain of the seed is the loss of the flower, which withers as the ovary develops. Surrender gains an inner substance that cannot leave us. It will invest the future as the spirit of the plant within the seed does.

Thus sexual commitment may be a deep and powerful and for-keeps kind of experience. For when one's intimate personal being is awakened in a sexual embrace and surrenders to its beloved in trust, a birth takes place in a spiritual realm. There is an alteration in the lifeline. It is bound with the fate of the psyche itself. When one's consciousness lives deep in the tissues like this, deep in the spirit-light of the blood, deep in the will that turns thus to the beloved as lungs turn toward the air, one's commitment is much more than personal.

In fact, this is part of why surrender is so at the heart of the human being. For surrender to love is more than surrender to another person of the same natural order as oneself. The human act of love is an expression of a deeper surrender — a relation to a being of love, or a power of love, in the world, entrusted to us. It is an awesome trust.

Human beings are inspired by serving a purpose larger than themselves. This is one reason why sexual love works so well to entice us. (Like . . . why . . flowers are so beautiful and smell so sweet: to attract bees — a purpose larger than their own existence! Larger than our pleasure in them!) For the period that passion and fascination endure, we feel ourselves supported by a larger purpose, a larger wholeness, our lives have meaning, we seem to have some function after all, to labor on behalf of the love that has been entrusted to us. Then the mood changes, and the "show" of love has the opportunity to evolve into conscious relationship, faithful in sickness and in health, for richer for poorer, in all the ups and downs of moods and conflicts. It is no trick to love when one is "in love," or in a state of innocence — there is no freedom there. One is free to love in the moment when one *falls out*, awakes from the spell, sees the other person nakedly, sees oneself, and reconfirms the union on behalf of the Love Whom one serves. It is an initiation, into conscious relationship, a necessity that awaits us as our soul's enterprise just as loving kingship awaits the amorous prince. It is the sacrifice of unconsciousness for separateness. At this moment devotion becomes possible. And when one reaches this moment, commitment to love is a serious matter indeed, rooted as it is in the very organism of one's spiritual self-awareness. Love of others quickens in the birth of the self. The capacity for loneliness and the capacity for love are counterparts in the human heart.

Peace can be thought of as a fusing of the opposites. It overcomes the one-sidedness of violence. For violence is a quality of natural energy when it is seized by its own fire and blind to consequences. (But the energies of violence are glorious and useful. The fires burning in us: our natural drives, our libido, raging in us. Like the great fires in the smelting furnaces or pottery kilns, or the glassblower's fire, the forge. The blinding desert storms, the cruel sun, cataracts. The slow stubborn relentless violence of falling snow, inch after inch, foot after foot, covering EVERYTHING, EVERYTHING.) When we harness and transform it, violence lights up a continent.

In the psyche, violence creates trauma: consciousness breaks down. We lose our memories; we become deaf, dizzy, disoriented, disorganized, non-functioning. A violent emotional experience pulverizes us in the same way that an avalanche or flood dissolves the structures of a lively town. But transformed from a ravaging force into a capacity for feeling, it is our warmth, it is our caring. It is the smile and touch that bless. It is our tears. It makes all the difference. And when it blows wildly and yet may be contained, it fills the forms of life with inspiration.

We can feel the energy that is in us. We can feel the violence, the thrust, the passion and its disregard. It is like a great horse we may learn to ride. To give direction to, to rein in. Yet to be carried by, where otherwise we could never go. It is a part of ourselves that we can understand if we pay attention to it and come into human relation with it. It can serve us if we serve it in a wise way, sensitive to the inner laws of how things work. Willing to listen, willing to be taught, through the inner ear. It is a trustworthy symptom of one-sidedness. Violence is self-absorbed and cannot surrender. We cannot surrender our power until we have ceased to identify with it. We can do this by allowing to arise into the inner ear, the voice of its opposite. Rage harkens to pity.

There is another violence than the hot gush that spills where it spills or the massive withholding. Another violence that neither spills forward nor locks, but regresses, demanding that there be no differences between us. For there is not only the forward movement of evolving consciousness, but a resistance to it. The claim that to get on together we have to be like each other, can be found in the columns of literary criticism, politics, art gangs, and personal relationships. At the level of gossip or tourism, differences are charming. In community, they discomfit. This is not a moral issue, it is how the energy works. When persons and experiences begin to differentiate, to separate and become individualized, this movement is felt as anxiety. Anxiety is the labor pains of consciousness.

When a new country begins to assert its own identity, to break away from "the parent," violence breaks out. When a new child moves into the neighborhood, violence breaks out until he is accepted. When we extend ourselves into a new vocation, violence breaks out: we burst into tears, are a prey to doubt, are aggressively confident and talk of nothing but our plans — the violence and disregard take many forms. We are going through a deep energy change, a spiritual change, and we are producing symptoms.

It is like when a baby starts to be made. The egg and sperm have been separate. Suddenly they come together, wham. Then the new union begins to differentiate: it divides into two cells, four cells, and the parts of the body begin to develop, the functions, the whole new being begins to be created in the physical plane by operations so extraordinary in their wisdom that we do not yet understand how it all works. It takes nine months for a tiny baby to get ready to come out into the air. Before, it's been all fluid and dark and cozy. Then wham, down the canal, out into the light, the umbilical cord cut, you think there is no violence there? For mother and child alike? Such violence that the tiny baby shrieks and the mother often goes into depression. These are reactions to *division*. To *separation*. Our shrieks bear important messages if we have ears to hear from the inside.

During labor, if we hold our breath, we will cut ourselves off. I find that if I exhale into the pain and anxiety and woe, I am able to contain it. To contain it is to honor it, to be its vessel so that it may perform its work. The bearing of pain is part of expanding consciousness, it is an inner discipline and need not lead to self-pity or isolation. It is, actually, like bearing any pure experience: pure sweetness, pure salt, pure air, it's all too much to bear. One exhales and thus is carried into the mystery organically.

We do not need to go with every gust of energy that rises naturally in us. We do not need to follow every lust. We can stay still, containing it. But the violence needs to be felt and handled. Lust is part of nature and can become a resource: it is like changing the form of energy from an erupting volcano to a diamond needle. For are not volcanoes and diamonds different stages in the same fiery process?

The invisible inner world is as specific in its contours as is the outer physical world. As our sense organs are adapted to the physical world, so inner spiritual organs perceive the supersensible world. We cannot know ourselves *from the inside* with machines, I do not think so. Machines do not pick up the feeling tone, nor do machines pick up the sensations themselves. They pick up the patterns, they do not pick up the real thing. We are not patterns, we are living persons. Living vessels.

Is it in the poetic imagination, where conflict is the basis of its truth, that we may find a clue to our new perception — in the altered consciousness and fusion of opposites that poetry achieves? Owen Barfield has illuminated this question for us, in his studies of romantic imagination, poetic diction, and "what Coleridge thought." Experience in the spirit is real. The dream of the fire is a real event. Inner experiences of loneliness and of love alter our substance. Little may show on the surface, the forms look much the same, only the color is deepened. The undergoing is richer. The tolerance for pain and ordeal is greater. The ability to undergo violence in the psyche, without discharging it, enables a transformation of behavior to develop. For physical actions have their source in the psyche, in "the voice of nature in the unconscious," which we may make into a human voice.

There is an impulse within the unconscious to seek itself in consciousness. How gladly we would agree to slumber if we could. But we can no more withstand the movements of our psyche and the evolution of our consciousness,

than we can withstand aging and renewal. Of course we can stand in the way.
We are free to do that. We can take potions to catch some rest from the dread
grinding of the divine mills. We can try to hide from the great inner eye.
Hide, hide. We can decide to think about all that later. And in this way we
can greatly affect what happens — we can imperil our safety and the safety
of others. Scriptures and legends tell of the efforts of humankind to deny relationship with spirit, to avoid the drastic contact from which there is no
escape. We will gladly betray if only we can be left to play as children,
manipulating our bodies and our concepts and our relationships as if they
were moves on a chess board: we call it "playing the game." Meanwhile,
back in the central nervous system, the spiritual powers are going about their
business, while the children play in the battlefields. We children know the
gods are in there, that there is another level of awareness we are supposed to
be preparing to enter when we are grown up enough. The gods call, the children do not obey. We must be free, the children cry, free to disobey. Okay,
sigh the gods, we can wait. But of course it gets harder and harder to obey:
postponement becomes a way of life. People get to rely on certain kinds of
postponements from each other, to save us all from face-to-face encounters,
when we let the gods come forward to dance in our faces and our limbs.
We may have to sacrifice our lives as we have so far made them for this to
happen. Make way, make way for the gods.

If we are not careful to sacrifice our games, we may die in childhood, aging
children, undone by our strategy. And the gods weep and cover us with leaves
and wait while we withdraw ourselves in death and school ourselves again in
the spirit. Perhaps the next time round we will be readier to let the holy voices
sound through us.

The divine Oneness has to be dismembered, an ancient wisdom tells us.
And then the god has to be reconstituted. He is reconstituted in His children,
in the differentiated aspects of His consciousness. The unconscious mind
grows into multiformity. Multiformity grows into ego strength. Ego evolves
as spirit-self. The gift of the inner self mediates the realms of Union and
Aloneness, and reveals them to consciousness in a bearable paradox.

We want this. Everywhere the cries rise, for the *One* World, the *United*
Nations, the People of the World *Unite*; and at the same time for independence, autonomy, self-rule. It is precisely because these are not mutually exclusive that people clamor simultaneously for them. The fusion of the opposites
is the way forward.

For some, it begins in self-confrontation: courage and fear, wholeness and
guilt; in efforts to bring about in the depths, "behind the brain," an intermin-
gling of those poles where energy tends to gather. Consciously we try to bring
the terrors into dancing interplay with tenderness. The weeping child into the
breast of the gift-giver. Bringing anger and woe into listening and offering.

Churning the cosmic milk, as the Vedas say. Churning, churning! For the "clarifying of the butter," the transformation of consciousness. The labor, the spiritual strenuousness. Come in, baby, come on in. Inviting ruin and destruction into oneself like a lover. Like a lover. Take me. Take all my beauty and my hope and my innocence; envelop them in your dark, cold, angry embrace, in the embrace of love, where love is transformed by having slept with its ruin, where the ruin is transformed by having slept with its love: where anger and hopelessness and guilt are transformed by having felt the orgasmic trembling surrender of a released power that moves through them in radiating waves, radiating waves. This is what happens, physically, psychically . . . the transforming power of the mutual surrender, we feel our Being *move* even as we dwell within it.

We seek to experience ourselves from the inside: as one experiences sunshine or cold or the taste of an apple or a lemon or the pinch of a shoe or the release of a cramp; to experience the Being within our Being, our spirit-self within our unconscious.

How may we practice oneness in a world where differences and oppositions and conflicts are the daily realities? How do we experience conflicts as the dynamic inner law of oneness? How may we wake up, grow up, see where we are, and learn to step aside so that the flow *both ways* through the center can take place? Both ways. One wind, two directions. What a tremendous mystery we live within. It is not enough to be alive, or wise, or willing to fight, or willing to love. These pass through each other like simultaneous impulses pulsing through a center so that what we feel is one throb, but its texture and resonance animate an awareness of many levels of body, soul, and spirit in an organic oneness. It is not like electric circuitry. It is not like multiple screen projections. It is not like watching ourselves have visions. It is like being a living word that is being spoken. A LIVING WORD. The word communicates past all bodily obstruction: even when our senses are blighted, we see and hear in the inner realm.

The dark is all about us. We light our little lights. Our candle flames, the sensible flame, the living flame. This brings light into the darkness, shows the darkness to itself, its terror abates, its ecstasy abates, the forms emerge, the dark forms turn into light; as the light moves, new shadows form, how beautiful it is, how stirring and formidable and unheard-of. Our consciousness changes. We step carefully. We know where we are going. We have been there before. It is a dark narrow passage to the inner chamber. There is the threshold, obstructed with a thicket of brambles, the narrowest possible passageway, the dark earth obstructing and at the same time opening. Our hearts are so full, so swollen with painful weeping and surrender, perhaps they will not be able to squeeze through the tight spots.

Into the dark chamber at last. The light is the half-light of the underworld, the twilight of the inner realm. Shadowy figures. The dark lady poet and seeker is there, checking to see who is coming through the dark passage, who is it I am bringing with me? A large soul is following us. Too large really for the tight places. He will have to go through the needle's eye. Will his largeness be able to be small as a mouse, or a worm, when the tight spots come? Able to slither through the narrow places? We cannot get everywhere on two legs. Sometimes we need four, or none! Sometimes we are fish out of water, and then we must be birds if we are to be able to swim in air. Strong feet, strong thighs, for the long climbs up and down.

How to come at it, how to come at it . . . by the serpent's path, indirectly, never straight on, head on. Picking our way through all that befalls us and besets us, all the experiences streaming toward us as well as those we initiate. For in the intricate mesh of our mutual involvement, we befall each other constantly. Weathering each other, by the atmosphere of our invisible being. Invisible as air. As wind. Visible only in its effects. We do not see the wind. We do not see the air. We see the plane mounted upon it. We see the leaves it stirs up; we hear its pressure against surfaces; the wind of the spirit, bloweth, bloweth. Befalls us everywhere, through the breathing kingdoms all about us, through the fiery exhalations from the planetary worlds.

How can we contain our own violence so that it does not explode or leak out prematurely? How can we hold it, with firm gentleness, so that the inner processes, the metabolism, can work? How can we bear the heat, the deep shifts in the world within?

It takes a special caring of our inner being. Often we are helped by solitude and silence, to hear our inner voice from the house of self. Certainly we cannot be always busy with something else. Sometimes it seems necessary to fall apart to begin from a new place, the way a seed falls apart to reveal a germinating center. It may well be the growth process that causes our conflicts in the first place. The bud, pushing from within, cracks the outer forms. It is these outer forms that feel the violence. They will be helped to contain their pain if they understand how they are a part of an evolving wholeness. What a vessel we have to be to hold the polarities of our experience together.

By awakening the feminine within our inner life, we may transform power into human being-ness. This is the Mary to Creative Spirit. And we do not bear the Son of Man without Mary. Here is something for us to think deeply about whether we are men or women. For women may be as estranged from the feminine function in the psyche, as doubtful of its importance, as men may be. The awakened feminine function turns like a tender woman toward the wandering unclaimed features of oneself, turns like a bride to soften the fiery powers of creative spirit.

For creative spirit is incomplete, unwhole, out of phase with life when it rules alone. A marriage is needed with the feminine, who lovingly receives, nurtures, and maintains. The feminine brings us capacity for relationship, brings spirit into earth. The union happens slowly because body does not wish to give itself up and spirit does not wish to be contained. What a muddle.

How can we come to feel what we do not yet feel? Know what we do not yet know? Perceive what we do not yet perceive? There are, of course, ways of meditation and spiritual discipline taught by initiates through the ages. But there is another idea I would like to suggest, which has to do with a middle ground, with play, and with theater.

Think of a middle ground, which has the quality of an actor's art. The actor remains himself, yet he invites emotions not his own to dwell in him. How much feeling other than our own are we capable of? What thoughts inimical to our self-respect can we bear to think? Indeed are we able to feel any emotion dissimilar to our own? Are we able to entertain seriously an idea that is incompatible with our habits? Do we have a power of fantasy — an imagination that enables us to have inner experience different from our own lives? Can we receive into consciousness an experience that is mediated through the body but does not lodge in the body, is not given authenticity by physical density, but rather by precisely its opposite, by its power to take hold of us, to enthrall, as a story does, to possess us and release us — can we be changed through an inner imagination?

The middle ground makes possible a rapprochement between conscious and unconscious realms, between light and dark. It is "a holy distance" between the sensations of our experience and our being who is undergoing them. We feel ourselves *within* to be separate from the whirlwinds and forces and temptations that beset us, separate and distinguishable, in a position to come into a conscious relationship with what besets us, to struggle and work with it, to become freer agents. For it is foolish to speak of freedom so long as we are captivated by our bodies, our feelings, our social attitudes, our accomplishments. These are our riches. Attachment to them is our poverty. In the space between, the lifeline evolves. Conflict can be viewed as artistic process.

Once this inner distance shapes itself in us, we are in a position to explore and search out the meaning of what we are feeling or thinking or doing. Masters in our own house, we may be less fearful of being overwhelmed by unconscious contents. We do not need to take other people's opinion of what is happening. We may discover that when we begin to look thoroughly in the places where we have been warned there is nothing to see, we find realms of great meaning. This is why I speak of pain as I do, and guilt, and anxiety, and violence, and death. Kingdoms, kingdoms, all of them!

So here we are, FREE AT LAST, only to find that if we are to live in peace, we are to live in conflict and in pain as well as in the easing of conflict and in joy. Peace can be thought of as a special way of experiencing difficulties, an "art of war." Can we learn to be artists of peace, at home in paradox? And to disarm "conflict" of its one-sidedly negative overtones? To see it as part of harmony and goodness? For every path we take is governed by its law: the law of polarities. It is hard to accept the fact that we are in a big league, that we live in the universe and not just on Maple Avenue. But that's the way it is. We do indeed live in the universe and we are potent actors in its future.

It will help us to look in this new way if we reconnect with the dynamic living processes working all around us. The vessel of our being evolves in fire, and, once formed, the fire is forever present in it. So it is with our pottery and our kilns as well. The fire turns clay into stone. Fire in the stone. The fire-tried stone. The fire-filled stone. Fire is changed and body is changed. Life-vessel may be experienced in imagination as a stage of evolving human inner form. It gives off both warmth and containment.

A sense of one's own form may begin to deepen: this, and not that. As our individual being evolves, a new social impulse begins to quicken. Within a full experience of person as unique being of body, soul, and spirit, there exists, as a polarity, a sense of infinity, a sense of otherness, an experience of community within one's own form. The question may then rise: how may I manifest this polarity in a wholeness of practice? How may I project both a contemplative integrity and a warm social impulse? To get to this question, we may go a path of separating and connecting, of war and peace.

IV

The Works of Owen Barfield

A BIBLIOGRAPHY OF THE WORKS OF OWEN BARFIELD

Compiled by

G. B. TENNYSON

The following listing is not exhaustive. I have excluded some early fugitive pieces, largely unsigned editorial commentary, and some letters to the editor, that Owen Barfield contributed to periodicals in the twenties. There were also a few items that proved impossible to trace in sufficient bibliographical detail to warrant their inclusion. Nevertheless, the following listing contains virtually all important works by Owen Barfield through 1974 and a considerable number of lesser works that will be of interest to students of his thought.

All works are entered under the first year of publication with subsequent reprintings listed under the same entry. Information given is as complete as known for each entry. The notation "Reprinted in *RCA*" refers to a subsequent reprinting in *Romanticism Comes of Age* (1944, 1966). All bracketed information has been supplied by the compiler.

In assembling this bibliography I was greatly aided by Mr. Barfield himself, who placed his files at my disposal. I also express deep thanks to Miss G. C. Bosset of the Rudolf Steiner Library, London, whose aid was indispensable, to Mrs. E. Lloyd of the Rudolf Steiner Bookshop, London, to Professor Clyde S. Kilby of Wheaton College and to Mrs. Janet D. Keyes at the University of California at Los Angeles.

1917

"Air-Castles" [unsigned poem]. *Punch* 152 (14 February): 101.

1920

"Ballads" [unsigned review of *Old English Ballads, 1553-1625*, edited by H. E. Rollins]. *New Statesman* 15 (2 October): 701-2.

"Form in Poetry." *New Statesman* 15 (7 August): 501-2.

"John Clare" [unsigned review of *John Clare*, edited by Edmund Blunden].
New Statesman 16 (25 December): 371.

"Oxford Poetry" [unsigned review of *Oxford Poetry, 1917-1919*]. *New Statesman* 16 (20 November): 204-5.

"The Reader's Eye." *Cornhill Magazine* 49 (September): 327-31.

"Walter de la Mare" [review of *Poems*, by Walter de la Mare]. *New Statesman* 16 (6 November): 140, 142.

1921

"Boswell." *New Statesman* 17 (13 August): 520.

"The Fourteenth Century" [review of *Fourteenth Century Verse and Prose*, edited by Kenneth Sisam]. *New Statesman* 18 (22 October): 78.

"George Santayana" [review of *Little Essays, drawn from the works of George Santayana*, by Logan Pearsall Smith, and *Character and Opinion*, by George Santayana]. *New Statesman* 16 (26 March): 729-30.

"The Scottish Chaucerians." *New Statesman* 17 (11 June): 273-4.

"The Silent Voice of Poetry." *New Statesman* 16 (15 January): 448-9.

"Some Elements of Decadence." *New Statesman* 18 (24 December): 344-5.

"Wilfred Owen" [unsigned review of *Poems*, by Wilfred Owen]. *New Statesman* 16 (15 January): 454.

1922

"John Drinkwater" [review of *Selected Poems of John Drinkwater*]. *New Statesman* 19 (15 July), 415-16.

"Nine Poems" [sonnet sequence]. *London Mercury* 5 (March): 462-5.

"Old English Poetry" [signed "O.B.", review of *Old English Poetry*, by J. Duncan Spaeth]. *New Statesman* 20 (7 October): 20.

" 'Ruin.' " *London Mercury* 7 (December): 164-70. Reprinted as " 'Ruin': A Word and a History." *Living Age* 316 (1923): 164-70.

"Seven Letters." *The Weekly Westminster Gazette* (4 March): 16.

1923

"Awake at Night" [verse]. *London Mercury* 8 (May): 7-8.

"Chronicle: Drama" [theatre reviews]. *London Mercury* 8 (July): 326-9.

"Dope" [fiction]. *The Criterion* 1 (July): 322-8.

"Idiom" [review of *English Idioms*, by Logan Pearsall Smith]. *New Statesman* 21 (30 June): 368, 370.

"Milton and Metaphysics" [review of *Milton Agonistes*, by E. H. Visiak]. *New Statesman* 21 (11 August): 524-5.

1924

"Changes in the Theatre." *Theatre Arts Monthly* 8 (September): 637-42.
Letters to the Editor. *The New Age* (20 March, 30 October, 4 December).

1925

Letters to the Editor. *G. K.'s Weekly* (20 June, 29 August).
The Silver Trumpet. London: Faber and Gwyer. Grand Rapids, Mich.: Wllllam B. Eerdmans Publishing Co., 1968.

1926

History in English Words. London: Methuen and Co. Second edition, London: Faber and Faber, 1953; Faber paperback, 1962. Rev ed., Grand Rapids, Mich.: William B. Eerdmans Publishing Co., 1967.
Letters to the Editor. *G. K.'s Weekly* (9 January, 13 February).
"Romanticism and Anthroposophy." *Anthroposophy* 1 (Easter), 111-24.
"Three Songs: 'Words and Music,' 'In the Garden,' 'Bliss.' " *London Mercury* 14 (August): 352-3.
"Metaphor." *New Statesman* 26 (20 March), 708-10.

1927

"Ophelia" [poem]. *London Mercury* 16 (June), 121.
"Speech, Reason and the Consciousness Soul." *Anthroposophy* 2 (Christmas), 537-54. Reprinted as "Speech, Reason and Imagination" in *RCA*.
"Suggestions for a Film Scenario to be entitled *Romance* or *The Professor's Love-Story.*" *The New Age* (4 August): 166-7.
"Thinking and Thought." *Anthroposophy* 2 (Easter), 48-67. Reprinted in *RCA*.
"Two Poems: 'On Reading an Elizabethan Lyric in the British Museum Reading Room,' 'Ritual.' " *London Mercury* 15 (1 March), 463-4. "On Reading an Elizabethan Lyric" reprinted in *Living Age* 333 (1927): 500.

1928

"The Consciousness Soul," Part I. *Anthroposophy* 3 (Christmas): 475-94; Part II. *Anthroposophy* 4 (Easter 1929): 43-59. Reprinted in *RCA*.

Michael Owen [pseud.]. "Mrs. Cadogan." *New Adelphi* (March): 233-9.

Poetic Diction: A Study in Meaning. London: Faber and Gwyer. Second edition, London: Faber and Faber, 1952. Reprinted with an Introduction by Howard Nemerov, New York: McGraw-Hill, 1964; 3rd ed. with Afterword by the author, Middletown, Conn.: Wesleyan University Press, 1973.

"Poetry, Verse and Prose" [review of *Collected Essays and Papers*, by Robert Bridges, vols. II and III]. *New Statesman* 31 (6 October): 793-4.

"Rudolf Steiner" [review of *The Story of My Life*, by Rudolf Steiner]. *The New Age* (8 March): 226.

1929

Danger, Ugliness and Waste. London: Privately printed [pamphlet].

"Financial Inquiry" [signed A. O. Barfield]. *Nineteenth Century* 106 (December): 774-84.

"Lesson of South Wales" [signed A. O. Barfield]. *Nineteenth Century* 105 (February): 215-22.

"The Problem of Financing Consumption" [signed A. O. Barfield]. *Nineteenth Century* 105 (June): 792-801.

1930

Review of *Convention and Revolt in Poetry*, by John Livingston Lowes, and of *On Reading Books*, by John Livingston Lowes. *The Criterion* 10 (October): 155-8.

"An Introduction to Anthroposophy." *Anthroposophy* 5 (Easter), 58-80. Reprinted as "From East to West" in *RCA*.

"Psychology and Reason." *The Criterion* 9 (July): 606-17.

Review of *Rudolf Steiner Enters My Life*, by Dr. Friedrich Rittelmeyer. *Anthroposophy* 5 (Easter): 121-2.

1931

Review of *Coleridge as Philosopher*, by J. H. Muirhead. *The Criterion* 10 (April): 543-8. Reprinted as "Coleridge's 'I and Thou.'" In *RCA*, 1st ed.

"The Form of Hamlet." *Anthroposophy* 6 (Michaelmas), 245-65. Reprinted in *RCA*.

Hermann Poppelbaum. *Man and Animal: Their Essential Difference*. Edited by the Natural Science Section of the Free High School for Spiritual Science at the Goetheanum in Dornach, Switzerland. Translated from the German, Parts I, II, III, and V, by Edith Rigby, Part IV by Owen Barfield. London: Anthroposophical Publishing Co.; New York: Anthroposophical Press. Second English edition edited by Owen Barfield, London: Anthroposophical Publishing Co., 1960.

" 'The Shepherd of New Gifts.' " *Anthroposophical Movement* 8 (5 July): 112-13.

"The Village Dance" [poem]. *London Mercury* 24 (June): 109-10.

1932

"Destroyer and Preserver." *Anthroposophical Movement* 9 (15 September): 145-7.

"Equity." *Anthroposophy* 7 (Midsummer): 134-56. Reprinted as "Equity between Man and Man," with a postscript. In *The Golden Blade* (1961): 99-116.

"The Philosophy of Samuel Taylor Coleridge." *Anthroposophy* 7 (Christmas): 385-404. Reprinted in *RCA*.

"Rudolf Steiner and English Poetry." *Anthroposophical Movement* 9 (12 May): 77-9.

1933

With C. S. Lewis. "Abecedarium Philosophicum" [verse]. *The Oxford Magazine* 52 (30 November): 298.

"The Relation between the Economics of C. H. Douglas and those of Rudolf Steiner." *Anthroposophy* 8 (Michaelmas): 272-85.

1934

"The Inspiration of the *Divine Comedy*." Supplement to *Anthroposophical Movement* 11 (22 February): 1-8. Reprinted in *RCA*, 1st edition.

Oudel, Solomon [pseud.]. "Introductory." *Anthroposophical Movement* 11 (26 July): 124-6.

Oudel, Solomon [pseud.]. "Reminiscences." *Anthroposophical Movement* 11 (25 October): 164-6.

"Sonnet on the Resistance in the German Evangelical Church." *Anthroposophical Movement* 11 (25 October): 192.

"The Threefold Commonwealth and the Press." *Anthroposophical Movement* 11 (9 August): 126.

1935

"The Anthroposophical Society." *Anthroposophical Movement* 12 (May): 85-6.

"Come out of Egypt" [verse]. *Anthroposophical Movement* 12 (December): 161.

"The English Spirit" [review of *The English Spirit*, by D. E. Faulkner Jones], Part I. *Anthroposophical Movement* 12 (May), 76-9; Part II. *Anthroposophical Movement* 12 (June): 94-8.

Law, Association and the Trade Union Movement. London: The Threefold Commonwealth Research Group, Pamphlet No. 2.

"May" [verse]. *Anthroposophical Movement* 12 (June): 102.

"The Present Age." *Anthroposophical Movement* 12 (December): 186-7.

Untitled obituary notice on the death of Daniel Nicol Dunlop [signed "O.B."]. *Anthroposophical Movement* 12 (June): 87.

1938

Letter to the Editor. *The Spectator* (23 September).

Letter to the Editor. *The New Statesman* (24 September). [Same as the above.]

1940

"Panic and its Opposite." *Anthroposophical Movement* 17 (October): 1-2.

"Some Reflections arising out of the War." *Anthroposophical Movement* 17 (May): 1-2.

1944

Romanticism Comes of Age. London: Anthroposophical Publishing Co. [Rudolf Steiner Press]. New and Augmented edition, London: Rudolf Steiner Press, 1966. Middletown, Conn.: Wesleyan University Press, 1967.

1945

"The Psalms of David," Part I. *Anthroposophical Movement* 22 (March): 1-4; Part II. *Anthroposophical Movement* 22 (April-May): 1-5. Reprinted in *The Mint*. Edited by Geoffrey Grigson. London: Routledge and Sons, 1946, pp. 139-51.

1946

"Barfield at Birchfield" [anonymous abstract of two lectures on *Hamlet* delivered by Owen Barfield to the Sheffield Educational Settlement]. *The Spark* 1 (Easter): 1-4.

1947

Rudolf Steiner. *Behind the Scenes of External Happenings*. Translated by Dorothy Osmond with the help of Owen Barfield. London: Rudolf Steiner Publishing Co.

"Poetic Diction and Legal Fiction." In *Essays Presented to Charles Williams*. London: Oxford University Press, pp. 106-27. Reprinted in *Importance of Language*. Edited by Max Black. Englewood Cliffs, N.J.: Prentice-Hall, 1962; and in *The Norton Reader*. Edited by Arthur M. Eastman et al. Rev. ed., New York: W. W. Norton, 1969; 3rd ed., New York: W. W. Norton, 1973.

1949

"Goethe and Evolution." *The Listener* 42 (1 December): 945-6.

"Goethe and the Twentieth Century." *The Goethe Year/Das Goethe Jahr*. London: The Orpheus Publications Co., pp. 24-7.

"Goethe and the Twentieth Century" [not the same as the above]. *The Golden Blade*, pp. 37-51. Reprinted in *RCA*, 2nd ed.

"The Kingdom in Space-Time" [review of *Descent into Hell*, by Charles Williams]. *The New English Weekly* 35 (21 April): 19-20.

1950

"Greek Thought in English Words." *Essays and Studies*, n.s. 3, 69-81.

Review of *Briefe von Rudolf Steiner*, vol. I, by Rudolf Steiner. *The Golden Blade*, pp. 107-11.

G.A.L. Burgeon [pseud.]. *This Ever Diverse Pair*. London: Victor Gollancz.

"The Silent Piano" [verse]. *Nine* 2 (May): 113-14.

"Sapphics," "Gender" [verse]. *Nine* 3 (December): 39-41.

"Two Poems." *The Golden Blade*, pp. 61-2.

1951

"Form in Art and in Society." *The Golden Blade*, pp. 88-99.

"History of English Poetry in the Second Half of the Twentieth Century" [verse]. *Anthroposophical Movement* 28 (July-August): 4-6.

1953

Letter to the Editor. *London Times* (2 August).

1954

"The Art of Eurhythmy." *The Golden Blade*, pp. 53-62.

"The Light of the World." Supplement to *Anthroposophical Movement* (February), 10 pp.

Review of *Briefe von Rudolf Steiner*, vol. II, by Rudolf Steiner. *The Golden Blade*, pp. 97-100.

1955

"The Time-Philosophy of Rudolf Steiner." *The Golden Blade*, pp. 74-86. Reprinted in *RCA*, 2nd ed.

1956

"Israel and the Michael Impulse." *Anthroposophical Quarterly* 1 (Spring): 2-9.

"Walter de la Mare." *Anthroposophical Quarterly* 1 (Autumn): 7-10.

1957

"The Apocalypse of St. John" [review of *The Apocalypse of St. John*, by Emil Bock]. *Anthroposophical Quarterly* 2 (Winter): 16.

"Insight about Ultimate Things" [review of *Nurslings of Immortality*, by Raynor C. Johnson]. *Anthroposophical Quarterly* 2 (Winter): 12-14.

"Introduction to Eurhythmy" [review of *Eurhythmy as Visible Speech*, by Rudolf Steiner]. *Anthroposophical Quarterly* 2 (Spring): 13-14.

"Positivism and Anthroposophy." *Anthroposophical Quarterly* 2 (Spring): 7-10.

Saving the Appearances: A Study in Idolatry. London: Faber and Faber. New York: Harcourt, Brace and World, 1965. Chapter 19, "Symptoms of Iconoclasm," reprinted in *Romanticism and Consciousness*. Edited by Harold Bloom. New York: W.W. Norton, 1970.

"Thomas Aquinas" [review of *The Redemption of Thinking: A Study in the Philosophy of Thomas Aquinas*, by Rudolf Steiner]. *The Golden Blade*, pp. 93-5.

"William Blake, 1757-1827." Translated into German by Dr. Konrad Sandkühler. *Die Drei* 27 (November-December): 305-10.

1958

"I See Science Heading Straight for Bankruptcy." *Church of England Newspaper* (3 October).

"Self-Deceptions or Stages to Reality?" *Church of England Newspaper* (14 February).

"The Son of God and the Son of Man." Mimeographed lecture delivered by Owen Barfield at Zeist, Netherlands, 31 August.

"Towards a Science of Man." *Anthroposophical Quarterly* 3 (Summer): 7-8.

1959

Review of *The British, Their Psychology and Destiny*, by Walter Johannes Stein. *Anthroposophical Quarterly* 4 (Spring): 16.

"The Fall in Man and Nature." *Anthroposophical Quarterly* 4 (Winter): 6-13. Reprinted in *RCA*, 2nd ed.

Rudolf Steiner. *Genesis: Secrets of the Bible Story of Creation*. Translated by Dorothy Lenn with the assistance of Owen Barfield. London: Rudolf Steiner Press.

1960

"The Meaning of the Word 'Literal.'" In *Metaphor and Symbol* [being vol. XII of *The Colston Papers*. Proceedings of the Colston Research So-

ciety, held in the University of Bristol, March 28th to March 31st, 1960].
Edited by L. C. Knights and Basil Cottle. (London: Butterworths Scientific Publications), pp. 48-63 [text: pp. 48-57; discussions: pp. 57-63].
Reprinted under the title "The Meaning of 'Literal.' " In *Literary English since Shakespeare*. Edited by George Watson. London: Oxford University Press, 1970.

"Mr. Walker" [signed "O.B."] [verse]. *Anthroposophical Quarterly* 5 (Summer): 18.

"Prayer" [verse]. *Anthroposophical Quarterly* 5 (Spring): 15.

"Speech and Drama." *Anthroposophical Quarterly* 5 (Summer): 17-18.

Rudolf Steiner. *The Work of Angels in Man's Astral Body*. Translated by D. S. Osmond with the help of Owen Barfield. London: Anthroposophical Publishing Co.

1961

Rudolf Steiner. *Anthroposophy: An Introduction*. Translated from the German by V. C. Burnett. Second English edition edited and with a Preface by Owen Barfield. London: Anthroposophical Publishing Co.

"Centennial — Rudolf Steiner (1861-1925)." *The Contemporary Review* 199 (February): 88-91.

"Davy on Snow." *Anthroposophical Quarterly* 7 (Spring): 17-18.

"Mr. Koestler and the Astronomers." *The Golden Blade*, pp. 94-103.

"The Rediscovery of Meaning." *Saturday Evening Post* 234 (7 January): 36-7, 61, 64-5. Reprinted in *Adventures of the Mind*, 2nd ser. Edited by R. Thruelsen and J. Kobler. New York: Alfred Knopf.

"Rudolf Steiner's Concept of Mind." In *The Faithful Thinker: Centenary Essays on the Work and Thought of Rudolf Steiner, 1861-1925*. Edited by A. C. Harwood. London: Hodder and Soughton, pp. 11-21. Reprinted in *RCA*, 2nd ed.

1962

"Man, Thought and Nature." *Anthroposophical Quarterly* 7 (Summer): 26-32. Reprinted in *RCA*, 2nd ed.

1963

Rudolf Steiner. *Wonders of the World, Ordeals of the Soul, Revelations of the Spirit*. Translated by Dorothy Lenn, assisted by Owen Barfield. London: Rudolf Steiner Press.

Worlds Apart: A Dialogue of the 1960's. London: Faber and Faber. Middletown, Conn.: Wesleyan University Press, 1965; Wesleyan paperback, 1971.

1964

Rudolf Steiner. *The Gospel of St. Luke.* Translated by D. S. Osmond with the assistance of Owen Barfield. London: Rudolf Steiner Press.

"Preface." In *The Mystery of Physical Life,* by E. Grant Watson. London: Abelard-Schuman, pp. 9-12.

"The Riddle of the Sphinx," *Arena* 19 (April): 121-8.

1965

"Introduction." In *Light on C. S. Lewis.* Edited by Jocelyn Gibb. London: Geoffrey Bles; New York: Harcourt, Brace and World, 1966, pp. ix-xxi.

"Literature and Faith" [review of *The Climate of Faith in Modern Literature,* edited by Nathan A. Scott, Jr.]. *Journal of Bible and Religion* 33 (October): 340, 342.

"Night and Morning" [signed "O.B.," verse]. *Anthroposophical Quarterly* 10 (Summer): 276.

"Philology and the Incarnation." *The Gordon Review* 8 (Spring): 131-9. Reprinted in *Anthroposophical Quarterly* 14 (Spring 1969): 9-13.

Unancestral Voice. London: Faber and Faber. Middletown, Conn.: Wesleyan University Press, 1966.

1967

"The Abortion Bill" [letter to the editor]. *Anthroposophical Quarterly* 12 (Spring): 24-5.

"Imagination and Inspiration." In *Interpretation: The Poetry of Meaning.* Edited by Stanley Romaine Hopper and David L. Miller. New York: Harcourt, Brace and World, Harbinger Book, pp. 54-76.

With C. S. Lewis. *Mark vs. Tristram: Correspondence between C. S. Lewis and Owen Barfield.* Edited by Walter Hooper. Cambridge, Mass.: The Lowell House Printers.

Speaker's Meaning. Middletown, Conn.: Wesleyan University Press. London: Rudolf Steiner Press, 1970.

1968

"Where is Fancy Bred?" *The Golden Blade*, pp. 41-55.

1969

"Opium and Infinity." *Anthroposophical Quarterly* 14 (Autumn): 59-61.

1970

"Coleridge Collected" [review of *Collected Works of Coleridge*, edited by Kathleen Coburn]. *Encounter* 35 (November): 74-83.

"The Disappearing Trick." *The Golden Blade*, pp. 53-66.

The Case for Anthroposophy. Selections from *Von Seelenrätseln*, by Rudolf Steiner. Translated, arranged, and with an Introduction by Owen Barfield. London: Rudolf Steiner Press.

"C. S. Lewis" [letter to the editor]. *Times Literary Supplement* (28 August), p. 951.

"Dream, Myth, and Philosophical Double Vision." In *Myths, Dreams, and Religion.* Edited by Joseph Campbell. New York: E. P. Dutton and Co., pp. 211-24.

1971

"Either: Or." In *Imagination and the Spirit: Essays in Literature and the Christian Faith Presented to Clyde S. Kilby.* Edited by Charles Huttar. Grand Rapids, Mich.: William B. Eerdmans Publishing Co., pp. 25-42.

"In Conversation" [i.e., C. S. Lewis in Conversation]. In *C. S. Lewis, Speaker and Teacher.* Edited by Carolyn Keefe. Grand Rapids, Mich.: Zondervan Publishing House, pp. 95-108.

"Nature and Philosophy." *Anthroposophical Quarterly* 16 (Spring): 11-12.

"Self and Reality." *Denver Quarterly* 6 (Spring): 1-28.

"Verse: 'The Year Makes Answer,' 'A Meditation.'" *The Golden Blade*, pp. 69-71.

What Coleridge Thought. Middletown, Conn.: Wesleyan University Press. London: Oxford University Press, 1972.

1972

"Barfield on Coleridge: An Exchange" [includes a review by Douglas Wilson of *What Coleridge Thought*, and Owen Barfield's "Author's Rejoinder"]. *Denver Quarterly* 7 (Summer): 61-71.

Review of *Coleridge, the Damaged Archangel*, by Norman Fruman. *The Nation* 214 (12 June): 764-5.

"Comment: 'The Politics of Abortion.' " *Denver Quarterly* 6 (Winter): 18-28.

"Giordano Bruno and the Survival of Learning." *The Drew Gateway* 42 (Spring): 147-59.

"Participation and Isolation: A Fresh Light on Present Discontents." *Dalhousie Review* 52 (Spring): 5-20.

1973

"Comment: Poetry in Walter de la Mare." *Denver Quarterly* 8 (Autumn): 69-81.

"Comment: Some Reflections on Iconology." *Denver Quarterly* 7 (Winter): 42-54.

G. W. F. Hegel. "Eleusis" [poem to Hölderlin]. Translated from the German by Owen Barfield, in "Ancient Wisdom and the Heralding of the Christ Impulse," by Rudolf Steiner. *Anthroposophical Quarterly* 18 (Spring): 2-3.

"Language and Discovery." *The Golden Blade*, pp. 38-49.

Review of *The Visionary Landscape*, by Paul Piehler. *Medium Aevum* 42 (Spring): 84-91.

1974

"The Coming Trauma of Materialism." *Denver Quarterly* 9 (Spring): 56-73 [followed by "A Reply to Barfield" by Theodore Roszack].

"Matter, Imagination, and Spirit." *Journal of the American Academy of Religion* 42 (December): 621-9.

NOTES ON CONTRIBUTORS

Adey, Lionel. Lecturer in English Literature, University of Victoria, British Columbia; author of "The Light of Holiness: Some Remarks on Wm. Morris by C. S. Lewis" in *The Journal of Wm. Morris Society* (1973) and of *The Great War: Disputations Between C. S. Lewis and Owen Barfield.*

Barfield, R. H. Consultant on induction heating and author of many papers on radio-wave propagation and direction-finding in scientific journals.

Bohm, David. Professor of Theoretical Physics, Birkbeck College, University of London; author of "Quantum Theory as an Indication of a New Order in Physics" in *Foundations of Physics* 1 (1971) and 3 (1973).

Brown, Norman O. Professor of Humanities, University of California at Santa Cruz; author of *Life Against Death* (1959), *Love's Body* (1966), *Closing Time* (1973), and the forthcoming *To Greet the Return of the Gods.*

Hardie, Colin. Fellow Emeritus in Classics of Magdalen College and Lecturer in Greek and Latin literature in the University of Oxford; author of numerous articles on Vergil and Dante.

Harwood, A. C. Former Scholar of Christ Church, Oxford.

Hocks, Richard A. Associate Professor of English, University of Missouri; author of *Henry James and Pragmatistic Thought: A Study in the Relationship between the Philosophy of William James and the Literary Art of Henry James* (1974).

Kilby, Clyde S. Professor of English and Curator of the Marion E. Wade Collection, Wheaton College; author of *Poetry and Life* (1953) and of various books on C. S. Lewis.

Meiners, R. K. Professor of English, Michigan State University; author of

Everything to be Endured: An Essay on Robert Lowell and Modern Poetry (1970) and a volume of poems, *Journeying Back to the World* (1975).

Nemerov, Howard. Professor of English, Washington University; author of numerous books of verse, fiction, and essays, most recently *The Western Approaches* (1975) and the forthcoming *Figures of Thought.*

Piehler, Paul. Associate Professor of English, McGill University; author of *The Visionary Landscape, A Study in Medieval Allegory* (1971).

Preyer, Robert O. Professor of English and American Literature at Brandeis University; author of "The Fine Delight that Fathers Thought': Gerard Manley Hopkins and the Romantic Survival" in *Victorian Poetry,* edited by M. Bradbury and D. Palmer (1972), and editor of *Victorian Literature: Selected Essays* (1970).

Reilly, R. J. Professor of English, the University of Detroit; author of *Romantic Religion: A Study in the Work of Owen Barfield, C. S. Lewis, Charles Williams, and J. R. R. Tolkien* (1971).

Richards, Mary Caroline. Poet, potter, philosopher, and free-lance teacher; author of *Centering: in Pottery, Poetry and the Person* (1964) and *The Crossing Point: Selected Talks and Writings* (1973).

Sugerman, Shirley. Academic Coordinator of the Aquinas Program and Lecturer in World Religions at Drew University; author of articles on psychology and religion and of the forthcoming *Sin and Madness: Studies in Narcissism.*

Tennyson, G. B. Professor of English, the University of California at Los Angeles; author of *Sartor Called Resartus* (1966) and editor of the *Carlyle Reader* (1969).